H

BREAK POINT

BREAK POINT

The Secret Diary of a Pro Tennis Player

VINCE SPADEA *and* DAN MARKOWITZ

ECW PRESS

Published by ECW PRESS
2120 Queen Street East, Suite 200, Toronto, Ontario, Canada M4E 1E2

LIBRARY AND ARCHIVES CANADA CATALOGUING IN PUBLICATION

Spadea, Vince
Break point : the secret diary of a pro tennis player /
Vince Spadea and Dan Markowitz.

ISBN 1-55022-729-7

1. Spadea, Vince. 2. Tennis players — United States — Biography.
I. Markowitz, Dan II. Title.

GV994.S68A3 2006   796.342092   C2006-901700-X

Editor: Kevin Connolly
Cover and Text Design: Tania Craan
Cover Photo: Rob Tringali / Sports Chrome
Production: Mary Bowness
Printing: Friesens

This book is set in Fairfield and Akzidenz Grotesk

DISTRIBUTION
CANADA: Jaguar Book Group, 100 Armstrong Ave., Georgetown, ON L7G 5S4
UNITED STATES: Independent Publishers Group, 814 North Franklin Street,
Chicago, IL 60610

PRINTED AND BOUND IN CANADA

ECW PRESS
ecwpress.com

Dedications

To my family for their unconditional love and support over the years. Your everlasting devotion to me will be infinitely felt and appreciated.

Vince Spadea

To Jeanne, with great love and gratitude.

To Robert, and my Mom and Dad, who had one of the funniest-looking, but effective, backhands I've ever seen. And to all the tennis bums, may you always find a good game.

Dan Markowitz

I'd like to thank all of my friends in Florida, California, and all over the world, for caring and loving me for who I am. I'm not going to list names because I wouldn't want to leave someone out. You know who you are. Since my job is constant travel and always being away from you, it's meant so much to have your consistent friendship. All of you have lifted me to be a better person and tennis player, especially my Christian friends who encourage me to be an example and leader for God. I also want to thank everyone in the tennis world. We have a unique and special bond. Tennis is an amazing sport, and has given me so much fun and heartfelt times. I have shared them with you all, the tournament staff, the volunteers, the coaches, the fans, and of course the players. My imperative note to my peers: all the great battles and players I've encountered over the years, I want to say that I appreciate all of you not only as competitors, but as people. Your talent and work ethic have taught me life lessons, and you are one of the reasons I wrote this book. I wanted everyone to know more about our game. For those who enjoy this book, I thank you; for those who I talk candidly about, I wanted the world to know what pro tennis, the players, and I are really like through my eyes. What we go through, what we say and feel, because I know the voice of a pro tennis player to the world has been lacking for some time. I know we players are not all the same, but I hope you have a place for understanding that tennis is entertainment as well as a serious sport, and I wrote this material with the intent of promoting the game. Also to my acquaintances, I'd like to thank each and every person I've ever met in my travels. At airports, on subways and side streets, from sponsors at tournaments to players to ball kids on center court, I take away a piece from all of you, and it makes me who I am today. I have learned so many things, and I'm grateful that I've been a part of your lives, hopefully making a positive impact in some way. Finally, I want to thank Jack David and ECW Press for making this project happen, for believing in this book, and Vince Spadea — and you know I ain't afraid of ya. Thanks again to everyone and God bless.

— Spadea

I'd like to thank Jack David, the publisher at ECW, for believing in this book and working with Vince and me on it. Crissy Boylan, at ECW, lent an able hand, as well. Peter Bodo of *Tennis Magazine*, did a great job in editing the excerpt of the book, "Sitting Duck," that appeared in the 2006 January/February edition. Greg Sharko, the ATP's communication director, and king of men's pro tennis facts and trivia, was a big help, as well as the ATP's Pete Holtermann. I'd like to also thank the media directors at the Masters Event in Indian Wells, the Hall of Fame Championships in Newport, Rhode Island, the Delray Beach International Tennis Championships in Florida, the U.S. Open, and the USTA Challenger at Forest Hills, New York respectively, Matt Van Tuinen, Kat Anderson, Lisa Franson, Jeanmarie Daly and Dina Ingersole, for allowing me access to the players and media. The men's pro tennis tour is played around the world, but the women and men who cover it for newspapers, magazines, television, and the internet, especially in the United States, is a relatively small, but passionate group. I have talked to a number of you through the course of this book and I'd like to thank you all for your insight. Richard Pagliaro of *Tennis Week Magazine* was particularly helpful by posting an excerpt of *Break Point* on the *Tennis Week* website.

— DM

DECEMBER 31, 2004

Welcome to outer Spadea. I'm 30 years old and I'm having these dreams.

I dream I'm playing in the U.S. Open finals against Roger Federer, the world's No. 1 player, and I'm battling. I'm the guy no one bothered to worry about, but here I am trying to win my first Grand Slam title after 12 long years on the pro tour. No one, with the exception of the great Pete Sampras, has ever won a U.S. Open title in the open era of tennis after the age of 30.

But hey! Spadea ain't afraid of ya!

I'm playing like the warrior I am, and the crowd is jumping out of their seats. There are tons of celebrities in Arthur Ashe Stadium. Spike Lee is sitting courtside, and as I go back to towel off after a long point, he leans over and says, "Hey Vince, win this match and I've got you in my next movie."

It comes down to a fifth-set tiebreaker. At match point — my favor — I hit a running, forehand passing shot that streaks by Federer's outstretched racket. The ball lands flush on the line. *I win the U.S. Open!* I fall to my knees in a *Rocky IV*-meets-Björn-Borg move, with real tears in my eyes as I look over at my family in the player's box. I know that every inch I ran in tennis practices and matches, every drop of sweat that came out of me, has gone into the glory of this one moment. I get up off my knees and moonwalk up to the net to shake Federer's hand. The New York crowd — all 23,000 of them — are on their feet going wild.

I dream I'm playing for the American Davis Cup Team in the 2005 Davis Cup finals against Spain. In the fifth and deciding rubber match, I beat the 19-year-old Spaniard, Rafael Nadal. I'm hoisted up onto Andy Roddick's, the Bryan Brothers', and captain Patrick McEnroe's shoulders, clutching the Davis Cup trophy in my hands.

I dream that my picture is on the cover of *Tennis Magazine*, and they do a special "Comeback of the Year" feature on me entitled, "Spadea: The Italian Gladiator." It's all about how I've become the oldest player in the history of the sport ever to win his first Grand Slam singles title and play on a Davis Cup championship team.

I dream these things. I really do. I have been a professional tennis player for 12 years — have played on six different continents in more than 500 matches — and have beaten Andre Agassi, Pete Sampras, Roddick, Federer, Safin, and 12 other players who've won Grand Slam singles titles. In 2000, including the Davis Cup finals and the Olympics, I lost 21 straight matches, the longest losing streak in the history of the sport.

My ranking dropped from a career-high No. 18 in the world, to No. 237, and for the next year and a half, I played mostly lower level pro tournaments until I made it back into the Top 100. In 2004, playing in the 223rd ATP tournament of

my career, I won my first tour title in Scottsdale, Arizona —
breaking Roddick's laser serve three times in the last set of
our semifinals — and made it back into the Top 20.

My father, Vincent Sr., taught my two sisters (both college All-Americans at Duke) and me the game, even though
he didn't pick up a racket until he was in his thirties. I was
an overweight kid who grew up first in Brockton,
Massachusetts — Rocky Marciano's hometown, my grandfa-
ther was his doctor — and then on the wrong side of Boca
Raton, Florida. Stan Smith, the former Wimbledon and U.S.
Open champ, told me I should forgo a pro career at 18 and
opt for college instead. I said thanks, but no thanks, and in
two years I became the youngest American ranked in the
Top 100 in the world.

At 24, in my sixth year as a pro, Agassi called me "a journeyman." I proceeded to beat him in two of the next three
matches we played, the last one coming in the round of 16 at
the 1999 Australian Open. Last year, even though I was the
third highest ranked American behind Roddick and Agassi,
Patrick McEnroe, the American Davis Cup captain, chose
Roddick and Mardy Fish (Agassi didn't want to play) as his
singles players against Spain in the Davis Cup finals.

I wrote a letter to McEnroe — which I also released to
the Associated Press — criticizing his decision. McEnroe,
feeling some heat from the media, invited me to come to
Spain as a team member, with the teaser that if I beat Fish in
practice the week before the tie began, Pat might change his
mind and play me in the No. 2 singles spot. But when I easily
beat Fish in two practice matches, McEnroe still opted to
play Fish, a guy who had won a total of three clay-court pro
tour matches in his career. I, on the other hand, had reached
the quarterfinals of the Italian Open, and the third round of
Roland Garros, the French Open, three times on clay.

So why am I still out here traveling the world, playing on the pro tennis tour when almost all the top players I grew up playing with — guys like former No. 1 players Yevgeny Kafelnikov and Marcelo Rios — have retired? Not a single American player from my generation made it except me. So why am I still seeking to win a Grand Slam and make my "U-Turn for Glory" a smash reality? Why don't I take a cushy teaching-pro job at a ritzy country club, or coach a younger touring pro and get to be the one who feeds the balls while the other guy runs and sweats after them?

Mostly, it's because I'd rather be a top professional tennis player than the President of the United States; because I've hit more tennis balls in my life than probably anybody on this freakin' planet. What's a return of serve? What's a backhand winner down the line? What's a topspin forehand cross-court? These are strokes I've spent my entire life perfecting. I won't let this sport dictate my life. I want to be the master of my own destiny, and I'm challenged by the emotional energy and hard labor required to be a top player.

I'm in love with the battle, and battling is the essential part of a long career in pro tennis. Once you lose your passion for fighting to win every point and digging deep, your days are numbered out here. This game stimulates my brain and requires every ounce of my competitive spirit, physical conditioning, and trench warfare mentality. I believe a pro tennis player has to battle more than any athlete playing any other sport out there. When Steve Nash goes out on the court, he's got the support of his teammates and his coach, who has just given him instructions during a time-out seconds before. He has that emotional lift.

In tennis, you have no teammates, and your coach can only sit in the stands with the spectators and make facial gestures. Coaches are not allowed to sit next to their players and give counsel during breaks. Tennis is the only sport where you truly go out and battle on your own. Even boxers have their trainers come into the ring after every round, and golfers can consult with their caddies before every shot. That's why I call tennis the ultimate one-on-one sport.

The pro tennis player must balance his personal life with the edge needed to play matches, win tiebreakers, get over jet lag and injuries, and compete for ten months of the year. That's right! The tour starts on January 3rd with Association of Tennis Professionals (ATP) tournaments in three cities in three different countries — Adelaide, Australia; Doha, Qatar; and Chennai, India — and it doesn't end until Halloween in Paris. A total of 68 tournaments are squeezed in over this insane schedule, as well as 578 lower level pro tournaments. Often there is a choice of three tournaments to play in any given week and most pros play between 25 and 35 tournaments a year. At year's end, the Top 8 players in the world also qualify to play in the Masters Cup in Shanghai in November, while the two top national teams play in the Davis Cup finals in December. It's all part of the battle.

The players on tour are constantly around one another. We fly in the same planes, sleep at the same hotels, eat at the same restaurants, and dress in the same locker rooms. At a certain point, seeing so much of your competition can get into your head. Boxers fight two or three times a year, maximum. We play ten months a year, take a short break, then start practicing for the next season, when the Australian Open — one of the sport's four Grand Slam tournaments — begins play in January.

The game has many charms, but perhaps most compelling is that one great shot can turn an entire match around. That's what players and fans love about it. You can have one week where you go out and play well in every match and win a big tournament. Like Gustavo Kuerten stunning the world by winning the French Open for the first time in 1997. Before the tournament, he was a "nobody," ranked No. 66. Two weeks later, he was a Grand Slam champion. If you can find a way to win, you can become a hero overnight. You can get a huge paycheck and change your career in an instant.

What keeps me ticking is that tennis is an instant-celebrity sport. Even the top dogs in the game — the Samprases, Agassis and Federers — were all once frustrated, "up-match-point-and-lost" players, too. They were all once on the outside, looking in. I've never been the man everyone comes out to see and admire, but the great part about tennis is that tomorrow there's always another match, another challenge.

I'm totally engrossed in the game. I'm trying to win ugly. I'm trying to win pretty. I'm trying not to lose at any cost. As a warrior and rapper, I'm going to tell you straight out what it feels like to not give up — to never be fazed by disappointment or failure, to try to find harder ways to win rather than easier ways, and most of all, to enjoy the battle.

So what follows, then — after two detour chapters that chronicle the close of my 2004 season — is not so much a book about Vince Spadea as it is about the players, coaches, fans, and women I encountered playing the 2005 season on the ATP circuit and the pursuit of greatness that has so far been elusive for me. At the beginning of the 2005 season, in addition to Agassi and Tim Henman, I'm the only player over the age of 30 to hold a Top 20 ranking. I have spent a lifetime in the game. I'm a tennis player first and second, and everything else last. And at 30 years old, I'm far from being done.

THE DR. JEKYLL and MR. HYDE
of ANDRE AGASSI

FALL, 2004
Madrid, Spain

In pro tennis, rankings determine everything: tournament
seeds, appearance fees, endorsement deals, the size of your
hotel suite — even, in some cases, the quality of women you
meet. There's a special halo that surrounds the Top 10 players in the world. Their names as I'm writing this are Roger
Federer, Andy Roddick, Lleyton Hewitt, Marat Safin, Carlos
Moya, Tim Henman, Guillermo Coria, Andre Agassi, David
Nalbandian, and Gaston Gaudio, and these men represent
the pantheon of the game. At 30, I'm in the midst of having
my finest pro season, winning a career-high 37 matches, with
still three tournaments left to play. Along the way, I've beaten
Safin, when he was ranked No. 2, and Roddick, when he
was No. 7.

The rankings are calculated using a player's results at his
18 best tournaments during a rolling 52-week year. (Masters

events and Grand Slams are always counted among the top 18 if a player has a main-draw result.) It is called the "entry ranking" system, and it determines which players get entry right into the main draw of tournaments. Four years ago, the ATP, the governing body of men's tennis, tried to spice up the ranking system by adding a "champions race" that charted players on their calendar-year performance, but the players, tournament directors, and fans still pay more attention to the old system.

A player earns more ranking points when he wins a match at one of the bigger Masters Series tournaments than he does at the smaller International Series events, and even more points when he wins at a Grand Slam. Winning one of the four Grand Slam tournaments — the Australian Open, French Open, Wimbledon, and the U.S. Open — is worth 1,000 points. Winning one of the nine Masters Series events is worth 500 points, and capturing an International Series is good for 175 to 300 points, depending on the amount of prize money in the tournament. I started 2004 ranked No. 29, and now, as Master Series Madrid begins, I'm No. 23, still 5,285 points behind the world's No. 1 player, Roger Federer.

Let me just say a few more words about rankings and perception before I tell you about Madrid. When I was 18, I really thought I was going to follow in the footsteps of Sampras and Agassi and become a consistent Top 10 player. I had the hunger, but I didn't follow through with the results. So when I turned 20 — even though I was at No. 80 and the youngest American in the Top 100 at the time — I thought, "Sampras won the U.S. Open when he was 19, a year younger than I am now. I'm pathetic." I felt like I was under-achieving, big-time.

Then five years later, when I'd reached No. 18, I kind of took it for granted. Even after all those years of struggling,

— with my ranking hovering somewhere between 40 and 80, I didn't think anything of it at all. Less than one year later, after I had endured my eight-month 21-match losing streak, and I was playing in a Las Vegas Challenger tournament — the upper minor leagues of pro tennis — I finally broke out of the torpor I was in and panicked. I was looking at a ranking list, and when I couldn't find my name I broke out in a cold sweat. I thought I had dropped to somewhere between Nos. 170 and 180, but I was actually No. 237!

I was in such a state of shock that I went out the next day and lost 6–0, 6–1, in the first round to Jimy Szymanski of Venezuela, ranked even lower than me at No. 294. The next tournament — in Burbank, California, the home of the *Tonight Show* — I started my long four-year road back to the Top 20. I beat Neville Godwin of South Africa and Thomas Zib of the Czech Republic, then lost to this 18-year-old kid from my hometown of Boca Raton named Andy Roddick. I remember thinking, "Roddick's doing really well. He's made it to the semifinals of a Challenger." In less than three years, Roddick would win the U.S. Open singles championship and become the number one player in the world.

Masters Series, Madrid

Madrid is the capital of Spain, a city of many outstanding features, but I arrive with one mission: Tennis Masters success. I want to advance to my first Masters final. I've already been in three Masters semifinals in Indian Wells, Miami, and Monte Carlo, so I'm seeking new heights.

Madrid has as much or more traffic than New York City. Cars are everywhere, gridlock as far as the eye can see. It takes 15 minutes to go a quarter mile, but it's got beautiful,

Old World architecture, and like New York, once you reach your destination the fun begins, whether you're going to a restaurant, soccer game, bullfight, or even the Tennis Masters Madrid.

I arrive at the tournament hotel, unfamiliar because it's not the one from last year, and I find it very modest. The rooms are small and not particularly fashionable, Spanish style. Some of the players are upset, calling it a decorated dump. My traveling coach, T.J. Middleton — a former doubles player on tour — and I go directly to the tennis courts. It's only the third year of the tournament, and the complex is a large, multi-building indoor structure lacking any glamour. It looks more like a construction site, and we have to walk over rocks and dirt to get to the entrance of the players' lounge, where we receive our credentials and a security photo-ID.

As we finish checking in, who do we see walking toward us but Mr. Andre Agassi, otherwise known as "AA," rockstar tennis hero turned family man, history chaser, Energizer bunny. At 34, Andre is showing scant signs of slowing down. He missed getting to a Grand Slam final in 2004 for the first time in five years, but he's still in the Top 10 — the oldest player to be in such rare air since Jimmy Connors was at 36, in 1988.

I've known Andre since I was 18 and I warmed him up for his quarterfinal match against Jim Courier at the 1992 U.S. Open (Andre was 22 years old). A couple of months later, Nick Bollettieri, Andre's coach at the time, flew myself and another top junior player Lex Carrington to Las Vegas. Our mission was to practice with Andre, and get him training and motivated for his upcoming Davis Cup matches against Switzerland. He had just had wrist surgery, and was feeling lethargic.

Andre had won Wimbledon that year, but then had totally lost his marbles. He started to tank matches, losing to Brad Gilbert in the first round of the Paris Masters, 6–1, 6–2. Andre's right-hand man, who was driving a Corvette, picked up Lex and me at the airport. It was funny. The guy looked (he had long, dyed blond hair with earrings hanging down from both ears), talked, and even walked (in pigeon-toed Nike-clad ministeps) exactly like Andre.

On the first day, we practiced for 30 minutes, and then Andre said he'd had enough, handed Lex and me three $100 bills each, and gave us the keys to an Acura — probably his maid's car — and said, "Go have some fun in the casino." Lex was this huge black kid who was 18-going-on-26. He used to hang out with Mike Tyson. He and I went down to the casino, and in one hour, lost all the money Andre had given us.

So Lex went back to Andre's house and asked him for more money, and this time Andre gave him eight $100 bills and the keys to his Porsche. At practice the next day, Andre cut it short after 15 minutes. Bollettieri was kissing his butt. Andre was trying out a new racket — a Yonnex — and he wasn't happy with it. He kept yelling at Nick, the racket representatives, and his parents, "Get the hell out of here!"

On our last day in Vegas, Andre got into more of a groove and practiced for a full 45 minutes, which apparently was a lot for him in those days. On our last night, Andre invited us back to his house, where we played pool, ate pizza, and he showed us his Wimbledon trophy. Being flown out to Las Vegas at 18 and meeting Andre was like letting a three year old go to Michael Jackson's spread, "Neverland." Whatever Andre did, I was like, "Go brother. You're the man." Vegas and Andre's house — his surreal world at 22 — felt like a Disneyland for adults.

T.J. and I greeted Andre and his coach, Darren Cahill, an Australian. I never know what to expect with Andre. Since meeting him that first time, my rapport with Mr. Nike has always been on and off, hot and cold, as unpredictable as the weather; so I am naturally on guard.

I have had a few other run-ins with Andre. I spent some more time with him when I was 19 and had received a wild card to play in the qualifying tournament of the ATP event in Scottsdale, Arizona, in 1994. We practiced before the tournament began, and then Andre took a couple of guys in his entourage and me to lunch at TGI Fridays. He was driving a big black Suburban he called the "Black Bitch," and I sat in the back watching *Aliens* on one of the three screens while Andre flew around Scottsdale like Jeff Gordon. At Fridays, Andre ordered a chicken sandwich and fried calamari, and I thought, "This guy's roots. He's worth eight million dollars and he's eating fried calamari at Fridays?"

Andre knew the waitress. She was a hot girl. I was eating something light because I had just consulted a nutritionist, and she had told me to stay off fried foods. Andre wanted to know if I'd ever eaten fried calamari before, and I said, "No."

Then he got this disappointed look in his eyes so I changed my answer, "Well, I might've tasted it once or twice."

"Here," Andre said, "have some of my calamari." When I declined, he started calling me a "wussy," and shaking his head like he couldn't believe I wasn't ever going to try the calamari.

After lunch, we drove back to his hotel suite and I went into Andre's room with him and watched a tape of him playing Markus Ondruska the previous year at Scottsdale. Agassi told me he was on a diet, but then he started eating Cheez

Whiz on crackers. After a while, one of his buddies came into the room and said, "Hey, Brooke's on the phone." Andre went into the other room and never came back.

Four years later, in 1998, after I'd just had my best win as a pro, beating Patrick Rafter, who was No. 4, Andre called me "a journeyman." It was in Miami, Florida, and we were to meet the next day in the third round of the Masters event. Andre had skidded to No. 141 in 1997, and was in the midst of making his great comeback to No. 1 by 1999. He had this to say about me: "If you've spent five, six years on the tour and haven't broken the Top 50, you're a journeyman. He should be ranked a lot higher than he is. I've always given him nothing but respect. I think he's a real good player. I think he would be a heck of a lot better player without his dad."

I thought it was rude of Andre to call me a journeyman. I had a lot of trouble with the meaning of that word. At the time, I was ranked No. 44 and I'd been in the Top 80 for four years in a row. I felt for him to call me a journeyman was degrading and arrogant on his part. And not just to me, but to every player ranked at my level or lower. A journeyman, to me, is a guy who's been on the tour for a number of years and has never broken the Top 100. Andre had an Oedipus complex. He'd had a lot of problems with his father, and I think he didn't like the fact my father was my coach.

But in 2001 — while I was in the midst of making my own comeback — Andre invited me to his new house outside San Francisco, where he and his new wife, Steffi Graf, gave me some pointers on the court, then served filets mignons and margaritas. We sat and watched *Jeopardy* on television, and Steffi kept telling me, "You have to be positive, Vince. Be positive."

So, like I said, I never know what to expect from Andre, but in the situation in Madrid — sort of like greeting people you're not sure about at a cocktail party — the good cheer overrides any possible friction, and we shake hands. The key here is that Andre and I are still competitive on the tennis court. We've played each other five times in our careers, and Andre's won three of those matches. But I've won the last two. So no matter the state of our personal history and relationship, there is always an outer guard we keep up. It's almost inherent as a professional tennis player. We exchange small talk on simple matters. I ask Andre what hotel he's staying at, because I certainly know it isn't the tournament hotel. Of course — where else? — Andre is staying at the Ritz.

Andre tells us about his arrival in Madrid, and how he lost his luggage at the airport. I think to myself, "Andre Agassi? Lost luggage? AA flying commercial airlines again?" All these particulars didn't add up, Andre must be telling us a joke. But no, Andre explains how he even had to go to the local Nike warehouse in Madrid, where he was fitted with bare minimum tennis gear. And bare it was, the sizes being so small I wanted to ask Andre if his three-year-old son had lent him the shirt he was wearing. Well, maybe that's stretching it a bit, but his shirt also needed stretching.

Our little visit ended with an agreement to practice the next day at 10 a.m. on the stadium court. Now, with the exception of uttering some faint hellos under our breath at different tournaments, I hadn't spoken or practiced with Andre in a few years. I had seen him in an exhibition event in the fall of 2003, where he brought his father, Mike, but I exchanged more words with his father than with Andre. Mike was telling me how great a comeback I was making, which was cool to hear coming from a legend's father. But now I steeled myself, because I knew that Andre in his resurrection had changed his practice habits. Stepping on the court to practice with Andre Agassi for one hour could be harder now than playing a best-of-five match against many players.

The next morning, I step onto the stadium court at 10 and Andre's already there. Andre practices now with more focus than the Canon cameras he does ads for. Even more focus than I had on the leggy models who were debuting that year as ball girls at the Madrid event. The new Andre is relentless during practice, almost never taking breaks, and drinking only water as opposed to energy drinks. He's like a machine.

We start by hitting down the middle of the court. I take pride in my ground strokes, as they are the main reason for my success, but against Andre, on this day, I feel like a hockey goalie deflecting a blizzard of shots with my ankles and hands. Except I don't have the padding, which I could use after Andre's balls hit the line and devour my every reflex. I try to change the pace using a lofty-type ball with more spin. Andre quickly takes it on the rise and smacks a winner, saying, "Don't throw that crap around here," a joking comment intended to lighten things up, but at the same time with some edge thrown in.

Hitting with Andre starts to weigh on my aerobic conditioning because of the power, consistency, and timing of the drill. After 30 minutes of grinding, we decide to hit volleys. Now, hitting volleys against Andre, that's an experience I hadn't had in a long while. Nobody generates drive on the ball like Andre. It's like taking batting practice at 100 mph plus, only you feel like you're standing on the plate facing a wired, crazed ball machine. There isn't much time to react. It's pretty amazing, actually. After I save my life a few times, we finally hit some serves and begin to play a set.

Agassi is a tempo player. He plays fast and viciously, cutting time from your life on court. He loves to ambush his opponents, getting off to a fast start and then punishing you continually. He goes up 4–1 in the set and is cruising, so I decide to get a little more physical and play more powerfully, and I turn the tide on Andre and get back to 4–5. At which point, Andre serves out two aces, and takes the set in a good battle, and great practice, overall.

Andre doesn't speak too much on court — he'll make the occasional humorous comment — but he gets the job done. He mentions the way I hit my backhand — he seems intrigued by it — and praises me for its simplicity of motion, and urges me to continue hitting it that way. But nothing else, and we exchange thank-yous and go our separate ways.

I've always been straightforward and courteous with Andre, but I've never felt totally myself. Again, I think it's because we compete against each other — and I know that he speaks his mind and can be somewhat harsh in his assessments. So "let it be," I've decided. Andre's cool, and has generally been good to me. So who cares if sometimes I'm not sure where he's really coming from. When all is said and done, I look for the good in people, and Andre's okay with me.

I shower and change, and ask for my lunch ticket at the hospitality desk. But when I go and drop off my laundry, something peculiar happens. Standing behind me in line, dropping off his laundry, is the Vegas slugger himself. Agassi again, like a marine standing in line for his eggs and grits. I've never in 12 years on tour seen such a sight. I've never really given much thought to how stars take care of their petty rituals, but I would've expected a housekeeper at the famed Ritz to dry-clean and iron Andre's every wristband. Lost luggage, manual laundry drop-off: the name Andre Agassi doesn't automatically pop into my head. But it's actually really nice to see; humility is a great gift.

I walk upstairs into the lunchroom. It's a nice setting — about 15 tables — only players and coaches and their close friends who have photo-ID credentials. I order my spaghetti and grilled chicken — good carbs and protein — and I go to the buffet table for some extra goodies. I take a piece of fruit and a mini box of cereal named Smacks. There are no bowls, so as I wait for my meal, I take a spoon and scoop up the cereal and eat it dry, just for kicks. Then I swear I hear an echo behind me, saying, "Hey, I've never seen anybody eating dry cereal out of a box with a spoon before." I turn around and guess who? It's the guy who's been following me around since yesterday afternoon, the compadre, the tennis Sinatra of our day, Andre Agassi.

I laugh and say I'm being stupid. Afterwards, I think there's no question Andre's got personality, he's always noticing something or someone and pointing it out in a humorous way. The locker room always perks up when Andre enters it. Another player told me later that he saw Andre taking his used lunch plate back from the waitress so that he could bring it up to the counter himself.

After lunch, I hit for another hour with my coach, then went for a massage. Later, I visit the players' lounge to check email and relax. The players' lounge, in a nutshell, consists of leather sofas, chairs, dim lights, Xbox video games, a pool table, computers, and flat-screen TVs for match viewing. Mostly it's the players' entourages — their girlfriends, wives, trainers, agents, and family — who occupy it. The players rarely hang out there, but it becomes the entourages' second home during the tournament, a place to interact, be in the scene, and talk business. Another player once told me that the players' lounge can serve as a gauge for how attractive a female is. For example, if you think a girl's pretty, is she so pretty that you would bring her to the player's lounge where all the players can scrutinize your conquest? It sounds crazy, but players are competitive from A to Z, and we are constantly thinking about our opponents — even how attractive their girlfriends or wives are.

I'm back at the hotel at about 5 p.m., and what do I do now? My match isn't until the following night, when I play the 7:30 p.m. headline match against the young and surging Spaniard, Rafael Nadal. I think, "Spadea needs a haircut." I always feel like I play and think better when I'm clean-cut and shaven. It's probably one of those superstitions, but once I think it, I have to follow through on it.

But five in the afternoon is also my snack time. Ever since I've been working with this new nutritionist, I eat five meals a day, and only particular foods. It's such a great way to live, knowing what's good for you and what's not. But here's the catch: I'm used to grocery stores stocked with American foods. Trying to get a turkey sandwich with a salad in Spain isn't easy. I surrender to a toasted ham and cheese with fries. I don't eat ham, but in Spain, ham is like our chicken or turkey. They eat it here for breakfast, lunch, and dinner. Even for 5 p.m. snacks, ham is the desired morsel, but I take the ham out and eat the good-old grilled cheese with ketchup. It's light cheese, not the healthiest, but it will have to do.

Following my snack, I race down the street to find a haircutting place, modest and efficient. As I walk up to the shop, a striking blond exits. I'm impressed. "Yeah," I think, "good enough to take to the player's lounge." So seeing as how I have been out of touch recently in the girl department, thanks to my focused tennis ways, I decide to practice my Spanish — or should I say Spanglish — on her. In a stuttering, unrehearsed voice, I ask, not so intelligently, where I can get a haircut. Seeing as how her hand is still on the door, and I am approaching it, it doesn't come out sounding either smooth or legit. But the question's so ridiculous, she laughs and points to the place we're standing in front of.

I tell her it was the only thing I could think of saying. Then I tell her I'm a tennis player here in Madrid to play in the big tournament. We exchange numbers, and I proceed to get my haircut. I go back to the hotel, happy with my little victory, and get ready for dinner. As I walk up to the elevator, I merge with Marat Safin, the 6-foot-4 Russian standout and 2001 U.S. Open champion. Marat is wearing a black leather jacket, jeans, and a Jack Daniels baseball cap.

He asks me who I play and I tell him, "Nadal, the 18-year-old Spanish sensation. He won his first-round match today." Both Safin and I, as seeded players, have a bye in the first round. Marat says everyone will be watching my match — as well as his — because he plays another Spanish upstart named Feliciano Lopez.

"We'll both have the crowd against us," Marat says. Then he says he is on his way to a big European soccer match — Real Madrid, with Ronaldo and many other soccer stars playing. I'm not up on soccer knowledge, but I'm surprised to see Marat off and running to a soccer game when the tournament has already begun. Typically, when you're prepping for a major tennis week, you don't do things like take in concerts, sporting events, or movies. But Marat marches to his own tune.

T.J. and I go out for an atypical Spanish evening: Planet Hollywood and Starbucks. Hey, I'm feeling deprived of my fajitas and American-style latte. I get to bed early and wake up late — I like to get in a good 10 hours of sleep a night, especially when I'm playing a match the next day. I'm not used to playing night matches, though, or being the headline match of the evening. Tennis players are creatures of habit. We like our matches to begin at the same time that we usually practice, in my case either at 11 a.m. or 2 p.m. The next day I practice at 11, go have lunch and then try to stay off my feet. At 4 p.m., I go back to the Starbucks — my favorite place to hang out before a match — and stay loose.

In Spadea vs. Nadal, we have old vs. new, unheralded vs. heralded, American vs. Spaniard, shorthaired vs. longhaired — and 10,000 Spanish tennis fans screaming for him to win. The only person in the whole place rooting for me is my coach. I've never played this kid, who is rising fast, already No. 42 in the world, but I'm a confident man and experienced. I take the first set, but every point is a grind. Nadal hits a very heavy ball, lots of spin, and it begins to take my legs out from under me. He's tired me out, and wins the second set 6–4.

The third set is a battle. I'm already fighting a bad cold that started a few days before, so I'm running low on fuel. I get down a break in the third set, but I refuse to back down — fighting even the crowd, including a famous soccer player named Raul, who is trying to intimidate me by standing up in his front-row seat and pumping his fist at me after every point Nadal wins. The atmosphere only gets me more amped to make a comeback, and I do. At 12:30 a.m. I close out the match with a down-the-line, backhand winner. At last, Spadea does it again.

I feel relieved and vindicated, especially when I hear later that after Nadal won his first match, he had already started talking about facing Agassi in the third round, completely looking past me in the second. If you mess with the bull, Rafael, you get the horns. Finally, Spadea vs. Agassi, the two comeback stories, the two elders, the two practice partners, set for the stage the following night at 7:30 p.m. Prime time once again.

I go through my same routine of the day before, and when nighttime arrives, the war is on: the A-Train against the Italian Gladiator. This is my chance to even the score in our series. After practicing with him, I feel it works to my advantage having seen his sharply hit and perfected strokes, especially on the indoor surface.

Court surfaces are one element in tennis that is unique in our sport. We play on rubberized hard courts, concrete hard courts, both green and red clay courts, grass, and indoor-carpet courts. I don't think many fans realize the tremendous significance each court surface has for an individual player's psyche or game. Surfaces make a huge difference in the way the ball bounces, in footwork adjustments, and in the favoring of certain shots, serves, volleys, ground strokes, slices, and topspins. Everything is affected by the surface, and players have to adjust their game accordingly. Every now and then you find the legendary player who can play well on all six surfaces, but for the majority of pros, the level of their game rises and falls on each different surface.

In Agassi, I happen to be playing a legend who has won all four Grand Slams on different surfaces, the only player in the history of the game who has done that. When Don Budge, Maureen Connolly, Rod Laver, Margaret Smith Court, and Steffi Graf won their Grand Slams, the Australian Open was played on grass and not its current hard rubberized surface. Indoors happens to be a surface that no Grand Slam event is played on, but Agassi still excels on it, and it is my worst surface because it doesn't give me much time to develop a point. It's bang-bang tennis, whoever draws first blood usually wins. Sampras, Boris Becker, Federer, and Agassi are the bangers who love playing indoors, but nonetheless, I'm feeling confident going into the match.

When Andre Agassi walks up to you, there is a certain aura about him right away that says, "star quality." First off, he is always wearing black — whether it's tennis clothes or street clothes, he drowns himself in all-black outfits. Adorning at least one ear — his left — is an earring. His face is freshly shaved, as are his head, legs and who knows what else. His eyebrows are the only evidence of hair follicles anyone can notice. It all creates a smooth vibe when combined with the hard edge provided by the all-black clothing, the earring, and the shaved body. The vibe is like Hollywood-meets-the-rock-music-world, and it lands with a tennis bag on its left shoulder.

He's not the tallest man I've seen. I'm five-eleven and I feel I've got him on the height chart. But physically, he is built like a rock, his upper body chiseled and substantially broad compared to his frame, and legs toned to match an anatomy poster. He has a thin body type, but he has benched and drenched himself in the gym until a fight-day Roy Jones Jr. popped out.

At 6 p.m., I'm on the practice court with Safin. Marat is fun and easygoing, making jokes, talking about parties, women, and how he's been cutting loose lately. It's just what I need — Marat's joviality — to keep me loose for the big match. Andre can be fun in practice as well, but he clearly draws a line between giving social commentary, like Marat does, and being a serious champion. When practicing with Andre, players know there is only a certain amount of wiggle room to navigate.

After a 30-minute practice session on center court with Marat, I go back to the locker room feeling under the weather. For the previous three days, I'd been suffering from a minor upper-respiratory infection, with a sore throat, excessive coughing, aches and weakness, and a general feeling of disorientation. But I'm playing Agassi for the first time in five years — and after the Category 5 hurricane my career had been through in the past four years, wild horses, as they say, couldn't keep me off of that stadium center court.

The previous night, after the Nadal battle, I got to sleep at 2:30 a.m. but as a pro tennis player, I've learned how to overlook, overcome, and push through adversity — whether it is a matter of health, equipment, or something else.

The Spanish television station broadcasting the match wants us to walk out onto the court at 7:30 sharp. I stand behind the A-Train and try to keep up with him as he walks in his usual hyper, fast-forward slightly pigeon-toed gait, glaring like Seabiscuit coming out of the blocks. Here I am, on the official walk out to the stadium center court, and I'm already playing catch-up.

Six security guards surround us walking down the tunnel, like we are in the line of fire, ready to make a presidential campaign speech, or like it's a U2 pre-concert walk. When we reach the entrance, they announce Agassi's name first, and he marches out to a cascade of deafening cheers. The follow-up announcing of my five-syllable name produces talk and anticlimax from the approximately 10,000 fans — with the exception of, again, T.J., and also, Maria, the Spanish blond from the hair salon.

I'm not exaggerating, she is A-level material. Maybe I wasn't Brad Pitt to her, but upon hearing that I was playing Andre Agassi in prime time, I had more of a Brad Pittish quality to me than the stumbling, dubious fellow who approached her on the street two days before. So, of course, she is fire-hot and totally in attendance tonight. Who knows, I think as I look over at her — maybe Maria is also secretly rooting for Agassi. Players on the tour have an opportunity to meet a lot of women from week to week. I don't make a habit of this — although I do have my stories. Tennis stars aren't like rock stars, but depending on the player and his personal motivation, whether you want to call them groupies, roadies, female acquaintances, or camp followers, there is an overabundance of fond female fans and ample opportunity to score off the court.

Back to the match. I am captured in the moment, my moment: shining lights, enthusiastic fans, a full crew of linesmen, new balls, all the water and energy drinks I can stomach, the works. Sometimes, when I'm on the practice court and sweat is dripping from my nose, and I feel sick to my stomach from the tortuous, monotonous drill and I feel like I can't run to another ball, I ask myself why it is I do this? Where is the justice? Where is the satisfaction? Well, it's times like these, playing Andre Agassi in the third round of a sold-out event in Madrid, a good-looking blond on my side, that makes all that work I do feel worth it.

And now, as I take my final step to my chair at courtside and lay down my bag, a stunning, flawless female runs up and asks me if there is anything I need. She is six feet tall, and her waist is about the width of a pencil; yeah, the infamous model ball girls — only in Spain. I'm impressed with the models' ability to learn the ball-girl system as quickly as they have. As a former ball boy myself, I know it's not rocket science, but there is an education to it, and you need to be smooth. The girls here are almost smooth — there's the odd delay here and there, but overall, they're a success.

I start the match with an easy service hold and I quickly go up break point on Andre's serve. But I miss an easy backhand, my best shot, and it turns downhill and treacherous from that point on. I lose six consecutive games. Andre is so skillful off both wings. He swings you wide with the serve, takes a backhand at the height of the bounce, and hits it aggressively to the other coast (what's known as "coast-to-coasting" you), and he puts me on a string like a yo-yo, with no defense but to try to hit with Pete Sampras–like running forehands and somehow get back in the point. But I don't hit running forehands as well as Pete Sampras, so I begin to drown in the punishing tide of Agassi's forehand inside-out winners.

Even if he misses once in a blue moon, and I win the point, I am fatigued and worn out, especially as the match moves on. My aggressive shots — struck prematurely — begin to sail long, and my defense, slow and inadequate and decreased further by my illness, makes me hit weak returns. They become perfect setups for Andre's crisp and brutal put-away shots. After 58 minutes of one-sided tennis, I feel like a wounded gladiator, with no shield, plastic silverware, and a baritone cough. My self-esteem feels lower than that, and as we shake hands at match's close — 6–3, 6–1 — Andre doesn't say much, something to the effect of "tough luck," and I walk dejectedly back to my chair.

Andre steps back onto center court to an Elvis ovation. He blows kisses and bows to the elated Spaniards. Meanwhile, I do my impersonation of the quasi-gallop Andre uses to get off the court. I'm frustrated, and as I make my way back to the locker room, I reach into my bag and grab my mobile phone so I can take a picture of myself at that moment. Later, I'll want to see what I looked like after Andre crushed me. It might serve as motivation so this will never happen again.

In the locker room, I hear the media organizer ask Andre how much time he needs before his press conference. Andre tells him five minutes. Agassi is known for never stretching before or after a match or practice — or for getting many massages — which are imperative for most athletes. I asked him once if he ever stretched, and he said, "Of course I do." Then he sarcastically took out his wallet, dropped it on the floor, bent over to pick it up, and said, "OK, I'm done stretching."

Andre had hardly broken a sweat during our match. After his interview, he just picked up his bag and walked out, disappearing into the Agassiland he lives in every day. I was sitting in the locker room, plotting my next move, filled with doubtful, pensive thoughts, as is usual when I lose. I still believe that one day I can achieve that quality that people look at and admire about Agassi as he walks out of a stadium. It won't be because I have a lot of money or fame, but rather, like Agassi, because I have something more, something deeper, more compelling. They will look at me with respect.

Oh, and if anyone is curious about what happened with Maria, after the match, she briefed me that I had mispronounced her name. It was really, "See ya! Wouldn't wanna be ya." Oh well, I guess everybody loves a winner.

Anyway, I got a lesson and a rap out of Andre blitzing me:

Hey, it was like a dream, center court against Andre Agassi, It's like coming out a limousine, used to read about him in Tennis Magazine, I took my time though, hit my forehand slow, rapping to girls on the road, is this life getting old? Living away from home?

Not at all, back against the wall, taking out Nadal, models throwing me the balls, they're six feet tall, waists are small, and Vince giving them a call, but first back to the compadre, Mr. Andre, turning in his laundry, the responsible padre, what is he like? Spadea on the mike, telling you the life, of a hero who's tennis's Robert DeNiro, making all the zeros, but now it's time for Vince's story, the U-turn for glory, from a dead end to the Top 10, I thought I told you in '01 that I'd be back on a big run, and I am, soon I'll have happier days than Richie Cunningham, you listening to the comeback kid, hasta luego, nice to know ya, Madrid.

Davis Cup Finals
(or Don't Sweat the Small Stuff)
Seville, Spain

I played the final two indoor tournaments of the 2004 season, winning matches in both Basel, Switzerland, and Paris, before losing to David Nalbandian of Argentina in Basel and Radek Stepanek of the Czech Republic in Paris, both in straight sets. It was a little disappointing because I had started off the fall indoor season strong, reaching the semifinals in the tournament in Lyon, France. My 2004 season did not end in Paris, though.

The Davis Cup is tennis's version of golf's Ryder Cup, except teams from every tennis-playing country — 134 nations in 2004 — participate. The elite World Group of 16 teams including France, Spain, Australia, and even small but competitive tennis countries like Belarus compete for the championship. Since 1900, the Davis Cup has been held every year except during the war years of 1915–18 and 1940–45. Until 1974, the finals had been held exclusively in the United States, Great Britain, Australia, and France. But over the last 30 years, Sweden, South Africa, Russia, Germany, Italy, Czechoslovakia, and Spain have also hosted finals.

The Americans have won the most Davis Cup championships (31) followed closely by Australia (28), but an American team hasn't won one since 1995, when Pete Sampras nearly single-handedly won the three clinching matches on red clay in Moscow. I was on that team as a practice partner — which was a big honor for a 21 year old ranked No. 80 at the time. I remember Sampras's father, Sam, a mysterious figure on tour because he was very rarely seen, came to Moscow and yelled constantly at Pete when he served, "Keep your head up!"

In 2004, Patrick McEnroe went to the Davis Cup with his young crew of Americans: Roddick, Mardy Fish, Robby Ginepri, and the Bryan brothers. They beat Austria, Sweden, and Belarus to make the finals for the first time since 1997. I felt that I should have been selected as the second singles player after Roddick, for the second tie against Sweden — played in Delray Beach, Florida, the town next door to my hometown, Boca Raton — because I was coming off winning Scottsdale (where I beat Roddick in the semifinals) and reaching the semifinals of the Masters Series event in Miami where I'd beaten Safin.

All of the Americans' matches in 2004 had been played on home soil, but now the team would have to travel to Spain — Seville to be exact — to take on the Spaniards in front of the largest crowd ever to witness a sanctioned tennis match — 27,000 stomping and screaming fans.

As McEnroe was getting ready to pick his two singles players for the Davis Cup finals starting on December 3rd, I sent him this letter, dated November 11, 2004. I also mailed the letter to the Associated Press and *Tennis Week Magazine* so that not only McEnroe but every American tennis fan would know how I felt.

Pat,

I am writing this letter to you to express my desire to represent the U.S. in the upcoming Davis Cup final. As the No. 19 player in the world and third highest ranked American (behind only Andy Roddick and Andre Agassi), I have earned the opportunity to represent the United States against Spain.

Throughout the year, I have expressed my desire to represent my country in Davis Cup, a privilege I felt I earned earlier in the year with respect to previous Davis Cup matches. For reasons never articulated to me, and despite my solid results throughout the year, you have consistently chosen not to select me to the Davis Cup. Earlier this year, after having won an ATP tour title and reached the semifinals of the NASDAQ-100, you declined to name me to the Davis Cup team for the quarterfinal match against Sweden, as well as the semifinal match against Belarus. In bypassing me in your selection, you stated in a newspaper article (which I have enclosed for your convenience) that in order for you to select me to the Davis Cup team, I would have to demonstrate significantly better results or a higher ranking than the younger Americans in contention for the Davis Cup play this year.

I have done that this year, and, but for Andy Roddick, I am ranked higher than all of the other American players interested and available to play Davis Cup. On this point, I would like to highlight my record as compared to the other young Americans currently in contention for the Davis Cup final on red clay in Madrid [sic].

2004 ATP entry ranking (as of 11/7/04): Spadea (19), Dent (32), Fish (37). 2004 year-to-date wins: Spadea (40), Dent (32), Fish (28). Top finishes in ATP European red clay tour events:

Spadea (2004 Italian Open quarterfinals, 2003 Monte Carlo semifinals, 2003 French Open 3rd round), Dent (2004 Monte Carlo 2nd round, 2004 French Open 1st round), Fish (2003 Italian Open 2nd round, 2003 French Open 1st round).

I hope and expect that you will honor your word, and my hard work and achievements this year, and name me to the team for the final in Spain. Further, with regards to the integrity of the process, I feel that the Davis Cup selection should be an equitable one in which members are selected based on merit. Other irrelevant and unjust off-court factors such as age and friendships should have no bearing on the team selections. Having ended the year in the Top 20 and ahead of the other, younger Americans, my performance and ranking this year clearly demonstrate that my age has no bearing on my ability to perform at the highest level of our sport. Further, my record shows that age, unquestionably, should not be a factor in deciding the Davis Cup team. I know that I have earned a playing position on the American team in the upcoming Davis Cup final. I hope that you will make a fair selection and give me the opportunity that I have worked so hard to earn by recognizing my professional achievements this year in a selection to the Davis Cup team.

I appreciate your time and attention to this matter.

Sincerely,
Vince

I felt it was necessary to speak up, so I wrote the letter. It was in my heart to do so. I know Pat read it because he responded by saying how he appreciated that I was having a good season, but that he felt Fish had more Davis Cup experience and more firepower than me. Even so, Pat opted to take me, rather than Ginepri, along with the team to Spain, and he told me I would have a real chance to play if I beat Fish in the practices leading up to the finals.

Pat told the press, "I told Vince, 'I'm leaning towards playing Mardy, but that's not a lock.' I told him to come over with the attitude that he can play. So that will be my decision. I will make that decision a day or two before the tie begins. But as I said, Mardy's had the Davis Cup experience, so I will be leaning towards picking him."

I decided to go on Pat's word. Since becoming Davis Cup coach in 2003 — taking over for his brother, John, who coached only one year — Pat had changed his mind and played Fish over James Blake in the 2003 World Group playoffs against Slovakia because Fish beat Blake in practice. Fish went on to win a big match — coming back from one set down on red clay against Karol Kucera to win the first match of that tie. Fish showed his commitment and drive, and that's where McEnroe's deep allegiance and faith in him developed. The American team won against Slovakia on the road, which prevented us from dropping out of the World Group.

The USTA initially booked me to fly coach to Spain when everybody else — Roddick, Fish, and the Bryan brothers — were flying first class. I was offered one-tenth the amount that Roddick and Fish were getting. When I asked for only a 10 percent increase to the rather paltry sum I was offered, the USTA would only give me 5 percent. Needless to say, the amount was not large and in monetary terms, I certainly wasn't being treated like a member of the team, much less an actual playing member of the team, which I should have been.

Pat said, "I think what you're getting paid is enough for being a practice player, but I'm giving you the chance to possibly play." I felt like saying to Pat, "If you're going to dock me on the playing situation, don't also dock me financially, because I'm ready to play." But I kept my mouth shut this time, although I did get them to change my airline ticket from coach to first-class. Then because I had this sixth sense that something messed up might still occur, I kept a daily log of the practice games and matches played during the week leading up to the Davis Cup finals and Pat's decision on whether to play Mardy or me.

One reason why I love tennis so much is that it is the truest form of democracy in sports. If you win, you rise in the rankings and make money. If you lose, you either ask your parents for more money — if you have rich parents — look for a sponsor, or quit playing and find another job. There are no judges, coaches, or sports writers voting on player rankings and there is no team (except in Davis Cup and with doubles players), so there can be no dispute as to who is getting the job done and who isn't. Unfortunately, Pat didn't pay attention to the rankings or who won in the practice matches when he selected his finals team against Spain.

On November 28th, a Sunday, our first day in Seville, I did two-on-one drills in the morning and then beat Fish in three 11-point groundstroke games. We started to play a set and stopped at 2–2 games all. On Monday, November 29th, I did two-on-one drills in the morning with Roddick and Fish and in the afternoon I beat Wayne Odesnick, one of the two young practice players on the team, 6–1, and then won two tiebreaks after the set. Fish beat Alex Kuznetsov, the other practice player, 7–6. Kutz was winning easily, but then mysteriously started to play strangely, hitting ill-advised drop shots and playing impatiently. Hmm. Fish had lost to Odesnick earlier.

Tuesday, November 30th, I defeated Fish 6–1, 7–6(4) in two sets. I was up a break three times in the second set, 1–0, 2–1 and 5–4, serving for the match. Either way, I was the better player as he was struggling to make a match of it. All during the playing of the match, Roddick was on the sidelines encouraging Mardy and questioning my line calls. I wasn't too thrilled about Andy openly rooting for Fish when we were supposed to be playing to decide who would make the team stronger by manning the second singles spot. Pat stood in the background, saying nothing. Wednesday, November 31st, I lost 6–2 to Roddick, but was winning 4–1 in the second set when Roddick just walked off the court without saying a word and quit. I knew there would be some natural animosity when I accepted Pat's invitation to come and play for a singles spot, but I didn't expect blatant conflict.

Pat made his announcement on Thursday, December 1st, that he would go with Mardy and not me. Pat explained to me that while I was the better player in practice, he still felt Fish had a better chance to win. I had a hard time looking him straight in the face. Call Einstein to see if he has any suggestions on this one. Don't bother calling the police because the mafia paid them off, too.

When I look back and reflect on the details of my practice matches with Fish, I still cannot fully understand how Mac decided to go with Mardy. I beat Fish fair and square, but I don't think I could've changed his mind because he was already sold on Mardy. It was a political and sentimental judgment on McEnroe's behalf. I didn't get a fair shake.

I hadn't anticipated a situation like this. But once everyone knew who was playing the matches, things settled down and I felt passionate about helping the team win, even if all I could do was root from the sidelines. This was the job Pat appointed to me. If I had known that he had no intention of actually playing me, I wouldn't have flown 2,000 miles just so I could be a spiritual supporter for the team.

But since I was already there — once the actual tie began — the team (including myself) came together to fend for one another in any way possible under the extreme circumstances. The mammoth crowd of 27,000 for each day of the three-day weekend — they were mostly Spaniards; there were about 600 Americans in the crowd — the kryptonite red clay courts, and the fierce, opposing Spaniards on the other side of the net, turned out to be overwhelming. Carlos Moya and Rafael Nadal pumped their fists, thrived on every roar, and were fiercely united. The three-day final cup affair went by fast and furiously. Fish went down easily to Moya in straight sets in the first match. Afterwards, in the press conference, Moya questioned why McEnroe had selected Mardy to play over me, saying that while he thought he would have beaten me, I was a far superior clay court player than Mardy.

In the second match on Friday, Roddick courageously went down to the animated and emerging star, Nadal. Their match had all the tension and high drama of a World Cup soccer match with hearts and fire dominating the venue, from the players' emotions to every fan in the dome stadium.

On the second day, the Bryan brothers left us some salvation and Boston Red Sox-hope by winning their match. But Sunday turned out to be the final blow as a rejuvenated Moya — whose performance, particularly on clay courts, had dropped since winning Roland Garros in 1998 — handed Andy a four-set defeat. It wasn't pretty to watch us lose. I felt like I was wearing a straightjacket the whole time I sat on the bench, with my only reprieve coming when I got to clap on big points won by my teammates. I yelled and stood up on ovation-worthy points, giving my emotional best, but to no avail.

Everyone seemed drained in the locker room after the tie. To make it all the way to the finals, and then lose decisively weighed heavy on everyone's mind. It was December 4th and finally time to hang up the racket after a long year. Pat gave us our farewell speech, "Well guys, it sucked that we lost, but let's look at the positive. We had a great run until this point, and we should be proud of ourselves in a lot of ways."

Bob and Mike Bryan stood up and started chanting their support and agreement with Pat. I was sitting on the couch alone, Fish was sitting on a chair next to the table of food, and Roddick sat in a chair next to him. Both of them were still looking glumly at the floor, when suddenly Andy stood up, grabbed his shiny silver Davis Cup finalist trophy, and walked toward me and offered it up.

"Here Vince, I wanna give you this for being a team player," he said. "I'll wait until we win this thing to keep my trophy."

I chuckled, but at the same time I appreciated Andy's gesture. It was a classy, cool move, but of course, I didn't accept it. "Andy, thanks for the thought and kindness," I said, "but you earned this and you deserve to keep it. I had a great time here no matter what."

Andy and I shook hands homeboy-style and everyone started loosening up. We started playing some music, laughing, and then walked into the trainer's room to get massages. Relaxed faces replaced the frowns and hurt. I didn't see such a kind gesture coming from Andy — but even though he has this side of him that appears tough and uncaring, he also is a guy who will watch your back.

I had traveled to Spain to be part of something that I felt I had earned. I did what I thought I needed to do to make the playing squad and be a real Davis Cup player — but when the decision went against me, I still wore the USA hat with style, regardless of the fact that I was sitting instead of playing. I don't think Pat hates me, but we do not have much of a personal relationship — and he hangs out with the younger guys — so perhaps he felt more comfortable playing Fish over me.

What goes around comes around in life. I know how that works in my life. When I'm corrupt, things come back to test me and I'm more accountable the next time. I'm not saying I have any ill will toward Pat McEnroe. What I am saying is people with power have to exercise sound judgment when making their decisions, and in this case, I don't think Pat did.

PART I

ON THE ROAD

Auckland, New Zealand

A Qantas 747 airliner sets tire marks on the Auckland airport runway. Sweat is dripping from my forehead. I have both a backache and headache. For the past 14 hours after leaving Los Angeles International Airport — 14 hours in a machine 30,000 feet above a deep blue sea — I've been crammed into a coach seat. Now I've finally arrived in New Zealand, my eleventh trip to this part of the Pacific.

This is crazy. I'm restless, anxious, barely self-contained as I realize how far I have just traveled to play in a tennis competition. When you're on the tour for 12 years, more than occasionally you have what can only be characterized as Trips from Hell. I had occupied the last seat on the plane, 72H, and it didn't even fully recline. I felt like a packed sardine, knees to my chest, no elbow room, limited food and drink offerings. When we finally landed, I was dehydrated and delirious. This is just two days after I'd celebrated New Year's in L.A. with friends and family, making this trip more sentimental and emotional than most.

Spadea arriving in New Zealand, on New Year's I was dancing on the ceiling, now I'm squealing, appealing, praying and kneeling, but 2005 has begun, Vince gotta continue the run, gonna have more fun than when I turned 21.

This is the unglamorous side of a tennis professional's life. The travel is one of the main reasons you see so few players over 30 years old on the tour these days. When players start thinking of retirement, especially champions like Sampras and Pat Rafter, who have earned more money and glory than they could expect in ten lifetimes, it's the excessive travel that curtails their careers more than anything else. The time spent in airports, on planes, in taxis — and the delays of missing luggage and drivers who get lost on the way to the tournament hotel or courts — wears on one's stamina and patience. Björn Borg retired for the first time at 25; Sampras retired for good at the "old" age of 31, and Rafter, at 29.

This life of being constantly on the road, away from family and friends for ten months of the year — that's right, ten months is the length of one pro tennis season — gets to you every now and then. It's getting to me right now, and I'm preparing to play just my first tournament of the season. I'd played my last tournament of 2004 at the end of October, and then I was on the American Davis Cup team that played the finals into December in Spain. So I'd had less than one month of an off-season — if you can call practicing twice a day for two of those weeks and working out every day in the gym downtime.

Okay, so you're thinking, "What a spoiled brat this guy is. He gets to fly to New Zealand and Australia to play tennis, and he's complaining about it." But what some of you might not realize is that there's a major difference between taking a relaxing vacation and traveling to "go to work." This journey is costing me around $7,000 in airplane tickets, hotel rooms, and coaching fees for three weeks in which I will play two tournaments, one here in New Zealand, and then the big one in Australia, the first Grand Slam of 2005, the Australian Open. Usually, I also play the tournament in Adelaide before Auckland, but this year, because of my short off-season, I decided to skip that one.

I've made this exact trip 11 times now — no questions asked — having missed it only in 1993 when I was just start-ing out on tour, and in 1997 because I had a back injury. In 2002, I made the trip Down Under, but my slump had dropped my ranking so low I had to try to qualify for the Australian Open. After I lost in the qualies, I flew to play a lower-level pro tournament called a Challenger in Hawaii, where I beat Michael Chang in the quarters. It was my first win over the former No. 2 player in the world in five matches, and I never played him again because he retired in 2003.

Once I get here, there's not a lot of time to sightsee. It's just basically back-and-forth shuttles between the hotel and tennis courts. It'll be that way in every city I play in now for the next 40-plus weeks, in cities ranging from Indianapolis to Tokyo. Believe me, this isn't exactly the trip to New Zealand you'd want to win on *The Price Is Right*. At this point, I cer-tainly would have chosen the other showcase, the one with the new car. But I just read a mission trip to Mars on a space shuttle would take at least six months, so enough with the crying.

The good news is that I'm here and I *want* to be here. It's a new year to pursue my 2005 goals of making a surge into the Top 15 players ranked in the world. I'm setting new sights, trying to move into uncharted territory for myself. The Top 20 is the best I've ever achieved — I'm No. 19 right now — but I'm looking forward to moving up and making an impact in the Grand Slams, possibly making the semis or the finals of one or two, and make people wonder, "Can you believe this kid from the dirty south of Florida? Who's had such a roller-coaster ride both physically and mentally? He went into this tennis season and would not go away. Spadea is not dying, he's not fading; he's getting stronger as he gets older. How does this guy do it?"

I'm starting out in the Kiwi nation, the city of Auckland to be exact, a wonderful, cosmopolitan capital city. I'm greeted A-list style, by a chauffeur carrying a sign that reads, "Spada." Okay, missed it by one vowel, but at least I got the driver, right? My new coach — there will be plenty of time to talk about coaches later, because I've had about 30 since my father, Vincent Sr., stopped being my coach about five years ago — is Greg Hill, one of Nick Bollettieri's main men. Greg played on the pro tour for a four-year stretch in the mid-1980s, and his claim to fame is that he beat Agassi when Andre was, like, 16 and first coming up.

Greg and I get situated in the picturesque tournament hotel, just minutes away from the beautiful Viaduct Harbour, which was home to the 2003 America's Cup. From my room, there are fantastic views of the water, yachts, and islands nearby. Dozens of hip bars and restaurants line the water-front, and crowds pace through the area even as the notorious winds and occasional showers blow and drip.

But I'm not here to get too comfortable. I take a short two-hour snooze and then we set out for the courts. How do you make it to the semifinals of the Australian Open?

Practice my friend, practice! Except my right shoulder is sore — I played 80 matches the previous season, including doubles, and I might have overdone it, so I can't hit for too long.

JANUARY 11

The Auckland Open is a cozy, well-run, fun tournament to start the year off. I'm still having mixed feelings being here because of the short off-season. In one respect, I'm confident and eager to continue my run up the rankings — in 2004 I rose from No. 29 to No. 19 in the world — and I want to pursue new and heightened goals. I'd worked hard on and off the court in November and December, improving tennis techniques, quickness, fitness, nutrition, and mental conditioning. But on the other hand, the last tournament of 2004 ended on November 7th, and here I was back in full blast mode on the 6th of January. I would have liked to have another month off.

Three years ago, I started training some in Los Angeles during the off-season instead of in my native Florida, where I own a home in Boca Raton. After my ranking plummeted in 2000, I started working with Dr. Pete Fischer, the architect of Pete Sampras' game, and he has played an important role in my comeback. I started to believe in my skills again when I went to Fischer. I needed something new — some new blood — and a fresh and interesting way of playing.

I've always been a backcourt grinder, relying on my ground strokes and legs to beat opponents. Fischer is famous for developing Sampras' nonpareil serve, and his great frontcourt volley game. He taught me Sampras' service motion, and coached me to take more chances and end points quicker. He provided me with more artillery and better mechanics.

Fischer focuses on hitting the ball wide to a certain depth area. He says it's stupid to miss long, because even if the shot lands in, your opponent will probably be able to return it. You hit winners by taking people off the sides of the court, rather than hitting balls deep toward the baseline.

Because Fischer had been a pediatrician and was convicted of child molestation in 1997 — serving three years in a federal penitentiary — we had to practice at the courts in his housing complex in Rolling Hills, because he was still under probation. I had to drive about an hour and a half from my sister Diana's apartment in Hollywood — where I was staying — to practice under Fischer's tutelage.

Everyone's a strange cat in tennis. When I sought out Fischer, I felt I was getting the best person in the game to help me. Like an actor struggling with his craft, I called the Stella Adler of tennis. (Adler was Marlon Brando's acting coach.) I knew about Fischer's past, but I was in no position to be choosy. Not only had Fischer developed Sampras' game, he had helped him develop his attitude — and I needed an attitude change.

As I traveled to Challenger tournaments in 2001, playing in places like Tulsa, Oklahoma, Tyler, Texas, and Granby, Quebec, I would call Fischer before each match and he would give me my game plan. In two years' time, I'd regained my Top 100 ranking and began playing the main tour events in places like Wimbledon, Miami, and Monte Carlo.

But recently I've noticed a change in Fischer. He doesn't seem to care as much about how I do. I'm not sure if it comes from the way I've operated with him or just the way he's started dealing with the situation. I almost feel like he's decided, "Y'know, I've been with this guy for a few years, and he's only going to be so good. And that's not good enough for me."

About eight months ago, I started working out at the IMG

36

Academy run by Nick Bollettieri in Bradenton, Florida. Nick revolutionized the game back in the 1980s by developing ground-stroke kings in Jimmy Arias, Aaron Krickstein, Agassi, and Jim Courier. He's in his seventies now, but he's still passionate about tennis.

Bollettieri's is like a military school for tennis. "We start at nine o'clock in the morning," Bollettieri says. I like to start about 10 or 10:30 for my first practice of the day. But Nick wouldn't hear of it. "Show up at nine o'clock in the morning," he told me. "You hear me? You hear me. Okay, son, okay boy." He's a disciplinarian. He easily flies off the handle. "Oh, what the heck, son. You can't go around with that kind of back swing. You want it right here. No higher, alright, you hear me? Alright, boy."

Nick believes I should play more like Andre, by owning the baseline and striking first, dominating with big forehands and backhands. He put me up against two of his teenage players at the Academy and stood behind me yelling, "Get your racket back, get it back faster. You take it back from 12 o'clock to 9 o'clock. That's too long, son. You're wasting too much time. C'mon, move, move." Nick's instruction is always short and sweet. It's 15 intense minutes, and then he walks over to another court and comes back 40 minutes later to make sure that you're doing what he told you earlier.

So I am now at a crossroads in my game, somewhere between how Fischer wants me to play and the way Greg Hill, my traveling coach and a Bollettieri disciple, is telling me how to play. When I talked to Fischer about it, he said, "We know Agassi's style can be successful when it's being done by Agassi. But I don't see anyone who has been able to imitate him and have success. You mention David Nalbandian, but Nalbandian can't hit a backhand like Agassi. The difference between Nalbandian and Agassi is that if

Nalbandian wins eight more majors, he'll be tied with Agassi.

"Agassi does what he does because he's inside the court. You might be able to pick up the ball as fast as Agassi on your backhand, but nobody's going to hit the ball to your backhand. It doesn't make a lot of sense to me for you to look to put away a forehand shot if the ball is one inch inside the baseline. I'd much rather see you wait until you have a high forehand and then go in and clock it. You've got to look for the chance to move forward, Vince. You can't say, 'I can stay inside the court like Andre,' because you can't. The only other person who did it was (Jimmy) Connors.

"I've already told you what I think. You've gone as far as you're going to get being a pure defensive player, and you're never going to be a great offensive player, because at 30, you're not going to develop a weapon. You've got to maintain your defensive skills, and get enough offense so you can win a few more points that will translate to winning a few more matches. You're never going to be Top 10 in the world. Staying inside the Top 20, like you are now, should be your goal for the next couple of years."

I never like to be told that I've reached my peak. Agassi won five Grand Slam tournaments (three Australian Open, one Roland Garros, and one U.S. Open) from the ages of 29 to 33. Rod Laver swept all four Grand Slam tournaments in one year — a Grand Slam (something only Don Budge and he accomplished in the men's game) — at 31. Rocky Marciano won the heavyweight crown at 30, and held it for four years until he retired. I respect Fischer's opinion, but I don't want to work with a coach who doesn't believe in my abilities or my potential to get better.

With Fischer's and Bollettieri's competing strategies playing out in my mind, I step out onto the hard courts in Auckland for my first match of the 2005 season against

David Sanchez of Spain. Sanchez is mainly a clay-court player, but he's feisty and fit, and there is never a sure thing in men's pro tennis. I'm the No. 4 seed in the tournament — only Guillermo Coria of Argentina, Tommy Robredo of Spain, and Dominik Hrbaty of Slovakia are seeded ahead of me — so my match is the feature of the night session.

From the second the umpire asks, "You guys ready to go? Good luck," I'm all business. But before a tennis match actually begins, it's scary. When I first came up on the pro tour, before my matches, I used to think, "I'm in a scary world right now, and I hope to God I win." You don't know what's going to happen. All the questions are unanswerable at that moment. "What if I don't win? Where am I going to go after this? Why am I doing this? What am I trying to accomplish?"

It's the element of the unknown that gets to you, the fear of being out there naked, not knowing how the match is going to go, what points are going to be crucial to win, and more importantly, whether you can hit the shots on those big points? Have you prepared and worked hard enough, punished yourself enough? How fit are you? How well are you going to focus?

It's a very scary thing. And it's no less scary today than it was when I was 17. I think I'll know I've lost my passion and fire to play the game when I no longer feel scared before a match. Now I like that empty feeling of fear in my stomach, because I know that I want to win — I need to win — and I'm going to do anything to win, at any cost. When I have the opposite feeling before a match — "I've been here, done that" — I know I'm going to get sloppy and lose my concentration out there. I might let up and not get off to a good start. I might get annoyed and have a bad attitude, and then I won't have a good result. No, it's good to feel scared.

The match starts at 7 p.m., and by the time it's 7:48 p.m., I'm shaking hands with my Spanish opposition, telling him "tough luck." Tough luck, I'm thinking, but not for me. I had just recorded a win in 48 minutes by the score of 6–0, 6–0. No typos in that score; I'd won every single game of the match! I'd never double-bageled an opponent in my 12 years on tour. Winning in this fashion in the first match of the year is extremely rare and pretty eye-opening. The ATP officials at the tournament said it had been more than a year — Doha, Qatar, in the first week of January 2004 — since a 6–0, 6–0 match had been played on the pro tour. I played well, and Sanchez had had an off day. I won all the big, close points and that helped to make the final score so lopsided.

I'm going to sleep well in Auckland tonight.

JANUARY 12

It's nice for my confidence to know that I can vanquish another pro player so soundly, still I don't start out with a one-set lead in today's second-round match just because I won the first one 6–0, 6–0. I wanted to appreciate my feat, but not dwell on it too much. I needed to prepare and focus for my next opponent, Robby Ginepri from the U.S. Robby is a friendly, easygoing dude, a 22 year old born in Fort Lauderdale, Florida. He'd made it to the round of 16 at both the Australian Open and Wimbledon last year, and reached a career-high ranking of No. 23, but had slipped recently to No. 63. I've played him only once, last year on a fast, indoor hard court, and beat him in straight sets.

Ginepri's age cannot be used as an explanation for his slide in the rankings. When I started my precipitous drop, I had just completed the summer of 1999, in which I made it to the finals at Indianapolis and the round of 16 at the U.S. Open. I had attained my highest ranking, No. 18, and at 25, I seemed on my way to bigger and better results. But then I lost in the first round in six of the last seven tournaments I played in '99, and that snowballed into not winning another match until Wimbledon 2000.

Some so-called experts came out then and said they suspected I had reached my plateau in my early twenties. There must be something innate in humans that we love to see precious, precocious teenage wonders conquer the adult world with early success. It's a novelty to achieve the seemingly "impossible" at such a young age. Maybe this fascination with young achievers comes from a lifelong personal dream of ours lived vicariously through the young, rich, and beautiful star.

The majority of us don't want to get old. Old is bad, young is good, and this sentiment is only heightened in a sport like tennis, where a Boris Becker wins Wimbledon at 17, and great champions like Björn Borg and John McEnroe never won a Grand Slam title after the age of 25. It's not a healthy outlook, but it's alive and well and passed down from generation to generation.

At 30, people in the tennis world I live in consider me to be like a broken-down racehorse, old and unexciting. I don't overpower my opponents with 140-mile-per-hour serves, or flex my biceps, pump my fists, or lambaste umpires over bad calls. I have the feeling that even if I were to perform spectacularly — say, win the Australian Open — the simple truth is I live in a world that cherishes the protegé, the wunderkind, the 15-year-old genius (Donald Young, who turns pro before graduating from high school, or the 17-year-old gorgeous, tall, blond, Maria Sharapova, who beat Serena Williams to win Wimbledon) would make it seem like an aberration rather than a feat of great perseverance.

I know that regardless of age, I haven't won enough throughout my career to become a household name. My name is not foremost in the minds of the world's — or even American — tennis fans. A lot of people still think I'm from Spain because of my name and how I look (my father is Italian-American and my mother is originally from Colombia). I know that if I won more, people would learn how to pronounce my name (Spadea rhymes with *afraid-a-ya*) and spell it correctly, no matter how difficult it might be.

Leaving such thoughts behind — they don't help me on the court — it's Spadea vs. Ginepri time, the unheralded vs. the still-heralded (but the clock is ticking), my second-round match. It starts out with me breaking serve in the second game — only to give it right back — and after fighting a highly contested first set, I lose in straight sets, 7–5, 6–3. Naturally, I'm disappointed, as I am after every loss.

It's a surreal feeling to win a pro tennis match, but when I lose one, I immediately feel like, "Oh my gosh, my life is heading down the tubes." It feels like clouds have suddenly arrived overhead, and everything has gotten really dark. I feel lousy, and no one else seems like they're at their best, either. It's just a very down feeling. I feel like my life has hit a slide and I have to figure out what I'm going to do about it soon.

All excuses out the window, I tried my best tonight, but I didn't execute as well as I can. Robby evened the score against me in our match tally, and played so strongly that I felt almost like there was nothing I could do about it except go back to the hotel at the end of the match, mind my business, and get ready for Australia. Robby has matches where he plays great tennis, and then he has times when he gets into funks, loses his rhythm, and can't win a match.

Today he was on, but who knows how he'll play tomorrow. He needs to be kicked in the butt by a strong coach. Success came easily and quickly for Robby, and he took it for granted. He likes to have a good time off the court (he dated the British movie actress Minnie Driver, nine years Robby's senior, for around eight months last year), and his motivation and training are sometimes questioned by other players on tour. Ultimately, he doesn't have any huge weapons. Tennis players and coaches love to talk about "weapons," meaning shots that are big, decisive, and win points instantly. Pete Fischer is constantly talking about developing "reproduceable weapons" like Roddick's serve or Federer's forehand, that can continually win points. Instead, Ginepri has to always be on the ball, like a Michael Chang in his prime or a Lleyton Hewitt today, to grind out wins. Basically, he's a defensive player — which is not an insult. One of the greatest champions in the game, Mats Wilander, won seven Grand Slam titles playing this way. And when Ginepri's on, he can push with the best of them.

Today, he was able to do that against me. Sometimes in tennis, you just lose matches because the other guy has an on day, and you are slightly bothered by the weather, or your shoulder, or whatever. When that's the case, you just have to shake hands at the end of the match and accept the beating. How you recover can be the biggest factor in how well you play in your next match. In tennis, there's always next week — especially after the first week of the season — and the Open starts in only five days.

We will see you in Australia, come on now sailor, you're not yet a failure, stay positive, Vince, you are still the prince, ever since, you were intense, you climbed up the fence, so stay up, stay up, Spadea about to erupt, so please don't stop, moving up the ladder, girlies are starting to chatter, besides winning, nothing else matters, no dream of mine will be shattered, scattered, my wallet needs to be fatter, so stay up, stay up, Spadea about to erupt, so please don't stop, Robby had me walking in the hotel lobby looking for a hobbie, but who will be winning in the end? I'LL BE! YOU'LL SEE! U can't stop me, even if you rob me, so stay up, stay up, Spadea about to erupt, so please don't stop.

JANUARY 13
Melbourne, Australia

Melbourne is home of the 100th Australian Open, the first of tennis's four coveted Grand Slam tournaments. It's summertime in the third week of January, Down Under, mate, and Spadea's ready to bring the thunder, make people wonder. This outback island is so far away from the rest of the world — 15 hours by plane from Los Angeles — but it's a beautiful country, in particular the pretty and friendly city of Melbourne.

Melbourne Park, once known as Flinders Park, is the home of the Rod Laver Arena, a grand, state-of-the-art complex with numerous courts with great seating and viewing capacity. The two feature stadiums, Vodafone and Rod Laver, are both solid white and contemporary-looking. They are also both equipped with a retractable roof, ideal for rainy days. Other Grand Slam sites have entertained the idea of adding this asset to their stadiums, and Wimbledon will do so over their center court in 2008.

It's a Friday, and after arriving the previous night from Auckland, I organize a courtesy car, provided for the players by one of the major sponsors of the competition, to take me from my hotel to Melbourne Park for practice. As we draw closer to the grounds, my first sight is of the hundreds of tennis fans gathering around the entrance. They are waiting in line just to watch the qualifying rounds, as the main draw doesn't begin until Monday.

Australians are big tennis fans. The people express a huge interest in supporting their top men and women players. The guys are all looking their best, and the girls are in their tennis dress. It's a summer fest (we're in the southern hemisphere where our winter is their summer) and this is their precious major; there're big wagers, children and old agers, face-painted ragers, and Spadea checking his pager. With huge ticket sales, advertisements all over town, and a constant buzz throughout the city, I know I have arrived at the main event.

Not only does the Australian Open attract their local patriotic, enthusiastic, Pat Rafter–squealing, Lleyton Hewitt and Mark Philippoussis–obsessed fans to the action-packed courts, it also brings out fanatics from all over the world, coming in groups, performing cultish cheering, fiercely supporting their compatriots with every shot struck. There's match-point level applause from the first to the last point of most matches, which creates drama in each individual court and match. It's a typical day of intense summer heat, yet I find it pleasant to walk through the grounds.

I walk into the player's cafeteria, filled with coaches, trainers, families and friends, and of course, other players. This area is restricted to VIP-credentialed individuals. It gives us a welcome escape from pressure-filled matches, locker-room tension, and the crowded public areas. As I get my toasted panini sandwich and sit down at a table, a slender man wearing Nike clothes and tennis hat with small round sunglasses, walks up to me and greets me in a warm and familiar way. His name is Yuri Sharapov (add an "a" to the end of his name and you have Sharapova). That's right, this is the father, mentor, coach, and driving force behind the best thing that's happened to women's tennis since Hingis's precocious prowess, Kournikova's dimensions, Steffi's intensity, and Chris Evert's concentration.

Yuri Sharapov is the only person I know who's hungrier than Maria herself. Their combined wills set a unique example of a kinship between father and daughter that was so adamant it made tennis success a reality. Every time Maria steps on a court and Yuri sits down to watch her, they both show that steely will, and express it through skill and determination.

Behind closed doors, Yuri and Richard Williams (Serena and Venus's father) share the same personality. They're both extremely driven, won't-take-no fathers who have a desperate drive for their daughters to be No. 1. Richard gets up with his flashcards at Wimbledon, and always has his camera out snapping shots of Venus and Serena. He keeps his distance from the girls at tournaments, but he's always talking to the tournament employees. Yuri is different. He's always glued to Maria's side. He wears his intensity much more openly than Richard.

I got a chance to see this firsthand back in 2002, when Maria and I were both playing the tour event in Tokyo. I became friendly with Yuri during the week as the men and women played separate tournaments at the same site. He had remembered meeting my father and me at a Florida tournament years earlier, and struck up a conversation with me. Then he asked me to join him as he watched Maria play her match.

Maria was only 15 at the time and ranked in the 200s, but as I watched Maria play and lose a closely contested match, it was obvious her biggest weapon was her desire, her will, her killer instinct. She was not quite developed physically yet, her serve was undernourished, and her ground strokes were erratic, but she seemed like she had just graduated from Connors–Hewitt High School (if ever one existed). She was clearly destined for greatness, especially, and most importantly, in her own mind.

Yuri was constantly asking me what I thought of Maria's game and asking my advice on what event she should play the next week, looking for any edge or insight that might improve his daughter's chances of making it to the top. Even today, after she has been coached by Bollettieri and Robert Lansdorp, the Southern California tennis guru who constructed Tracy Austin's game, Yuri asks me about Pete Fischer and whether he could help Maria's serve. He's obsessed with Fischer. He'll always ask, in a sarcastic way, "How's Fischer doing?" I think he's pursued Fischer to work with Maria, but at the time, Fischer had an exclusive deal to work with no other woman player but Alexandra Stevenson.

As I finish my lightly toasted panini, Yuri and I exchange some more friendly tennis talk, but as soon as Maria arrives from the massage room, Team Sharapova (my former junior sidekick, Michael Joyce, is now Maria's hitting coach), swiftly moves its campaign out of the cafeteria and back to their hotel. I leave soon after, and brush past Mary Pierce and her brother, David, who are coming in. I virtually grew up with the two of them, spending countless hours on court with their father, Jim.

Mary has a calm and happy look on her face. She's a very positive person, but I know how hard she has worked dealing with all the blowups and demands of her controversial father. I have had some great tennis workouts and fun dinners with Jim, and found him to be a hardworking and confident man with a passion for his family and tennis.

Parental support is big in tennis, but it can lead to stardom or disaster. Tennis has gotten a bad rap for all of the domineering parents on the woman's side of game. But it's not the only game where parents go overboard. Hollywood's even getting into the act now, with Michael Lohan, the father of Lindsay, reportedly threatening to kill his family, and Joe Simpson, the creepy father of Jessica and Ashley, embarrassing himself.

There's a real discrepancy in professional tennis when it comes to the upbringing and early coaching of women and men players. Basically, the difference between how girls and boys develop into pros is like the difference between Borg's and McEnroe's court temperaments. In women's tennis, the parents are often overzealous, and in some cases, crazy. But it works. Girls usually need more nurturing growing up, and several big-time champions have been produced with domineering fathers serving as coaches for their daughters. In men's tennis, the guys are usually a little bit more independent emotionally, and that leads them to usually want to travel separately from their fathers.

I'm one of the few exceptions. My father coached and traveled with me for most of my junior career, and then as a pro until I was 25. It worked for a while, but then I needed to start calling more of my own shots. Taylor Dent's father, Phil, a former Australian Open finalist, coached Taylor for a while, but then Taylor moved on. His father has worked with many great players, including Michael Chang, and I'm sure he's a great coach, but when you're coaching your own son, there's always potential friction that builds up.

Jim Pierce, who also coached Mary, was reportedly often verbally and physically abusive to her during practice sessions and after defeats, although I never saw it happen. He was a tough dad and in 1993, was ejected from the French Open after he punched a spectator. The Women's Tennis Association (WTA) later banned him from all events until 1998.

But Jim Pierce is a classic man. I once asked him how he learned how to play and coach tennis and he said, "I went into a bookstore one day in North Carolina and picked up a book on tennis. I read the techniques, bought the book, and started teaching my kids tennis." There are times where he has gone way too far, but that is also probably the case with other tennis parents like Peter Graf, Stefano Capriati, Melanie Molitor — Martina Hingis's mom and coach — and Andrea Jaeger's dad, who was a former boxer like Andre Agassi's dad, Mike.

Chris Evert's parents came to every single big match she ever played. They didn't have a reputation for being bombastic, but they were sticklers for reserved behavior and tennis achievement. Karolj Seles appeared jovial and smiling in the crowd, and there were heartwarming stories about how he used to paint animated figures on Monica's tennis balls when she practiced as a kid. Monica developed her furious focus because of her dad's determination and his relentless practices. It's not always so black and white when it comes to who's a good parent and coach.

When I worked with Jim Pierce, he didn't encourage belligerence and confrontation. He was a great motivator, preaching about being a fighter on the court and never giving up. He believed in physically and mentally conquering your opponent by being in better shape, being stronger, and hitting deeper shots. Every conversation we had, Jim talked about what a dream it would be for me to win the French Open. He was obsessed with winning the French Open. He always used to yell at Mary and me to hit our backs with our rackets on our follow-throughs.

I briefly say hello to Mary and David and continue with my busy day. I've got two practices scheduled, at one o'clock, and again at five, massage and trainer appointments, a gym workout, some equipment refining, and a laundry drop-off. Then I hope to chill some. It's a nice job if you can get it, right?

I figure most people strive for economic security so that they can do whatever they want: retire, play tennis or golf, travel, get massages, and have other people do their laundry. Basically, that's my job description, and it just reinforces my appreciation of the good fortune I have had in life. I get to do what I love for a living and get paid to do it. Though there is a little more to it than just that, for sure. There are pressures, adversities, and challenges to overcome but I love taking them on. I've spent 25 years practicing to get to this, my ninth Australian Open, and I want to exceed my best showing, a quarterfinal appearance in 1999.

JANUARY 14

Before the Australian Open begins in a couple of days, I feel compelled to say a little bit about the three big Australian men's players of the last decade: Lleyton Hewitt, Pat Rafter, and Mark Philippoussis. They have dominated the headlines of Australian tennis because, since the 1960s and '70s — when the two great Aussie women players, Margaret Smith Court and Evonne Goolagong Cawley, patrolled the tennis scene — tennis has been pretty much an all-male affair here in the land of Oz.

I played against Hewitt in the 1998 quarters at Adelaide, his hometown in the south of Australia, when he was a 16-year-old wild card. Everyone was wondering how he got a wild card in the first place, because he was like No. 500 in the world at the time, and nobody had ever heard of him.

Some of the other Australian players were even mystified. He had just played a Satellite — an even lower pro tournament than a Challenger that has since been mostly phased out in favor of "Futures" — the week before Adelaide, and had lost to a nobody.

Anyway, it's a night match, center court, and I see this little guy with long blond hair who looks like a surfer walk out onto the court. I figure, "I'm in the semis. This kid is 16 and he looks weak, inexperienced, unrehearsed, and unpolished." The match begins and he's holding his own. He keeps on hitting balls in the court. I wasn't playing strongly or consistently enough to overpower him, even though I've got him outweighed by about 40 pounds.

I end up losing the first set 7–5, and now I'm thinking, "What does this kid think he's doing?" He didn't miss one shot long the entire set. My dad, who was coaching me, said after the match, "He missed into the net and he missed wide, but he never missed past the baseline." Whenever Hewitt won a big point he screeched out, "C'mon!" and punched the air with his fist. I thought that was a little annoying and cocky of him, but I didn't let it bother or intimidate me. I won the second set 6–3.

I had been working with Jim Pierce, so I was in great shape. I had been killing myself in training. I expected to steamroll the kid in the third set, but instead, he put his game into another gear and beat me soundly, 6–1, to win the match. The next day I was sitting eating breakfast with my dad in the players' cafeteria, and Brad Gilbert walked up to us and completely ignored me. He approached my dad and said, "Your son had Hewitt last night, but he choked. Andre will show you how to handle the kid tonight."

Brad was Andre's coach back then, and Agassi was playing Hewitt in the semis. I didn't listen to Gilbert much, because once, when I was walking off the court after losing a match 6–0, 6–2, he'd come up to me and said, "Good going. Good job, Vince." I thought he was either being really spiteful or maybe he got it wrong and thought I had won the match. Gilbert was always digging at my father, too, because he believed "you have to play the game before you can coach it," and my father had learned the game in a country club in Brockton, Massachusetts, when he was north of 30 years old.

Gilbert and my dad would go back and forth over who knew more about sports. Gilbert would tell him, "You're not in the same league as me," but my dad has a photographic memory, and could recite the batting lineups and averages of the Boston Red Sox, or tell you every statistic you ever wanted to know about Bob Cousy. There's this warped macho mentality on the men's circuit, even the coaches are constantly testing each other to see who knows more about tennis coaching or even arcane sports trivia. Getting back to Hewitt and Agassi, 16-year-old Lleyton playing in his second tour event (he had qualified at the 1997 Australian Open and was beaten badly in the first round), straight-setted Andre 7–6, 7–6, and then went on to win the tournament.

Hewitt has gone on to win more than $14 million in his career, along with a Wimbledon and U.S. Open title, and he's a true warrior on the court. He doesn't get fazed by disappointment or failure. He doesn't worry about whether he's hitting the ball great, or if he's winning or losing, he just enjoys the battle. The only other player who battled as successfully as Hewitt was Connors. Lleyton will never give up and he doesn't mind if he has to win hard or easy. He's inherently one of the greatest competitors in tennis. He comes off well every time — even if he's in a funk, he's able to beat guys he should beat. He's just 23 and I think he still feels optimistic even though he's starting to see a slight decline in his performance. I don't see him winning any more Grand Slams. The mileage on his legs and on his head is just going to increase; his weapons are going to weaken.

He looks like he's ready for the Australian Open. He won the tournament in Sydney last week, dropping only one set in five matches. It doesn't look like his wedding engagement breakup with Kim Clijsters is affecting him negatively. I never thought it was for real. I saw them around a lot together, but I never saw them in any romantic exchanges. I heard that Hewitt got caught sleeping with a young female tour player — this same girl had supposedly slept with her coach, too — and Clijsters dumped Hewitt. He's rebounded nicely, dating an Australian soap opera star. Clijsters is very flirtatious around the tour now.

Philippoussis is another matter. He was comeback player of the year in 2003, but last year he won only 11 matches and dropped to No. 106. I remember when he was in the Wimbledon finals in 2003, and he gave a speech where he said, "Dad, I want to thank you for everything. But this is just the beginning." But it wasn't. He had an injury-plagued season, and he faded again.

I'm sure he's hoping to rejuvenate his career here, and possibly win the Wimbledon title he so dearly covets and has so far eluded him — not unlike another big eccentric hitter, Goran Ivanisevic, who made good on that desire in 2001. Philippoussis is still saying his best tennis is in front of him, but he's just being politically correct. He's media-trained, and he knows they want to hear that sound bite from him. He needs to say something optimistic to convince himself. That's the only way it's going to happen. You have to say it to believe it. But he's been injured so often, and his mental toughness is suspect.

Philippoussis moved from Australia to Miami a long time

ago, but then he tried to escape the nightlife of South Beach by moving up to Boca Raton. Although, I heard he just bought another house in South Beach and he's back to his old carousing tricks. That's definitely not a good sign for his tennis game. Maybe he's settled down and has a girlfriend. He needs to get married, but it doesn't always help players' games when they do get married. It's almost like it makes them want to live the home life even more. The Rafters and Sampras's, and Agassi in his first marriage, once they hooked up with a steady woman or got married, they started going downhill. The best thing that happened to Agassi's game seems to have been his divorce from Brooke Shields. Andre won four Slams in the span of 20 months after his divorce in April 1999. His success since marrying Steffi Graf in 2001 and having two kids is an aberration for most tennis players, but since then Andre has only won one Slam, Australia in 2003.

Rafter was the most popular Aussie, a two-time U.S. Open champion and Wimbledon finalist, but he retired three years ago. He was always a man who traveled with a girlfriend. I remember the summer he shocked the tennis world and won his first U.S. Open in 1997, he had traveled the whole time leading up to the Open with this Dutch model. Right as the U.S. Open began, he broke up with her and sent her home — turning his focus to triumphing at Flushing Meadows.

The first time I ever played him was in 1994 in New Haven. I was a rookie pro rising in the ranks, coming off two consecutive Challenger titles. Pat was already a Top 20 player and he beat me 6–4, 7–6, in a good match. After the match, we merged at the lunch line and he gave me his opinion.

"Yeah you played well, mate. You should be a Top 50

player for sure. You have the talent." I came away thinking, "I wish he'd said I'd be a Top 10 player," but either way, it was a classy gesture and a generous comment to a young kid who was trying to get to the top. That was Pat. He always played with good sportsmanship, and was well-liked by the public and his fellow competitors.

JANUARY 15

I practiced with Greg Hill today working on a few tactics and strokes specific to playing against Radek Stepanek of the Czech Republic, my first-round opponent. These last few practices before a big match are really just warm-ups and fine-tunings. The real work has been done way before, when I developed my game as a junior and then a young pro, and tinkering with it in the off-season.

The most difficult part of playing professional tennis is the preparation process. You can't win unless you actually prepare right. There are always times when I don't want to get on the practice court and work on certain drills that are physically and mentally draining, but make me tougher. For some reason, I'm upset or just dragging it and I don't feel like pushing myself. There are times in the gym where I'm working with my trainer and I can't do that extra sprint or pedal the extra rotation on the stationary bike; it's too much pain and my heart's going too fast. We're all hanging on a wing and a prayer out here. Our wing is our training — doing everything we can control in practice to facilitate winning matches. Even when I have trained and prepared well, I then have to execute and be aggressive in the key points.

My warm-up with Greg today consists of hitting some ground strokes down the middle for about five minutes and then hitting into each corner for a few minutes at a time. Stepanek likes to rush the net so I have to get my angle shots grooved. Then I run into the net and bang some volleys, trying to miss as few as possible while working on depth and hitting targets. Then Greg comes to net and makes me move around a little, waking up my feet and forcing me to hit my shots with less preparation.

We're hitting on a back court at 9:30 a.m. so the atmosphere is pretty dead. A few other players are hitting too, but there are no fans watching because it's Sunday and the qualifying tournament is over. The grounds don't even open until 10:30. It's breezy out and all I hear is the wind and Greg's voice from the other side of the net, "More legs and racket speed." He's talking about my backhand that I just missed into the net. He wants me to bend my legs lower which helps me get under the ball, increase my racket head speed and allows it to accelerate and hit the ball with more velocity and early timing.

"More follow-through," Greg belts out, breaking my early morning sluggishness. Extending my follow-through helps me keep the ball inside the baseline, especially on windy days. I hit some returns of serves with Greg standing at the opposite service line, cranking them at full throttle, giving me a shorter time than usual to reach the ball. I turn, pivot, and hit my returns early and aggressively. It's an unrealistic approach, but an effective practice tactic for preparing to return Stepanek's big serve.

I hit some serves next. Starting at the deuce court, I hit about ten serves down the middle tee, a few at Greg's body, and several more out wide. Then I kick some second serves around the box, and repeat that routine to the ad court. Greg finishes the 30-minute practice session off by feeding me balls out wide so that I have to hit running forehands. Then he lofts balls into the center of the court so I can hit sitting forehands. This is called the "killer forehand drill." Finally, he slices backhands at me and rushes the net and I hit passing shots. We gather our gear and head back to the locker room while Greg talks to me about some match tactics — taking my time before I serve and using my forehand to dictate points while hitting my backhand down the line to keep Radek moving. We feel good. We're ready for war.

JANUARY 16

Another easy practice day. It's important not to peak on the practice court so I'm easing down for my first-round match in two days. I thought I'd talk a bit on the decline in the development of players' physical games — their techniques, mechanics, and styles of play — over the past decade. You can count on one hand the number of good serve-and-volleyers who have come onto the pro tour in the last ten years. Besides Federer and Henman, there are no really good serve-and-volleyers anymore. The overall full-court games, the creativity and smoothness of play has suffered. The equipment — the rackets and strings — the overabundance of clay-court specialists and ground-stroke kings, and the slowing down of court surfaces have all contributed to the decline. Bollettieri reduced the dimensions of the type of game people thought could win at the highest level, and his one-dimensional baseline style of play is now pretty much the norm on tour. Fischer once told me that if I learned to serve-and-volley, I'd move up into the Top 10.

That's part of the reason why Rafael Nadal, the teenage wonder who is already ranked in the Top 50, and who dismantled Roddick in the decisive match of the Davis Cup finals last year, has been so successful so quickly. There aren't many crafty all-court players around anymore who can break down Nadal's game. But he will never achieve what Federer will in the game, because he doesn't have nearly the skills, options, and creativity of Federer. Nadal's kind of robotic. He is getting a lot of attention because of his muscles, good looks, and his flamboyance. There is a real problem on tour today with the players' charisma, or lack thereof.

Agassi was once the King of Charisma, but he's turned that way down, and now he's the family man who only wants to win. If he didn't still sport an earring, no one would ever know he once went by the motto, "Image is everything," wore dungaree shorts and wildly colorful shirts, and had sun-bleached hair down to his shoulders. Hewitt has hit a plateau. He's still doing well, but he's not a No. 1 player anymore. Marat Safin is so unpredictable that he is predictable. Federer is great and predictable, and Henman, well, Henman is Henman.

Physically, the best player in the world is Safin. He's better than Federer, but he's not mentally tough enough. If he was as mentally tough as Michael Chang was, he'd have won more Grand Slams than Federer. Right now, Federer has won four and Safin has won just one.

Federer is the heralded one now, but he doesn't serve like Sampras, his volleys aren't Stefan Edberg's, and he has a volatile mental game. When things are going well for him, he hits the ball great. When things are bad, his backhand becomes iffy. His forehand might be the single greatest shot in tennis because it's heavy and it has weird spin on it. He can blast a winner on any given point with his forehand.

So who's going to win the Australian Open? It's Federer's world, and anyone who wants to enter it has to beat down his door first.

As I'm walking out of the Grand Hyatt Hotel in Melbourne, I'm hungry and it's dinner time. It's opening day of the Open, and my coach is at the courts getting my schedule organized — I play tomorrow against Radek Stepanek of the Czech Republic — and watching a night match, so I'm flying solo. I don't mind occasionally being alone. It gives me some time to reflect, think about other things, and people-watch. It can be therapeutic getting away from the tennis scene for a few hours.

I'm not close to any of the other players on tour, and I like to keep it that way. I don't try to alienate anyone, but I purposely divorce myself from the scene in the locker room and the players' lounge. I never saw Sampras or Agassi hanging out and being buddies with everyone. I know I'm seen by some of the other players as an outsider — like Michael Chang was — still, that doesn't make me want to be one of the boys.

A lot of the other players seem to hold it against me that early in my career, my father and my mother traveled with me. Sometimes, they still do. Some of the other players are insecure with their own relationships with their parents — many of them have had run-ins with their dads — and it makes them defensive to see me hanging out with my parents. It doesn't bother me. I'm not out here to form close relationships with people I most likely will never see after I retire. They're my competition, and I'd rather keep my distance from most of them.

I've always tried to emulate the most successful players: Ivan Lendl, McEnroe, Connors. These were not guys known for running down to the locker room and telling jokes. They didn't interact with the ATP officials or fans much; their focus was on the bottom line: winning tennis matches. I have my own moral character and ideas about friendship, but I really focus my tennis life on the bare principle of how to be great. I think the impression from the outside is that I'm not being as friendly as I could be, or that I'm not overly interested in making connections with other players or fans. But I was always aware that I was playing pro tennis to try to make a better life, to get mine. Still I try not to impose on anyone else or treat them badly.

The Spanish language dominates the locker room. The Spanish and Argentine players are very bold and free-wheeling, characters that hug each other freely and love to talk. They're not offensive, but they can get a little bit over-the-top by taking over the couches and computers in the players' lounge.

When I'm in the locker room, I'll say hello to Jan Michael Gambill or Ginepri for a minute. I'll say, "What's up?" to Paradorn Srichaphan, Max Mirnyi, or Xavier Malisse. But I don't believe in bonding in the locker room. It's not like we're a Major League baseball team and we're all in it together. Although most of us do see each other week in and week out, it's a competitive environment. We're not a mutual admiration club all trying to help each other out and be friends. But we're certainly not enemies either.

Most of the time when I'm in the locker room, the other Americans are talking about other sports. I hear them going on about Derek Jeter, Kevin Garnett, and Tom Brady. I like going to an occasional baseball or basketball game, but for the most part, I don't follow other sports. There are lots of different languages floating around the locker room and although I can understand a little Spanish, the rest is Greek to me. Most of the other talk that I can understand is about women. If I'm sitting in the trainer's room waiting to get a massage, and there are five guys in there being boisterous and talking smack, I don't need to tell a dirty joke to prove myself. Why should I try to break some other guy's balls over something? I just try to tune it out.

The other players may think I'm either aloof or shy, but I have an entertaining, storytelling, joking, rapping, foolish side of me, too. I can do the locker room ripping as well or better than anybody. But I leave that to Tim Henman or Andre.

Henman has that Sampras reputation for being very sub-dued, but in the locker room, he's a real cut-up. Say I come in wearing a beret; he'll say to me, "Hey Vince, what happened, did you lose a bet?" And I'll be like, "Dude, just because it's not your style — conservative plaid — doesn't mean I can't make a fashion statement around here." Tim likes to dish out the barbs, but he doesn't like to receive them.

Agassi has his Las Vegas street mode, where he talks like he's street-wise, and wears a lot of black. He's definitely got that rebel in him, and it's not contrived. He likes to act tough sometimes. I was traveling with him once to a tourna-ment, and at the airport he gave me a sleeping pill. He said, "You better take that because I don't have that many left." He was afraid I would ask for one (which I did) and then throw it away (which I also did). I just wanted to possess something that was Andre's. But he and Henman will cut it up. When Todd Martin was on the tour, he was kind of like the Jay Leno of the locker room with his sense of humor and grey hair. Andre will joke with Fernando Gonzales about the best leg-shaving technique.

Federer is very humble and respectful to everyone. He won't go out of his way to say hello, but at the same time, if you walk past him he'll look up and say, "Hey, how are you, Vince?" That's the weird thing about tennis. The players don't talk too much, except in passing. Americans are particularly strange that way. We'll say, "What's up, what's up," in passing, but we don't hug each other like the Spaniards or Argentineans, or give each other three and four kisses on every body part like they do. When I see that I'm like, "Damn, brothers! You guys better be packing some Tic Tacs with that kind of greeting. Stay away from me, too, because you're not even going to get a handshake. I don't know where you've been."

Anyway, back in Melbourne, I'm just going out for a quick bite alone and to think about what lies ahead. On my way to dinner, I make my usual stop at my own very American 7-Eleven. The one here is not as big as the ones back home, but it's nice and convenient for picking up snacks, water, Gatorade, juices, and bananas. As I spring through the automatic door, I notice the three people inside shopping and recognize one who's wearing a baseball cap, pulled down low, as the classic, everlasting Martina Navratilova, maybe the greatest women's tennis player to ever pick up a racket.

"Yo, what's up?" I say, sarcastically and loud enough for everyone in the small store to hear me. Martina hesitates to look up, but when she sees it's me she says, "Oh hey, Vince. What are you doing?" I met Martina when I was still a junior player, and at 17, her coach Craig Kardon — who later became my coach — asked me to hit with her before one of her matches at the U.S. Open. She has a fun-loving nature, and even though she's a legend, she easily lets down her guard when you get to know her.

"What's going on Martina? What brings you to 7-Eleven?" Martina was cashing out with a few items and I noticed specifically three bars of pure Swiss Chocolate. "Martina, is this the secret of a champion? You eat chocolate during a major tournament?"

I was intrigued, as I currently work with a nutritionist who has told me to limit my sweet intake. I also remember Martina's prime, when she was setting new standards and ideals on how people practice, train in the gym, and eat. "C'mon Martina," I prod her, "let's hear it from the horse's mouth."

"Yeah," she says, "I always have a little chocolate at the end of the day — just a little. These three bars will last me a couple weeks." Hmm, I think, that would take almost more discipline than not eating any chocolate at all. Who can open a bar of chocolate and eat only a quarter-piece, put it back in the wrapper, and make it last a couple weeks? Not me, but it's an insight to see a tennis great who is a stickler in every aspect of her training let some things slide. We're all human, even the lean, mean, fighting chocolate machines.

"Cool, Martina," I say. "Have a good night, and good luck in the tournament." She mentions that she's playing doubles the next day with Daniela Hantuchova, a woman 27 years her junior, and she's pumped to win. She even made a fist and pumped it right there in the good ole 7-Eleven, and piped, "Come on, baby."

What a wonderful, pleasing, unimaginable sight to see a woman at 48 years of age — who has won 167 singles titles and 174 doubles titles in her career — be as humble and friendly and as excited and alert for her first-round doubles match as if she were playing in her first Grand Slam. She is the quintessential example of a person who truly loves what she does, feeding off the pure enjoyment of a challenge, and her motivation to still be the best. Without a doubt, Martina genuinely believes she has the best job in the world. She has set an elite standard to strive for, above and beyond financial windfalls, match wins, bragging rights, and any other ulterior motives, and I'm honored to have had this unexpected chance to learn from such an overachiever.

I proceed to my dinner with increased zest and a better perspective on things. When I get to the local Italian restaurant, I order: "spaghetti with tomato sauce, add chicken please, a Sprite — no ice — and oh, do you have any desserts with CHOCOLATE?"

Bon appetit, mate.

JANUARY 18

The first round of a Grand Slam can be as tough as any match in a Grand Slam — granted I've never been past the quarterfinals, so my experience is somewhat limited. But I've played in and witnessed tough first-round matches in Grand Slams that proved pivotal in a player's rise to the finals and even the champions list. I'm thinking of Rafter as defending champion in the 1998 U.S. Open, when he was down two-sets-to-love in the first round against Hicham Arazi of Morocco. Rafter came back and won that match, and went onto repeat as U.S. Open champion.

I go into my first round of the Australian Open confident. I'm up against an improving 26-year-old named Radek Stepanek. Radek is a nice guy off the court — always shaking hands and saying hello and being courteous — yet when he steps onto the court he changes 180 degrees and becomes amazingly annoying to play against. He tries to find every possible advantage and in doing so he starts to get under your skin. He stalls when you serve, pumps his fist in your face, and questions line calls religiously. Actually, he drives me nuts, and I've been on the tour 12 years and have seen players do it all. I once had a guy take a bathroom break before the match even began, then take a shower, and put on new clothes and shoes. It was totally against the rules, but somehow the umpire allowed it.

Stepanek on the court is plain in your face — but enough about that. This is a tough draw for the both of us. We are closely ranked. I have slipped down to No. 23, and Radek is only ten spots behind at 33. Radek missed getting seeded by one spot, since Grand Slams only seed the top 32 players. It should be a good, entertaining match between two highly ranked players, but the tournament officials put us on one of the least desirable courts in Melbourne Park — way in the back — a 12-minute walk from the locker room if you already know where you're going. There are minimal bleachers, and since it's the first match of the day, an 11 a.m. start, there's hardly anyone around to watch. By putting us on the worst court for the earliest match of the day the tournament is basically saying to us: "Hey, if we could pay you less and treat you worse, we would, but any more than this is against the rules."

The simple fact is that the names Stepanek and Spadea just don't ring a bell for most people, but they will end up missing out on two hungry warriors trying to put food on the table. At the end of the day, I couldn't care less what court I play on. I got to be No. 18 in the world by overcoming bigger obstacles than how many people are watching me play.

I get off to an "I got up on the wrong side of the bed" start. No Wheaties, no spark in my movement, no punch in my shots, erratic serving, and it's a struggle from the get-go. I lose the first set in sluggish style, 6–3. I thought I had warmed up properly, but three out of five sets gives me some room to come back, so I'm not panicking yet.

Radek has an unusual but effective style of game. He serves quite well — pretty big and consistent — but he's streaky. He can ace you at any time, take you off the court for a harsh wide serve, and he follows it up nicely with a volley many times. He doesn't always serve-and-volley as a rule. He mixes it up with a clever, somewhat consistent, groundstroke game. His forehand is capable at times, yet vulnerable, and he has a sound two-handed backhand he combines with a consistent slice for variety. His flat stroking on both sides, and his down-the-line backhand can hurt you. He's got a well-rounded game with above-average foot speed and fitness, not to mention his tunnel focus and good work ethic.

In the second set, I aim to move him side to side so he can't get comfortable on the backhand side with his topspin down the line and crosscourt slice that he enjoys maneuvering like he has a remote control Nintendo, daring you to overhit or hit short so he can press the fire button and take you off the court with a volley or overhead winner. Returning serve well is paramount against Radek. If you give him no free points except the ones he earns with an ace or unreturnable serve, he becomes frustrated and presses on his second serve — which is fair at best — and he starts to miss. His favorite shot is a deft drop shot that lands nicely in between the sideline, the net, and your racket as you struggle to get a good play on it. The key to countering this is to hit the ball heavy and deep enough so that he can't hit the drop shot. Otherwise, you're running in all directions when you play him.

I hang in during the second set, get pumped up and stay even, holding serve to get to two-all, and three-all in games. I'm beginning to execute my shots and he is starting to get annoyed — uttering shrieks and screams — employing his delay-of-game tactics more and more in an attempt to break my rhythm. This is just stirring me to beat him even worse, but he somehow gets the advantage on me again. I'm serving at 5–6, 30–40 — break point, set point for Stepanek, to go up two sets to love.

As I step up to the line, I mutter to myself under my breath, "There's no way I can lose this point, first serve in and just battle." I miss my first serve — not part of the plan — so I just kick the second safely in and go to battle, hitting heavy crosscourt percentage plays, high-clearance, high-depth shots, all the time looking for a short ball to attack. After five rally balls, Radek shanks a forehand way wide, and it's finally deuce. I sigh briefly and continue going forward. I win the next two points and it's tiebreak time.

Tiebreakers are nerve-racking. You have to have more poise and hit with more care, yet with confidence — but no steering or hoping, that's a dead end. I start great in the tiebreak, and finish it off convincingly to even the match. Now it's my turn for a fist pump to the crowd. The third set proves to be another dogfight, but my confidence keeps rising, my arms are loose, and I'm freewheeling it, breaking serve, walking with that believing attitude — the tennis strut — like I won Melbourne Park, or I'm looking to buy it. I win the third set 6–4, and I'm rolling, strolling to the next set, feeling like I've got a sure bet on winning the match now.

So I take a bathroom break, much needed, and it gives me a chance to gather my thoughts and rhythm. The fourth set feels straightforward. I'm hitting like I have the momentum, but Radek keeps plugging away, serving big when he needs to get out of trouble, being slippery in the rallies, consistent yet aggressive. Up 4–3 on serve, I get up 15–40, double break point on Stepanek's serve. I'm just five points from winning the match. Boom, ace, 30–40. Boom, I prepare for a forehand return and hit it fat and too high, and he rushes the net and smacks an overhead winner. Deuce. Geez, momentum changes so fast, I get another break point and devour a return, hitting it low and hard off his first serve. He hits up a volley to my best and favorite shot, a backhand, and I nail it down the line, but slightly higher than I wanted it, and he anticipates, closes off viciously, and ricochets an angle volley winner. I feel the breath explode out of my lungs, taking my spirit out of me for the moment in a big way.

Radek holds serve to even the score at five-all, and then breaks me and I feel even more deflated. "What a dodgy service game," I think to myself. "I didn't dictate the points." He potently serves out the fourth set and screams out like a kid in a candy store, wanting more. I'm ready to deck him to the floor, and my anger causes me to fall apart in the fifth set. I lose my serve again right away, then lose my flow and my chance to break him. He serves well, backs it up with sound volleys, ground strokes and fist-pumps as he looks on to his entourage of coaches and friends, whoever they are. He marches though me like a soldier who is a little fitter and stronger. I compete well in the fifth set, but I've lost a lot of my ammunition and come up short. It is a hot day, and after more than three hours of warfare, I come in second.

There's no worse feeling than sitting in your chair by the side of the umpire's stand at the end of a losing battle. I'm 12,000 miles away from home, and I've battled for hours to settle for second place. It's just one of the harsh realities of being a pro tennis player. Hey Vince, stop crying with a loaf of bread under your arm. Look at the bright side: in two weeks you'll be playing another tournament in Delray Beach, Florida as the No. 1 seed. You made some money, so cheer up.

But no, this was the Australian Open, the first major tournament of the year. Dang it!

Melbourne is a small and comforting city with many suburbs surrounding it. Pro tennis players, especially at a major event like the Australian Open, don't get to see much of the city we're playing in. We usually just make the rounds from our hotel to the courts — maybe venture out to a nearby restaurant, and then it's right back to our hotels. But in Melbourne, there is an attraction that draws players, the famous Crown Casino, which is gaining popularity as a place to spend time and wind down from the hot-and-heavy demands of the tennis world.

A casino offers a chance to roll some different dice for a change. I'm not a big gambler, but I enjoy watching. Basically, I'm pretty much a casino prude. I limit myself to the slot machines and one or two hands max at the $10-ante blackjack table. The air-conditioning makes it feel cold in the Crown Casino, and the place is polished, a nice reassuring comfort, like I'm back in America.

The reason I don't like to gamble is simple: I hate playing cards, a pastime most male pro tennis players use to while away the hours. I've never seen Agassi gambling, but I guess when you're born on a craps table — Andre's father, Mike, used to work at the MGM in Vegas — you're not apt to hang around too many casinos. I look at a casino as too easy a place to blow through hard-earned money quickly. Unfortunately, people who like to gamble are usually risk-takers, and if they happen to have a lot of money handy — say a pro tennis player with his tournament winnings fresh in hand — it can turn addictive and ugly very fast.

But the promised rush of winning quick money does not lure me to the tables. If I'm gonna drop $1,000, I'd rather

69

spend $200 in the casino and $800 on a nice Prada jacket.
I've heard it said by people who work in casinos, that unless
you're a professional, if you spend any longer than 20 minutes at any of the games, the house will win every time. So
I'm just a spectator here.

I've made almost $4 million in prize money over my
career — starting the year I'm No. 91 on the all-time total
career prize money leader list, right behind Björn Borg —
but I still worry about not having enough to retire on. I can't
even say what I'm worth now, because, frankly, I don't know.
I trust what my financial people are doing with my money; I
don't ask them many questions.

Of the $4 million I've made, a lot of it has gone into
investments, but I also bought a house, and I have a lease
out on a few cars. I'm not like Philippoussis, who owns
something like 12 Harley motorcycles. My parents live in my
house in Boca, and my father drives my silver X5 BMW when
I'm not around. I just bought a small share of a new restaurant in Los Angeles called Providence, but I stay with my
younger sister, Diana, in her apartment in Hollywood. My
family didn't come from a lot of money, so my money has
always been their money. Both my sisters are lawyers now,
but my younger sister didn't start making money until a couple of years ago, and she had loans to pay off. So I was the
rainmaker for a while.

I was passionate about making the lives of my family
and myself better. Now that that's been accomplished, I'm
buying nicer things. It makes life a little bit smoother, but
money doesn't change anything really. Having money hasn't
changed who I am, and it hasn't changed how I feel about
most things. It makes some things feel more exciting, but in
actuality, if they weren't exciting before I had money, they're
not that exciting now, either.

So I'd rather wear my nice jacket at the slot machines or $10 minimum blackjack table, than be the guy sweating at the baccarat or poker table, thinking he might have to cash in his own jacket for more chips. But I've heard the craps table is where a player has the best chance to win, so I'm working on learning the rules. I want to hear a casino employee say, "Cashing out the $50 chip is the male in the nice black jacket . . ."

Still, I enjoy the liveliness and grandeur this money haven brings, and the Crown in Melbourne is established, with a nice hotel and many levels of shops, movies, nightclubs, and entertainment. So after my disappointing loss to Stepanek, after dinner, Greg Hill and I decide to liven up our stay with a visit to the world of risky game-playing. Greg spots his territory at the roulette table and settles in with a few Australian bills converted to chips, so I tell him I'm gonna wander and check out the scene: the high-rollers, the different kinds of games, so much action.

I pass Robby Ginepri, my doubles partner this week, sitting at a blackjack table and losing badly. Robby's taking it easy, though, only betting at the $20 table. I run into Dean Goldfine, a fellow Floridian and a cool, amiable guy, who's also the new coach of Andy Roddick. Goldfine traveled on the tour for years as Todd Martin's coach. Martin, while not a household name in tennis, played 16 years, retiring after the 2004 season with more than $8 million in prize winnings. Unfortunately, he's still best known for blowing a 5–1 game lead in the fifth set of the 1996 Wimbledon semifinals to MaliVai Washington, then losing the final set 10–8.

In his usual warm style, Dean says to me, "Hey Vince, we have our own table over there: Andy, Serena, Venus, and Mark Knowles. We're gambling, come join us."

"Thanks, I'll be over there in a few," I tell him.

Sounds like celebrity poker, with the young and rich American stars having a powwow at the poker table. Andy Roddick is very outgoing — he has a good sense of humor and enjoys fraternizing with his fellow players. I am not as social as Andy or most other male pros, but I enjoy seeing my compatriots coming together, relaxing and having a good time, socializing in spite of the fierce competitive demands of preparing for a Grand Slam. As I walk up to the table, Serena spots me and yells out, "Hey, Vince, I wanna hear a rap."

As I'm known as the "tennis rapper" — unlike pro basketball players, there aren't too many pro tennis players who like to rap, so people request random poetic artistry from me at the drop of a hat. Mostly, I thrive on it, stringing together some rap lines that tell a joke about how broke or crazy I am. My usual banter goes something like, "Gosh, I was so broke, I used to be on the street selling loose M&M's."

I go way back with Serena and Venus, from their early days in Palm Beach, Florida, before they were even teenagers. I met them when Serena was nine and Venus ten — they were these two little girls who practiced all day long at Rick Macci's Academy on Linton Boulevard in Delray Beach. They both would be screaming as they hit the ball, the beads in their hair flying all over the place.

All you heard when you were playing on the same row of courts as Serena and Venus was grunting. You knew the Williams Project, the Williams Show, the Williams Campaign was over there. They had their two courts separate from everyone else. They had two grown junior boys on one side, and the girls would be on the other side, hitting ball after ball after ball, and playing like maniacs, wanting to kill, hitting every ball to the target with deadly intentions.

They've always played with a lot of heart and emotion. I've even seen them break down and cry in a press conference or two. They wear their Compton, inner-city Los Angeles past and their vicious style of play on their sleeves. Each one goes out on the tennis court feeling: "It's me against the world. I'm going to break you down and I'm going to beat you. I'm going to heckle, grunt, and do whatever it takes to take you down. I'm going to dominate you and go out and be a street-fighter, and play like someone you've never, ever stepped onto a tennis court with before."

That's their attitude, and I think it stems from the father, Richard Williams, proclaiming to the media from the very start just how good his daughters really were. He got them all these amazing sponsors, years before they ever played on tour. Richard created so much hype, and he had this divine story of teaching his daughters on the public courts in Compton. Then, miraculously, all the hype came to fruition. It was like a movie playing right out in front of our eyes. Venus and Serena both lived up to the advance billing and that's a pretty amazing thing to actually do. They were nobodies at the beginning — Richard really put a lot of pressure on them — but they've fulfilled his proclamations of their amazing potential by winning ten Grand Slams between the two of them. [Editor's note: after the 2005 season, their cumulative Grand Slam total had risen to 12.]

Back at the casino, it's comforting to see the familiar faces of my fellow Floridians, who grew up playing on many of the same courts I did. You'd think Florida would be the breeding ground of many top professional tennis players, but until Venus and Serena, and Andy and Robby, came onto the tour, Jennifer Capriati, Corina Morariu, and I were the only Floridians out here.

By now, a crowd of curious tennis fans and gamblers is starting to form around the Williams sisters and Andy's table.

I back off a bit — no one recognizes me; their eyes are all glued on the stars — and tell Serena to "give me a minute to think of something tight." I know she wants something authentic, classic, and spontaneous with a hip-hop delivery, otherwise known as a "free-styling" slang rap.

My cell phone starts buzzing just as I'm coming up with some lines. It's these two girls from New Zealand I had met a few days back at the airport in Melbourne. I often go up to hot girls I see in places like airports and tell them I'm a pro tennis player playing in the local tournament that week. In this case, it was the Australian Open, which practically everyone in Melbourne is excited about. We exchanged numbers at the airport. These two Kiwi girls were skeptical at first, but they kept calling me, curious to hang out, and eventually they came out to see me play.

I'm interested in one of them. Her name's Victoria, a 5-foot-7-inch blond with swirly, snowy locks and a thin but toned body. On a scale of one to 10, she's about a 36 DD. Ha Ha. OK, well I would say an eight, but a rock solid eight. She has flawless skin tanned to the color of golden grahams, curves fulfilling every promise, a face that is hard to replace, nose perfected as if Michelangelo came in as a plastic surgeon and created the exact slope we'd all want to ski off to land directly on her bottom lip, which could also have been created by a computerized model collage, and fully complements the upper.

She looks like a product of the Rachel Hunter breed, a youthful version. If Pamela Lee Anderson has a long-lost twin sister, tell her to look in New Zealand. Victoria's possibly the closest I'll get to seeing paradise on earth. I don't know what she sees in me, but hey, I don't fear anything when it comes to meeting women, or people in general. Remember, "Spadea, ain't afraid of ya." I'll talk to you whether you're President Bush, the homeless vagabond on the sidewalk, or the hottest thing since fire, the ultra-hot Victoria.

The girls wanted to meet up, so I suggested they come over to the casino. They were game — pardon the pun — and came right over. So I had to abort my rap performance for Serena and meet the girls, who arrived promptly, dressed in their Sunday best. I have to confess, they are beauties. I had to stare, compare, there was no glare; just two revealing Kiwi girls, appealing and dancing on the ceiling, high on life, standing right in front of me.

"Hey there, nice to see you again," I say. "Let's go check out the casino."

I'm a little hesitant to bring them back to the table with Andy, Venus, and Serena, as I'm not into showing off, or trying to impress girls with who I know. But I told Serena I'd be back with her rap, and as a man of my word, I start walking the girls in that direction. Victoria has heads turning even during the final drop of the roulette ball at the high-rollers table.

All of a sudden, I see several security officers and a crowd of dozens of adoring fans coming our way. Walking at the core of the huddlers is the featured Sister Act Two, Venus and Serena — or is it Serena and Venus now? Given their respective rankings, who knows?

"Oh hey, I was just looking for you two," I say. "Are you done gambling already?"

"Yeah, we gotta play tomorrow," Venus replies, "We're done. Who's this?"

I introduce the two girls, and Venus is more than nice, greeting them and telling them how cool I am. Then they scoot right along through the masses. I don't want to halt their schedule so I move on with the girlies to play some billiards and jukebox tunes, much more economical and practical than the brutal betting and losing going on in the next room.

Needless to say the Kiwis give me the thumbs-up. I know I said that I don't like to cash in on knowing famous people, still it always amazes me how getting the approval of two icons like Venus and Serena can win you a lot of admiring stares. As the night draws to a close, we play some pool and watch people making fools of themselves singing karaoke.

As much as I don't want to have to say goodbye to Victoria and her friend, I do shortly afterwards, because I'm playing doubles tomorrow with Ginepri against the Bryan Brothers, the No. 2 team in the world.

JANUARY 19

Robby and I got our butts kicked by the Bryan brothers, losing 6–2, 6–1. Both Robby and I were out of the singles — Robby having also lost in the first round in five sets, to Gaels Monfils, the 18-year-old black Frenchman, who along with Nadal, Richard Gasquet, and Tomas Berdych of the Czech Republic, are expected to cause quite a teenage sensation on tour this year. I could sense that Robby was not so keen on playing doubles — perhaps he had even already scheduled his flight back home by the time we stepped on the court.

"Tanking," purposely losing a match as fast as possible to get it over with, is done all the time on the pro tour. Everyone, including the top players and legends in tennis, has done it. Even though there is money riding on every match, sometimes it's better to conserve your energy and tank a "less meaningful" match so you can conserve your resources for a "more meaningful" match. But players tank for all kinds of reasons. They can be under the weather, angry with their coach, or just not want to play. It seemed to me that Marcelo Rios tanked his matches more blatantly than most. Agassi used to sometimes semi-tank if you met his level early in a match and he didn't feel like killing himself. It wasn't like Robby and I blatantly failed to put forth an effort, but our spirit clearly wasn't there. We had no pop in our serves.

The Bryan brothers are doubles specialists, meaning they do not play singles. Even though they are one of the best doubles teams in the world, they don't receive the respect — or earn anywhere near the money — as the top singles players, because doubles is undervalued in pro tennis. In doubles, players don't cover as much court, they don't need to work as hard or be as emotionally present, and there's not as much demand placed on their concentration skills as in singles. That's just the way it is.

Singles is far more challenging, and in the last 15 years, most of the top singles players have stopped competing in doubles altogether. I'm one of the few Top 20 singles players today who still plays doubles. Mikhail Youzhny of Russia, the 15th seed here, and myself, the 19th seed, are the only Top 20 singles players also competing in the Australian Open doubles tournament. The only time doubles ever really matters in pro tennis is during a Grand Slam event or in Davis Cup. But comparing the importance of a singles player to a doubles player is like asking, "Who sells a blockbuster hit, Brad Pitt or the unknown actor playing his distant cousin?"

I asked Victoria and her friend — I don't like playing the "third wheel," but it seemed as if they were a package deal — if they wanted to hang out again after the casino rendezvous and their having watched me lose to Stepanek. Victoria said they had to work.

"Work in Melbourne?" I said. "I thought you two were

from New Zealand and were here on vacation."

"Well, we work at a nightclub on Wednesday nights," replied Victoria. "You should come. It's fun."

Wednesday night is my last in town before I fly back to Florida. I still have almost two weeks to prepare for my next tournament, and I don't usually watch the clock on an "exit" night, but I still like to keep a good schedule. Even if I don't have a match the next day, I want to reserve the option to possibly get up in the morning and practice, get a massage, and have a good off-day's rest before boarding the plane back to the States.

I don't really want to go out with a girl who's working at a nightclub, have a drink, and go to bed in the wee hours of the morning. I usually like to get right to the point, but I can't just say to her when she gets off work, "Should we shag now or should we shag later?" That kind of night usually winds up ending between two and six in the morning.

But after dinner, I hail a taxi outside the hotel and give the name of the nightclub to the driver. As I step out of the taxi and up to the entrance of the club, a bouncer greets me with "$20 please."

"Twenty bucks on a Wednesday night?" I'm thinking. This must be like New York or L.A., but it isn't, it's only Melbourne. I walk around to the side of the building, deciding if I want to plunk down $20, and I see windows that are filled with silhouettes of curvaceous women dancing. Yeah, I'm starting to see the truth, the naked truth, literally. The place is a strip club.

I'm turned on by the idea of naked women, but not with seeing my Victoria dancing. I mindlessly walked back to the front of the club, and the bouncer barked, "Hey mate, are you gonna pay or what? You're holding up the line!" Confused and disappointed, I stuttered, "Actually, I think I have the wrong place. I'll be going now, mate."

I don't feel bad in saying that ultimately, Victoria was not my type. I don't judge people, I just have certain criteria I follow when it comes to women, and I wasn't going to change my standard even for a woman as beautiful as Victoria. All that talk about her having the exquisite face . . . well, I've been down that road once or twice before without walking away with the gorgeous girl on my arm.

I text-messaged Victoria the next day and let her know why I didn't come in to see her. She was sort of embarrassed, and she said, "I'm just not into this at all. I'm so sick of this. I don't even do the dances anymore. I just do it for the cash I get for dancing and the tips."

Peace to all that. I had a better encounter later on in the day when I ran into Serena in the lunch line at the player's cafeteria. Yeah, we all have to wait our turn for a sandwich, even the diva of women's tennis, Serena Williams. While we were waiting, I broke out some lyrics for Ms. Wonder Woman.

Have you seena playing in a sold-out arena? She's leana and meana than any fighting Myskina, Born western, but more Easton than Sheena, Name is Serena, She got more millions than Christina (Aguilera), No one's more Williams than Serena. Yo, can you hook me up with Angelina (Jolie)?

JANUARY 20

It's a long, multi-flight trip back to Florida, and along the way I remember a night out I had with Roddick that ended at the Melbourne Casino in 2002. Roddick's had three or four public relationships already, the most visible being the one he had with the actress Mandy Moore. But Roddick is not a womanizer. He tries to do the dating thing, the girl-friend thing. It's hard, because he's on the road all the time. We're all on the road all the time, but he takes a bit more advantage of his status. I heard a story where he had a run-in with an actress on a sitcom.

Safin is another guy who likes his share of women. Carlos Moya, who all the women love with almost the same fervor they once reserved for Patrick Rafter, is not much of a wom-anizer. Mariano Zabaleta and Feliciano Lopez have their share of female admirers. Jan-Michael Gambill and Taylor Dent are not hounds. Basically, no one's getting laid every week unless they're No. 1 in the world, and Federer has a steady girlfriend who travels with him to every tournament. But anyone who doesn't have a serious, serious girlfriend is going to dabble. And some of the guys with girlfriends might be worse than the guys without girlfriends.

But getting back to that night out with Roddick, he was just coming up — 19 years old and ranked about No. 13 in the world. We were both out of the Australian Open early that year. He had hurt his ankle and lost to Ivan Ljubicic, and I was in the qualifiers that year, still on my comeback, and had lost.

We were at the player party in the ballroom at the Melbourne Hyatt and we met two girls, both models. Tennis players and models go together like Donald Trump and young Slavic beauties. It's human nature to want something beautiful, and we're like a mutual admiration club. We seek them out and they seek us out. We're both on the road a lot in major cities for short periods of time, and we both tend to have money to spend.

Anyway, I was sort of along for the ride. We were out to all hours in the morning. Roddick's a very smooth operator with women. He knows what he's doing. He's very smart, funny, and outgoing. He's mature, yet he's got a little flavor, a hip style, and he knows how to move on the dance floor.

We went out club-hopping. I'm not much of a dancer — I've got 12 moves and they're all good, but beyond that, I get stale and I just start chilling out at the bar, looking for stars, and for a car to take me home. We ended up at the casino at 5 a.m. It was time to make a move. I'm thinking, "Let's booze, cruise, or someone's going to lose." I was ready to go, but Roddick was still hustling.

"Well, are we going to see you again?" he asks the girls. "You guys should just come over to Florida sometime." It was sort of a figure of speech rather than a serious offer. I mean, it was 5 a.m. But the girls took him seriously. They got on their cell phones right there and started calling Qantas and they made reservations for a flight to Florida the next day. Roddick was in a pickle. I hadn't invited them, and they didn't like me, anyway.

I told Roddick, "These girls are actually serious." But Andy thought it was all a joke on the girls' part. I left to play a Challenger tournament in Hawaii the next day. When I returned to Florida a month later, I went down to South Beach to meet some friends, and as I'm walking, I bump into the two girls. I say, "What's going on?" They told me they'd been hanging out with Andy for a while, but then he had to leave to go play some tournaments, so they decided to stay in South Beach.

The thing I don't like is when girls become traitors, so desperate in their search to hook up with players that they move from one player to the next as it suits them. I've heard that one top Swedish player's wife was once another Swede's longtime girlfriend. That type of thing — or a version of it — happens more than you can imagine on tour.

I went out with a woman — a German model — in

Hamburg once. I picked her up in a taxi and took her out. We had dinner and started making out, and then I said, "Hey, why don't we go get a drink somewhere?" But she said, "No, I want to go to the players' party."

I said to myself, "This girl's obviously the biggest tennis groupie of all time," but I relented. We get to the players' party, and I have to go to the bathroom. Within five minutes — it was a No. 1, it was like a three-minute pit stop, I checked my eyebrows and that was it — I come out of the bathroom, and this girl's in the arms of James Blake. Well, not exactly in his arms, but close enough, in that "we're talking alone" zone. She ignored me when I walked by, and I left the party 10 minutes later. I wasn't interested in her anymore, or anyone else there, and I assumed she left with Blake. I don't know what happened for sure, because I don't talk about that kind of stuff with the guys.

The story doesn't stop there, however. One year later, at the same tournament, this same girl had hooked up with Feliciano Lopez. When I saw her at the players' party again, I said to her, "I know your story. You can just keep walking. If you see me on the same side of the street as you, don't stop, just keep on stepping. I don't play that game."

I don't blame Blake. She was a beautiful girl, and I doubt he knew that she came to the party with me. I probably would have made a move on her too, if I'd seen her alone at a party. Pro tennis players have an advantage, in that we meet hot women more easily than we would if we were just single guys with steady jobs. I don't think of it as an unfair advantage; it's an advantage we've earned.

I see hotter women ranked No. 20 in the world than if I were out of the Top 100, but I don't see as many as the superstars of tennis. It's ironic, though, that I saw almost as many beautiful women — or more — earlier in my career when I was ranked lower, because of my pick-up skills. I was able to beat that curve.

If you approach enough women, it's easy to get some phone numbers. Not everyone's going to have a green light. Some might be involved or married. I try not to approach married women; I try to show a little restraint. I won't try to pick up every woman who walks the earth. I make sure they're my type. I make sure that it's the right situation. But the average male goes wrong when he doesn't have confidence. Jennifer Aniston is attainable. Every woman needs a man who will tell her what he wants, and who makes her think. Women are just what they are. Did Britney Spears have a baby with Justin Timberlake? No. If Britney Spears married this guy, Kevin Federline, there's not a girl on the planet I couldn't get. And that's how every guy should think.

That's why a number of years ago, when I was on this same flight from Australia back to Florida, I devised my own rules for guys who don't know how to approach women and get their numbers, and what to say and wear on a first date. I call it The Da Vince Code and I use concrete research and tactics as well as emotional, psychological, and verbal assessments in my coaching. I'm a pro tennis player — not a relationship doctor — but I had problems with women in my early adulthood that left me frustrated. So I figured out these basic guidelines with the idea of creating a self-help book for men whose best line is normally, "Let's get drunk."

It encompasses physical appearance (what to wear — belts, shoes, specific shirts, types of pants, jeans, etc., as well as how to style hair); psychological and emotional strategy (what to say, when to say it, how to use tact and directness, and have conviction); and momentum and timing (it should happen inside one or two minutes — there should be an accelerated process of asking questions so the girl doesn't have time to think: "What's your name?" "Do you want to go out for a drink?" "What's your number?").

It's all about combining the right look, the direct approach, unpredictability, and execution. Women want a dependable guy, but they also want one who has some mystery and who keeps them slightly off-kilter. I'll give you guys out there a few examples, and then you can just follow the lead and trust it.

Step 1: Appearance

Hair: If you have shorter hair, gel the top upwards to create an Elvis or Brad Pitt appearance. Longer hair should be combed back and lightly gelled to create body and shape. Men with no hair should tell girls that they're Andre Agassi's cousin, or look for a really dark bar. Girls like guys who take care of themselves and who pay attention to detail. Regardless of what fits, be neat and stylish.

Shirt: Button-down, long-sleeved is essential. Must be white, with minimal design, stripe, whatever. You're creating a tone for a classy, yet fun and stylish evening. Remember, don't go to extremes in color or prints, and button your shirt to at least one button from the top, two maximum.

Pants: Jeans are essential. Take your pick of brand, but a lighter fade is the way to go, because it has a casual but chic appearance. If jeans aren't your fashion, go with a dark, slim-fitting pant with no pleats — conservative, yet elegant.

Belt: This is an important element, underrated by men. The belt you wear needs to be fun and cool. I like snakeskin; it catches the eye, especially in a dark room. If snakeskin isn't you, go with a telling belt buckle — silver is always good.

Shoes: They should match the belt. I like black shoes that are rounded with a boot bottom. It shows you have class, but also know the trends.

Accessories: It helps to put a nice fun chain or wristband on, something that shows you pay attention to adornments. If you're conservative, go with silver or gold. Hipper people should try an island necklace or leather wrist ornament.

Cologne: Go with Cool Water by Davidoff. It just works; it's an oldie but a greatie.

Gum or candy: Always keep a piece in your mouth. It'll keep you relaxed and excited. Chewing gum makes you look happier and more confident. It can help you, if the girl rejects you, to continue to chew. It shows that you're still confident and have everything under control. In extreme cases, you can just blow a bubble in her face and move on.

Step 2: Conviction

Girls can sense when guys have it. Don't be obsessive or possessive. You have to catch girls off guard. Girls like a guy who treats them like a lady sometimes, but throws them to the floor and makes love to them at other times. You have to keep the different sides of your personality available and use them at the right time.

Step 3: The Approach

How you walk up to a girl, where you put your hands when you talk to a girl, different hand gestures you make during your conversation — this is all very detailed important information I don't have the time to go into right now.

Step 4: Hooking Up

How do you get a girl's telephone number to set up a first date? Start out by asking her, "Hi, where are you from? Are you from around here?" Everyone takes pride in where they come from, their heritage. Make them feel comfortable by focusing on this first. A guy just can't call this out in passing;

he must literally walk straight up to a woman and ask this question looking straight into her eyes. Don't be afraid to approach her. I look at every girl and think, "I might get sick of this girl at some point, so why should I be afraid of her now?"

Step 5: Assertiveness

Don't give women time to think. You have to be assertive and call the shots. Assertive but flexible, that's the key. Beautiful girls are used to getting compliments. You have to spark their interest by telling them what you want, not by fawning all over them.

If the average guy goes up to ten beautiful girls following The Da Vince Code, I say he gets three to five phone numbers, and that's a lot. But the average guy has to put his head, hair, belt, and charisma and assertiveness together and follow this formula. It's not using smoke and mirrors. It's using concrete consistent tactics that work.

The Da Vince Code is a way to get women's phone numbers; then once you have them, I'm in the process of devising a whole new system for you to follow to make the relationship work. But this system will only work for the first two to three dates maximum, and then you're on your own. It's hard to design a protocol for a lasting relationship, because every one is so different. It's not just putting together five principles.

The Da Vince Code is just about the initial clicking and getting a date with women the average guy didn't think were attainable. It's about rising above your expectations and history. Use it and good luck, guys. But I don't want anyone coming up to me after you try this saying, "Hey Vince, you made me buy these expensive jeans and cologne. Now I'm broke, I got no girl, and I'm gonna give you a hand gesture."

PART II

COMING HOME

JANUARY 27
Boca Raton, Florida

These days, I only get back to Boca for a month or so during
the year. I'm spending more and more time in Los Angeles,
and intend to buy a small apartment there. My parents live
in my house here. I don't feel like I need the space, or that
I'm in town enough to put out a lot of money and buy
another place in Boca. So it's convenient to live with them
when I come home.

So many memories flood through me when I come back
to Boca. I just drove by Veterans Park on Palmetto Park Road
— when I was a kid it was called Pinewood Park — and I
played there every weekend night with this guy named Al
Holden from the time I was 14 until I was 16 years old. He
was like so many guys, some would call them "tennis bums"
(a guy who hangs around a tennis club or park and just can't
wait to play), who lived in Florida and worked in the tennis

87

business. He wasn't a tennis pro — he worked as a court attendant — and he rented a room in a trailer. He loved to hit, he loved to battle. He helped inspire me to be a warrior.

We would play from eight to 11 at night, when the electronic lights would automatically shut off. We'd hit crosscourts. It was a way of life, we lived just for it. Al Holden would call me out at 7:30 by saying three words, "Go for it?" A lot of people saw us play then, and when I became a nationally ranked junior player, parents started to seek Al Holden out to hit with their kids. He was said to have taught Roddick the motion for his serve. Veterans Park was just across the street from my house in the Logger's Run section of West Boca.

My dad, Vincent Sr., was my first and best tennis coach, but he wasn't a trained tennis player. He went to Cornell, and actually trained to be an opera singer. He wasn't one of these guys who just fell off the truck. When he graduated from Cornell, he asked his parents — his father was an orthopedic surgeon and his mother a psychologist — if they could stake him some money, because he wanted to move to Italy and study opera.

His parents gave him only enough for two years, but he traveled to Milan and studied at La Scala, the world's most famous opera house. He studied with Pavarotti's voice coach. At first, he did not think of himself as a singer, but rather a connoisseur of opera. At Cornell, he had studied all the operas of the past. He knew the names of all the tenors. Then he discovered that he also had a good voice. But when he got back to the United States, he couldn't find a steady job in opera. He met my mother, Hilda — who is from Bogota, Colombia, but was studying in Boston — and they married and moved to Brockton, Massachusetts, the hometown of Rocky Marciano.

After my parents got married, they drove up to New York City to see Pavarotti perform at the Metropolitan Opera House. My mother didn't believe that my father knew the famous tenor. Before the performance, as my parents were waiting in the crowd outside the theater at Lincoln Center, Pavarotti saw my father and called out, "It's Vincenzo!" They were ushered into his dressing room.

My father idolized Rocky Marciano. His father had been Marciano's doctor. My father knew that Marciano had become heavyweight champion of the world at age 30, so when my father was about that age and I was eight, he abandoned all thoughts of a career in opera, and decided to start over and move the family to Florida. He had this idea that he would groom my two sisters and me to become professional tennis players. He had just taken up the game and was fascinated by it. He liked watching tennis on television — it was tennis's heyday in the early '80s with the Borg-McEnroe rivalry — but my dad was just an average club player.

We settled in Boca Raton, but not the ritzy part of Boca Raton. We were on the wrong side of Route 441, the highway that divides West Boca from East Boca. West Boca is a different world: a far lower social strata than East Boca. Marilyn Manson grew up in West Boca. When you cross 441 going from East Boca to West, the best restaurant you'll find now is Chili's — and that wasn't even there when I was a kid.

We didn't live next to alcoholic, trailer-park psychos; it wasn't Eminem's 8 Mile. But at my middle school, some of my classmates were living in trailer parks. This wasn't uppity Boca Raton at all. I got excited if my parents bought me a new pair of shorts at Winn-Dixie. On Halloween, one family in our neighborhood only gave out pennies. A lot of cops lived on my block, but some of the families had Mafia connections, too. Some had really nice cars, but all of the houses were plain and small. There were a lot of tough kids and fistfights, and I did my best to steer clear of all that.

My father worked as a substitute teacher, and then as an entry-level technical writer at IBM. He always had a side gig as a piano player at this club in Boca. We didn't go on vacations to Miami. We would only go there for junior tennis tournaments. Gas up the car in Boca with $5 to start the trip, and on the way back — if the gas tank was running low — stop and fill it up with $5 more in Hollywood. My parents drove a Toyota Corolla station wagon.

When I got a scholarship to attend a private high school in Boca Raton, St. Andrews, I saw everyone rolling around in Mercedes and BMWs, and it dawned on me, "God damn, this is different from what I see driving around my neighborhood. I can't conceive of this. Where the hell's the bike rack?" When my dad dropped me off at school, I had him drive me around to the back, because I didn't want everyone to know my father drove a Toyota Corolla.

We didn't have enough money for tennis lessons. My mother would pick up my two sisters, Luanne (who is 18 months older than me) and Diana (who is 18 months younger) and me from our grade school and drive us to the public tennis courts. She usually brought us Burger King to eat as she drove, and sometimes she'd stop at home to let us watch cartoons for a half hour.

Then we practiced from 3:30 to 6, doing drills my father had taught my mother how to run. My father would get to the courts at 6 — coming straight from his job at IBM — and for the next hour he'd really drill us. When I would complain or not practice hard enough for his liking, he would yell across the net, "If you don't like practicing, Vince, how would you like flipping burgers at Burger King?"

My dad was tough, but he wasn't verbally abusive or physically intimidating. He was just animated and passionate. My dad has never been able to watch a complete match when I'm playing — not as a junior, or as a pro. His emotions get the best of him, and he has to walk away. Richard Williams is like that with Venus's and Serena's matches. He's known for walking out right in the middle of their matches.

My dad was my coach from the time I was eight until I was 25, with a few years off from 15 to 18 when the USTA selected me for their junior national team, and assigned their coaches — Stan Smith, Nick Saviano, and Tom Gullikson — to work with me. Sometimes my father would yell at me while I was playing a match — something loud and negative about the way I was playing — but he didn't do it every match. He would get on the umpires, too, and sometimes the tournament director would walk out to the court I was playing on and ask my father to leave the grounds.

After a match, he could be very negative. He believed in acting like a football coach, getting very emotional and issuing stormy critiques, then rousing pep talks. When he said something, I listened, because I knew — for the most part — that he was intelligent and rational. If he didn't like the way I, or one of my sisters, had played in a tournament match, he would take us right back out onto the court and make us practice for a few more hours.

It felt like torture at first, but later, the extra practice actually made us feel better. We improved, even though we weren't aware of it at the time. My dad would get really worked up in the first hour after one of us lost a match — the excitement and anger just building up. But then he'd go to a store and buy us a couple of boxes of Oreos, and he'd change the subject and start talking and laughing about something else as he drove us home.

Whatever my dad is talking about, he exudes a tremendous amount of passion. He's expressive and animated, there's a lot of juice in him; maybe it's his Italian heritage. His theory is that we had to fight for everything we got. Nobody was going to give the Spadea kids junior championships. He raised three national junior champions from modest economic means, and he did it by instilling discipline, desire, and a grinder's mentality in all of us.

Luanne was thin and small, but she never missed. She was like a ball machine. I was a very husky kid and at 5, I could hit baseline to baseline. Diana beat Chanda Rubin in the juniors and was a national semifinalist in the 18's. The neighbors used to ask my mother why we were never out playing in the yard, and she told them, "None of us are ever home. We just come back to sleep." We were busy every weekend playing tournaments, and my parents gave every ounce of their energy and minute of their time to us kids.

I never had a lesson until I was 14 and started working with the USTA National Junior Traveling Team coaches. My dad was a self-educated, natural teacher. He was a stickler for work ethic, practice, and repetition of ground strokes. He loved the Connors-Borg-McEnroe era of tennis and he observed that most of the pro players in that era had much better forehands than backhands . . . except for Connors, Borg, and McEnroe. They were the three best players in the world, and their backhands were all better than their forehands. So my father made sure that all of his kids had solid backhands. My sisters' and my best shots became our backhands because we practiced them so much.

My dad never believed in playing sets in practice, and he never pitted us against one another. He believed in hitting tennis balls back and forth, and in drilling. He didn't believe in playing every Tom, Dick, and Harry and losing 6–2 in practice, then being in a funk for three days because you lost and thought you didn't have a chance of making it. My dad always believed in positive energy.

"You're the best," he'd tell us while we were practicing. "You're hitting the ball great."

When I was 12, I flew out to San Diego for my first national championship as a seeded player, the 12-and-under National Hard Courts. Samantha Stevenson, the journalist who would later become a noted intense tennis mom with her own daughter, Alexandra, wrote an article in *World Tennis Magazine* that bashed my dad for his behavior. But my dad was no different from Peter Graf, Jim Pierce, Andrea Jaeger's dad, or Jennifer Capriati's. Even Karolyi Seles, who appeared jovial and was always smiling, drove Monica hard. Clear and simple, a kid does not become a tennis champion without a parent — usually the father — to drive him or her on.

When I was 14, I had a magical season. I lost one match at the beginning of the season to Brian Dunn — a local rival of mine in Florida — and then went undefeated the rest of the year. I went 59 and one, and I won all the three big junior national tournaments for my age group — the hard courts, clay courts, and indoors — as well as the Easter and Orange Bowls, which were international events. I became the No. 1 player in the country in the 14-and-under category.

It was incredible; I was this boy wonder. I was so nonchalant, so relaxed, and so confident and free-flowing, I was sort of unconscious. I was this overweight kid with this extreme Western grip. But people who saw me play back then said, "Wow! That's an amazing athlete. He's so smooth and he doesn't muscle the ball. He's so confident, smiling and laughing out there on the court." All I did was win, win, win. I was impossible to beat.

I became this mini junior-tennis legend in the South

Florida region. Elton John, who's a big tennis fan, saw me play once around that time and said, "I'd give up one of my gold records for that kid's backhand." I hit with Ivan Lendl, who had dropped to No. 2 in the world, and he said afterwards, "That young kid I just practiced with today — if I had that kid's backhand, I'd still be No. 1."

My father likes to tell the story of how once, when I was practicing with the Palm Beach College tennis team, this older man came by and asked my father, "Is that your boy? He hits the ball well. How old is he?"

My father said, "He's 14."

"Do you think he can hold his own against that college boy?"

"Yes," my father replied.

"Does he have a national ranking?" the man asked.

"Yes," my father replied.

Finally the man asked my father, "How would he do against that Spadea kid?"

The USTA picked me as the youngest player on their junior national team. I was 14, playing against 16 and 18 year olds. It was a big honor, but it was also kind of sad for me, because I knew the USTA had taken my dad out of the picture. He was happy for me, and probably a little relieved that he didn't have to shoulder the financial and coaching burden anymore, but sometimes I wished — and I still do — I had never got the USTA's support. I wonder how far I would have gone if my father had continued to coach me.

My dad had a higher standard of success than any coach I've ever worked with — and I've worked with Pat Cash, Peter Lundgren, Jim Pierce, and Pete Fischer, to name a few. He always asked more from me, and that's why I never paid attention to the people like Samantha Stevenson, who felt sorry for me when I was a kid. They'd see my father yelling at me — cursing me out — but a lot of people also felt sorry for Martina Hingis, Andre Agassi, and Steffi Graf when their mothers and fathers were tough on them. How many of those people feel sorry for them now? Bill Gates is known for yelling at his employees, but do people feel sorry for them or the end result at Microsoft?

I don't want to sound conceited, but anyone who hasn't experienced a high level of achievement cannot relate to my situation. To make it in the crazy competitive world of professional tennis, a major price has to be paid. I'd rather be a high-ranking professional tennis player — making millions of dollars over a career for playing a game — than be President of the United States. But no one becomes a Top 20 tennis pro without battling and struggling a lot.

Looking back on the way my father trained me as a kid, in some ways, I think he wasn't tough enough on me. I haven't won any Grand Slam titles, the U.S. or the French Open. Maybe if he had been harder on me, I would've been more successful. I'm not interested in what the average Joe who hasn't strived for the top thinks. I'm interested in the opinions of successful people. Even my father admits he was never as hard on me as Mike Agassi was on Andre, before he handed over the job to Nick Bollettieri.

My father became my coach again when I decided at 18 not to follow the USTA's and Stan Smith's advice to go to college and turned pro instead. Some of the other players and coaches — particularly Agassi and Brad Gilbert — criticized me for keeping my father as my coach for so long. Tennis is a very incestuous game, and although everyone would admit that, people are uncomfortable with the reality of it, especially when it's father and son in the roles of coach and player. Other players would ask me, "Why is your father always with you? Do you two stay in the same room?" What made matters worse was that my father wasn't a stoic like Paradorn Srichaphan's dad, who also coached Paradorn for many years on the pro tour. My dad wasn't afraid of speaking his mind.

When Agassi called me a journeyman — "I've always given Vince nothing but respect. I think he's a real good player. I think he would be a heck of a lot better player without his dad" — my dad had a few choice words for Andre. I had just beaten Rafter at what was then the Lipton Tennis Championships (now the NASDAQ-100 Open) in Miami, and was playing Andre in the next round. I was ranked No. 44 in the world at the time, and my dad said, "Will Andre say that if Vince beats him today?"

At 25 — when I decided to drop my dad as my coach — it had gotten to the point where my father's passion was out of control and it became too much for me. I hadn't won Wimbledon or the U.S. Open, so I wanted to change things. I thought to myself, "I'm 25 years old and I need to take charge." My dad and mom had been such strong supporters, and they had taken care of most of my big responsibilities. I needed to stand up for myself and see what life was all about.

My dad was getting too worked up. He thought I needed to be tougher on the court. He'd tell me things like, "You've got to get your serve stronger and come to net more," or "Your opponent didn't hit his backhand strongly, but you let him get away with it. You didn't press him." The bottom line is that he felt I was quitting. I didn't agree with him. I'd ask him, "Are you serious? I didn't think I quit in that match."

I needed a change. But for the last five years, I haven't found one coach who has really helped me improve as a player. Last year at the U.S. Open, I was in between coaches, so Karel Novacek, once a Top 10 player and now my financial advisor, served as my coach for the week of the

Open. After I lost in the second round to Jurgen Meltzer, Novacek said to me, "Your intensity could have been higher," but he didn't say, "You quit."

The following week, I focused on Novacek's comment and made sure my intensity was higher. I moved my feet faster, increased the energy level in my body, double-checked all my playing cues: "Am I moving my feet? Am I taking enough time on my serve? Am I hitting my inside-out forehand and moving this guy? Am I playing the right strategy?" I made it to the finals of the tournament in Delray Beach, back when it was held in September.

Looking back on it, my dad was a great coach, but he didn't always know how to express himself in a way that was positive and could help me. As I grew older, I needed to be treated more as a man, not as the kid I used to be. I couldn't listen and learn from many of his comments because there was an anger and disappointment in both of us that I had not achieved better results as a pro player.

If I asked my father to coach me again, he'd go out on the road again with me tomorrow. I still talk to him a few times every week — not so much about tennis, but about my career. He still follows the game religiously. He watches the Tennis Channel nonstop. He threw away the remote because he never needs to change the channel. When I was a kid I was my father's remote; he'd bark, "Vince, get up and change the channel."

It takes a certain uniqueness to play tennis for that long, to practice nearly every day for hours, a certain eccentricity which I call a talent or passion. We're talking about hitting a tennis ball over the net. Who's going to stay out there and hit balls over years and years and years? You'd better have a passion for it. You'd better love it.

Why do you think Martina has kept at it for so long, or

Agassi, or Connors? Do you think Martina or Andre needs the money at this stage? People say, "It's for the money," but you'll see if it's for the money because there are one-hit wonders in tennis, just like in the music business. They are a hit for one season, then they're out of the game and you never hear about them again.

It takes that extra level of love to get you out of bed saying, "I need to do better and I want to do better." My father gave me that passion. I would never have become a pro if it weren't for my mother and him. They gave every ounce of time to their kids. They never had a weekend free when we were growing up because of our tennis lives.

My sister, Luanne, was the first star of the family. She beat Monica Seles in the finals of a big junior tournament, and played in her first pro tournament at the age of 14. But my family didn't have enough money to send her out onto the pro tour unless my father traveled with her as her coach. He made the decision to stay behind because of me. He told us, "You all have the talent to make it as pro players, but it's who wants it most inside. The girls have kind of lost it."

It was true. For my sisters it was like, "tennis is cool and fun, and we're good at it, but there are other things in life." For me, once I got selected to the USTA Junior National Team, tennis became my priority.

I felt like tennis was going to be my life. When I was a freshman in high school, my first day at St. Andrews, all my classmates thought I was a completely ignorant kid. But I thought, "I'm not really into this school or any school. This is not me. I'm going to be a tennis player. That's what I'm going to do." And I put all my energy into the game.

I'm in the second round in the Delray Beach tournament, playing a complete nobody qualifier. I didn't even know his name — until I just looked it up — let alone know how to pronounce it (Teimuraz Gabashvili, a teenager from Russia who upset James Blake in the first round). But knowing everyone is dangerous, I'm hoping to get through this match somehow, someway.

Regardless of whom I play, I always plot my day out to facilitate winning. Athletes are all about creating routine — habits formed around our idiosyncrasies which we stick to like white on rice. Maybe we tap into superstitions, but it makes sense to us to never budge or deviate from a winning formula. During tournaments, Borg used to eat at the same restaurant, request the same table, chair, and meal, right down to the very grain of salt, *every single night*. Call it monotony, superstition, psychosis, obsessive-compulsive, or even scientific, but it worked for Borg, most importantly in his mind. Athletes and their coaches work hard to figure out that successful formula. It's not a very exciting life. It's a waiting game, but it's the price you have to pay for fame. Maximizing what you get out of every day is paramount.

I'm the No. 1 seed for the third time in this tourney's history. The reason why Agassi and Roddick aren't here is that after a major tournament like the Australian Open, the top players usually take the next couple of weeks off. In Delray, I'm the feature match every night, playing prime time at 7:30 p.m. Last year, I developed a pattern here that got me to the finals, and I'm sticking with it on an everyday basis this year, too. I'm sleeping in my own bed at home in Boca Raton instead of staying at the tournament hotel. I get up every morning at 11, usually getting to sleep at 1 a.m. after the previous night's match and aftermath. I usually need 10 hours of sleep to feel alert, sharp, and energetic. Agassi is rumored to need even more sleep. I've heard he can't play top-level tennis unless he gets 12 hours sleep. Wow, and I thought I was a beauty.

I eat the same breakfast every morning, so my stomach, digestive tract, and overall body knows what it's getting — no surprises! Here I follow yet another Rocky Marciano pledge: "No new foods before a fight." I eat a bagel with strawberry jam, one bowl of corn flakes with skim milk, a cup of flavored yogurt, and four sips or four ounces of orange juice. I have another cup of yogurt and four ounces of OJ two hours later.

After chillin' in my house all day until three, I drive to a local Italian restaurant and have lunch — spaghetti with tomato sauce, add grilled chicken, a Sprite, and a little bread if I'm still hungry. I eat alone, and at 4:30 I pick up my traveling coach at his house. He drives us to our old faithful Starbucks, and I drink a tea and chill some more. At 5:15, we go for our pregame mini-dinner, so I can stock up on carbs two hours before the battle. When we finally arrive at the Tennis Center, it is sixish and I get ready to practice for 30 minutes. On the way to the tournament site, we pump up our usual rap music on the stereo: Jay-Z, Kanye West. The music is a must for me. I'm like Pavlov's dog — when I hear my music, I go into battle mode.

Our practice isn't until 6:30, an hour before the match. I like warming up just before I play, because that way I'm still sweating when I walk out onto the court. I've gotten through the day meeting all my preparation guidelines, and now it's smooth sailing. I've got my rackets ready, a change of clothes, my Gatorade and energy bars in order, and I'm set once again, in *Groundhog Day* fashion, à la Borg, to charge to the title. Play ball.

Teimuraz turns out to be a heavy hitter, and at 18, with nothing to lose, in the first set he's hitting all his shots for the lines and torching them, winning the set, 6–4. But I haven't been on the tour for 12 years without learning how to slow down a torrid youngster. I begin to make the points longer, induce him to hit more shots, and work harder, and he begins to break down. The result is a 4–6, 7–5, 6–3 win.

Early in my career, I beat a number of top-ranked players, starting when I was 21 with Yevgeny Kafelnikov in the 1995 U.S. Open, Thomas Enquist and Richard Krajicek at the 1996 Miami Masters, and almost Michael Chang — when he was the No. 2 player in the world — in the third round at the 1996 U.S. Open. I was serving for the match at 5–4 in the fourth set, when the wheels fell off my game. I even beat Pete Sampras — when he was No. 1 — at Indianapolis in 1999. We had split the first two sets when Pete retired from the match with an injury.

Last year, I beat Safin and Blake at Miami when they were ranked No. 2 and No. 15 in the world, respectively, and Roddick at Scottsdale when he was No. 7. But since I defeated Rainer Schuettler of Germany (No. 19 at the time) in the first round of the Rome Masters in May of last year, I haven't beaten a player with a ranking higher than mine. I haven't set out to beat the top guys with a real conviction lately. It used to be a rush to go out and beat the top guys. Now I'm focused on trying to beat the players I should beat — the ones with lower rankings than me — because I used to get a lot of flak for not doing that.

I'm in the semifinals, after toughing out a quarterfinal match against fellow American, Kevin Kim, in three sets. I want to win this, my hometown tournament, so badly, especially after making it to the finals just five months prior. I can see myself giving a storybook-ending speech in front of all my family and friends, thanking everybody for being part of my dream, but then I hear the ATP trainer ask, "How bad does your back hurt, Vince?"

I'm propped up on the trainer's table this Friday night after my quarterfinal victory, a two-and-a-half-hour, back-breaking match. "It's just really sore," I say, "especially when I rotate." It's midnight, and I have a two o'clock semifinal against a Belgian flare of talent named Xavier Malisse, who is enigmatic and quiet off the court, yet has serious ability, with heavy ground strokes off both sides, a formidable serve, relaxed hands, and fearless shot selection. On the flip side, Malisse has been heralded as the next Real Deal Top-Tenner since the age of 18. He's now 25, and has yet to win even one tournament.

The match is set for the feature of the day and it prom-ises to be televised and adrenalin-filled. I have my game plan — hitting aggressively enough so that Malisse can't dictate to me side to side. The key to playing a big hitter is to keep him from having a good strike at the ball. That means I need to vary my spins, depths, angles, and targets. Xavier has a solid backhand crosscourt, and likes to surprise you by hit-ting it down the line at times. He combines it with an effective and consistent slice backhand that keeps you on your toes and out of rhythm. The main thing for me to focus on is to keep the ball moving and not let him hit more than three backhands in a row.

What makes this difficult is Malisse's ominous forehand. He can take you off the court on a single strike, but he can also be erratic with it. When I change direction to hit to his forehand, I have to hit the ball with enough pace that he can't hurt me. I have to look for a short ball to attack, but Xavier has good foot speed, although his conditioning is sometimes questionable. Another one of my tactics is to attack his weak second serve.

We get it on and it's toe-to-toe, grinding, scrapping, slashing, slicing, looping, ground-stroker-savvy points. We trade service breaks a couple of times — similar to when I play Blake, both our return games are superior to our service games. My back is holding up after extensive treatment and hot creams used to numb any pains. All of a sudden, it starts to rain. On a hard court, rain affects the surface instantly, so play is postponed and we are sent off to the locker room. We sit there for about 15 minutes, and I collect my thoughts. I'm down a break at 2–3. Greg and my friend, Karel Novacek, come in and offer some encouraging words, "Just keep at it, you're doing OK. Stay focused, go for your shots." Novacek makes a funny face to try and relax me a little. "What am I doing wrong?" I ask him frantically, as I'm insecure as to why I lost my serve so easily. Greg says, "Don't sweat it. The match has just started. Get the break back now, and you'll be all right." It's encouraging advice — not stern, just positive.

When the rain stops and we resume playing, we continue to try to break each other down, rallying crosscourt, then down the line, an angle shot here, then I approach and stiff a volley into the net. "Make it!" I mutter under my breath, discouraged at duffing a volley after setting up the point perfectly.

"Game and first set to Malisse, 7–5," the chair umpire shouts out. I become frustrated and start reflecting on how he's beaten me twice before, at Wimbledon and the U.S. Open in prior years. Not the kind of thought to get me motivated to come back and win. I block off any negative thinking. I know I can play better, and I focus on the next game. Malisse is tough when he wants to compete. He can fly off the handle — which has proven to be his downfall — but today he's outhitting and out-toughing me. I can only adjust, sustain my effort, and hope for a favorable turn-around. My motto is: "Never give up on any points."

We hold serve to two-all in the second set, and yet again, a rain spell hits, sending us packing to the clubhouse. I'm trying to keep my back loose by doing stretches and jumps, and we momentarily get called back to play. Again it's back and forth, back and forth. It's exasperating tennis, but I tell myself I love the adversity of this match — or at least tolerate it. I'm looking for any sign that Malisse is starting to crack, but he doesn't let up. He continues his backhand-crosscourt attrition shot-selection, throwing in the occasional down-the-liner.

My muscles aren't responding, and my shots are going shorter and becoming weaker. The power on my serve and forehand is letting me down. He combines consistency with effortless power, and keeps his composure enough to take a 5–4 lead. All he needs to do is win his service game to end the match. I don't give up. A lot of times I feel I can claw myself back into a match — turn the momentum when my opponent is on the brink of winning. He might get anxious, and I relax more with my back to the wall and start to hit with abandon.

This is exactly what happens. I take a 15–40, double-break-point lead, but before I can blink, Malisse bombards me with two big serves, an overhead, and a couple of fore-hands, and quickly dismisses my hopes of an encore. I'm left with no choice but to walk up to the net and shake hands, wish him good luck in the finals, walk to my chair, and sit still and take it. Yet another year gone at the Delray Championships, another shattered vision, another victory speech on hold.

As I sit in the locker room in my usual pensive, post-match loss mode, I close my eyes and think about myself at age seven, playing at Delray tennis clubs, hour after hour with my family, day after day, weeks and years. I hardly ever went to parties when I was a teenager. My parents were fairly protective. They didn't like what they'd heard about high school parties. I never had an idol growing up. I never had a poster on my wall of any tennis star. My favorite TV shows were *Diff'rent Strokes*, *Leave It to Beaver*, *The Brady Bunch*, and *Love Boat*. I dreamed a lot of being a pro tennis player.

And here I am, still playing in Delray Beach, contesting for top-level titles now as the pro I always wanted to be. The feeling of being edged out for yet another title is disappointing. But I have no reason to be discouraged. I'm playing and striving not only for myself, but for the thousands of kids and adults I hit balls with growing up in this very city. There is a piece of every one of them in me when I compete, and I can't stop now, for them or for myself.

FEBRUARY 6
San Jose, California

Just arrived in San Jose, a day later than I should have. I wanted to stay one more day in Boca to just rest after my semifinal loss to Malisse. There's not much time to prepare for this indoor tourney. Indoor is not my surface. I just flew across the country, and now I find out from the tournament officials that I have to play tomorrow. That's just great. Oh, I'll manage, but I would've liked a little more time. Usually, when you make it to the semifinals or finals of the tournament preceding the current one, they give you an extra day off. But I guess I'm just going to have to "grip it and rip it." That's indoor tennis: serve, return, and volleys.

When I walked off the plane this afternoon, my back was stiff from sitting for what seemed like forever. I dislike flying. I don't care too much for being in a huge metal machine filled with gas, 30,000 feet above the ground I play tennis on. Whatever; I'll get over it. But it's the part of my job I could most do without.

After grabbing my backpack, filled with goodies like my iPod, candy, hats, mini keyboard, mini studio recorder, and more, I yank my racket bag — filled with eight Prince rackets — from the upper bin. Then my traveling coach and I walk to the baggage claim to pick up my two duffel bags filled with clothes. We get our carts ready and wait, which is an every-week affair for us. It's a good time to check cell phone messages.

"You have no new messages." . . . It's the story of my life. Well, not always, but everyone has those days where nobody loves them. Anyways, my coach checks his cell phone, too, and turns pale in the face.

"Hey Vince, the sheriff in Tampa just called me, I may have a problem," he says.

I look at him like he has to be nuts. "Not here, man, not now," I say.

"I may have to go back to Tampa," he says.

I think, "What in the heck kind of luck is that?" For him and for me. One of my bags doesn't show on the carousel, so we have to wait forever and then report it. This is turning into a great trip so far.

The Mercedes car service for the tour picks us up and drives us to the hotel. It's a very nice one. Generally, they are, but every once in a while you get a real fleabag. In the lobby, I see Ginepri and his coach, Francisco Montana. We just say "What's up?" to each other and go our own ways. Walking up to the front desk, the legendary Jim Brown, the football Hall of Famer, walks by me and I holla at him. He smiles back, but I can tell that, besides recognizing I'm a pro tennis player because of the racket bag on my shoulder, he doesn't know who I am.

Mostly, I get noticed in public only when I'm in Boca, or a diehard tennis fan recognizes me in a big city. I've been playing pro tennis since the age of 18, but besides appearing on *The Today Show* with Katie Couric during the Olympics, I haven't appeared on national television very often. With pro tennis in America, if you're not Andre Agassi, Andy Roddick, or maybe James Blake, very few people know who you are.

My room is very nice, clean, and big. I stay in a different hotel pretty much every week. If it's a nice room I say, "I'm home!" If it's a dodgy room, I say, "You're kidding, right?" But once I check it out, I just want to jump in bed and chill, always feeling exhausted after a trip. I say, "Whoa, put the lime in the coconut, and mix it all up." It's just a saying I use to make me relax — like I'm in paradise.

I begin to doze off, but the phone rings. It's my coach, who just learned his sheriff in Tampa call wasn't so urgent or perilous, and he wants me to meet him down in the lobby for tennis practice in 30 minutes. I don't argue with him, even though I was hoping for sweet dreams, not hitting another tennis ball. I've played four matches in the last five days.

A word here about coaches. I've had probably 25 in my last five years on tour. A lot of times I've gone without a coach — as Federer is doing now with great success. I would just travel with a buddy, this younger friend from Boca, Jason Applebome, or I've gone out on tour with only a trainer.

Pete Fischer believes all traveling coaches are overrated. Their roles are not that significant. He tried to convince me that I could go out on tour with the guy who is cutting my grass right now and win, as long as I worked with Fischer on parts of my game during the off-weeks. He believes that everyone Sampras worked with after him was pretty much a plumber. Fischer had shown Pete the technique, the mechanics, and that was the key. It's obviously a biased opinion, and most likely incorrect, but to Fischer, most coaches are basically security blankets.

I was coached by Peter Lundgren — Federer's coach when he won Wimbledon for the first time, and Safin's coach now — but only for two weeks. I hurt my back and he started coaching the Swiss Davis Cup team. I've been coached by Craig Kardon, Navratilova's coach during part of her heyday, and Gavin Hopper, who also coached Seles and Philippoussis. But I've never had a coach for a long stretch who was once a Top 20 player, and who really knows what it's like to play at the highest level of the game. I definitely need a new coach. I'm not going to retire until I find a good coach. I'll be 38 before I retire.

My traveling coach is only with me on a temporary basis. He will coach me through the first quarter of the year, ending in Miami at the end of March. I'm looking for continuity in a coach, but it's not easy. A lot of the big-name coaches, like Brad Gilbert and Larry Stefanki (who coached Marcelo Rios to No. 1) aren't working with players right now. But they want in excess of $100,000 a year, and they want to hitch their wagon to an up-and-comer, not a guy who they think is at or near the end of his career.

I think that if I could just clone myself, I would be my own best coach. A good coach will scout upcoming opponents, construct a game plan, and make practice sessions important. A good coach, especially at the beginning of a player's career, can make the difference in a player making it to the Top 10 or falling back to the Challengers. Where would Sampras have been without Fischer, Gullikson, and Annacone? Where would Agassi be without Bollettieri and Gilbert? Do you think Safin would have won the Australian this year if Lundgren hadn't pulled him back from the abyss?

When a good coach watches a match, he can see what is right and what should be improved, what needs to be better, more dynamic, and faster. The player might feel he's doing the right thing, but a good coach can see what he's doing wrong and set up drills that enable his player to hit a better stroke, a faster shot, to move faster on the court, or to correct his technique. What's right is right, and what's wrong is wrong. Like Fischer says, "In is good, and out is bad." That's why videotape is so important. But the best thing is for a player to have a good coach who knows what he's doing, and who can analyze and change the player's game accordingly.

At the end of the day, the player-coach relationship is a business. We're not out here like family members, we're just helping each other out. It's like collateral out here. For most traveling coaches, the life is not that hard. They get paid about $1,500 a week — bonuses if their player does well — and most get their expenses (travel, hotel, and food) covered by the player. They usually don't have to get up before 10, and they usually don't even practice with their players because they find another player to do that. Active coaching is not allowed in pro tennis, with the exception of Davis Cup, and then only the Davis Cup captain can have the player's ear — so during matches, they just sit on the sidelines and clap, make signals, and work on their tan.

For the player who is struggling, paying a coach can be like adopting three kids. And many of these coaches — unless they're an esteemed player from the past or a guy who works very hard — are not worth their salt. Anyone can say, "I want to be a coach." I could go up to Madonna and say, "Hey, I want to be your personal assistant. What do you want me to do?" Some of the guys out there coaching are charlatans.

Before Scottsdale last year, Kardon and I parted ways, and my mom asked Sam Aparicio — a longtime coach who used to be Pancho Gonzales' hitting partner — to travel with me. Right afterwards, I won my first pro tournament. I don't remember him giving me a ton of advice. He's a very smooth, relaxed guy — very generous and responsible, but not domineering. He stayed with me through the French Open — eight tournaments — and I went 16 and 7 with him, winning Scottsdale and getting to the semis of Miami and the quarters of Rome. But I was disappointed with my clay-court results, which were better in 2003.

I felt that in the short term, Sam was a good coach, but in the long term, my game would suffer. He was a feel-good guy who facilitated the game I already had, but I was beginning to block out what he said and not believe in him enough. So I hired my old Florida tennis buddy, Lex Carrington, as my coach for the grass-court season, and I made the round of 16 at Wimbledon, a first for me. But then Lex quit because he was offered more money to coach a top female player. Before the Open, Marcos Ondruska — who had been my coach for the summer — quit to go coach Jennifer Capriati. The all-time bail-out a coach gave me came from Gavin Hopper. He was coaching Amanda Coetzer at the same time as he was coaching me. At the 1998 Australian Open, I was in the third round, about to play Petr

Korda, and the day before the match, Hopper came up to me and said, "Listen, Vince, due to contractual obligations I have with Amanda, I have to go home."

I know I have a reputation for not sticking with coaches, but not everyone knows the full story of what's gone on. For example, I had one coach get stopped at customs in Montreal for having cocaine in his bag. They're checking my bags, when all of a sudden, I hear my coach yelling behind me. They found traces of cocaine on or in his bag, but it turned out not to be enough to convict. We ended up being detained for three hours — missing our flight — before they let him go. I had to fire him.

I had another coach who, when I asked him whether he thought a hostess at the restaurant where we were eating was pretty, and whether I should ask her out, said, "I don't care what they look like. Listen, they're all pigs. The other night I was with these three pigs, right? So, you know, I'm taking care of them for a good two-three hours . . ."

Luckily the waitress walked up with our food then, interrupting his story. Another coach of mine served jail time for having an affair with an underage female player. Tennis is a game that attracts some strange and rebellious folks, and if you play long enough, one of them is certain to become your coach.

FEBRUARY 7

The tournament is played in the arena downtown where the San Jose Sharks, the NHL team, plays. The ATP-sponsored Mercedes-Benz drops us off in the back, which looks like a loading dock for trucks and minivans bringing in equipment for rock concerts and other special events. As we enter, we walk past a small media room where journalists are preparing their stories, and where I must return for a press conference after the match — but only if one or more of the journalists wants to talk to me. I usually don't get many requests for interviews, unless I go deep into a tournament or it's the U.S. Open.

There's a buffet table set up in the players' lounge holding peanut butter and jelly sandwiches, fruit, cookies, and some chicken and pasta that looks catered. I have a flashback to my middle-school lunchroom where I would try to trade the two hard-boiled eggs my mother had packed for some kid's Doritos. I walk into the locker room and it's spacious. I peek out onto the center court, which is beautiful. Half of the arena is covered with a drape, which makes the tennis capacity 7,500 spectators instead of the full arena's 15,000. There is only one court, so every match is played on it, and you feel the excitement and you feel important.

I remember playing a quarterfinal match in 1996 against an unknown Slovakian player (his name was Jan Kroslak) and holding match point in the third set. If I won the point, I would play Sampras in the semifinals. But I lost the point and then the match, and when I walked off the court disheartened into the locker room, there was Sampras watching the television monitor. He hadn't even played his quarterfinal match yet, but he had been watching the final points of our match to see who he was going to beat in the semis.

You could always see the confidence in his eyes; he exuded it even in his silence preparing for his match. He would jump up and down, and wind his right serving arm into his service motion a few times, but that was the extent of his warm-up. Other players go through extensive warm-ups prior to their matches — riding a stationary bike, running in place, stretching like yoga instructors — but not Sampras. I never saw him overextend himself before a match. His confidence was his best warm-up.

I played Sampras five times and the only time I ever won a set, the second set of the last match we played in Indianapolis in 1999, Sampras retired from the match. But Pete was the best player I ever played against because he took me out of the match and, at times, made me feel like I wasn't even competing. Courier was the hardest worker, a pioneer in playing better than what his God-given skills should have allowed. Nick Saviano once told me, "Jim Courier is naturally one step slower than you, Vince, but he plays two steps faster."

FEBRUARY 10

I've reached the semifinals for the third time here in San Jose. I beat Anthony Dupuis of France in the first round, and James Blake in the second, taking the second set, 6–0. I'm going to play an unknown Frenchman, Cyril Saulnier, this afternoon, but I wanted to write a few words about Blake before I go out to the arena.

Few players in the history of the sport have received so much attention as James, and except for 2003 when he reached the fourth round at the Australian Open and achieved a career-high ranking of No. 22, his play really hasn't merited it. I get more reporters coming up to me and asking me my opinion on James than I do about my own game.

Fischer likes to talk about players having "reproduceable weapons," meaning shots that are consistent assets, and James doesn't have those. He's got a flashy game. Blake's backhand isn't a beautiful, flawless shot, it's an element-of-surprise shot. He keeps it deep, and he kind of surprises you with it down the line. He also slices it and comes in sometimes. But it's not a Tommy Haas backhand. If you move Blake around and keep the ball deep to Blake's backhand, he's not going to hurt you. Sometimes he'll go for broke on his running forehand, but if you hit authoritative shots and you move well, you'll be fine.

His serve also lets him down. He'll run through some of his service games impressively, but there are always one or two service games a match where he just folds or double-faults. Blake's forehand is supposed to be his money shot, but he doesn't extend enough with his right arm. He turns it over too fast and has a wristy follow-through, whereas Federer gets that little extra extension, then finishes off like Blake does. I think if Blake extended his forearm at least three-quarter's length — you don't want it straight because then it would be stiff — he'd have a more effective forehand. He gets a lot of action on it, but he doesn't get a lot of consistency out of it.

Biomechanically, from an anatomy and physics standpoint, his forehand is not correct with its geometry and the way he finishes. If you ask an expert, there's no way in the world he's going to tell you that Blake's forehand is rock solid. The players with the best forehands are Nadal, Federer, Agassi, Moya, Roddick, and Fernando Gonzales. Blake's forehand is a dangerous shot if the ball's high and he's on it, but it's not like my backhand, where I can play perfect defense with it, then go on the offensive. People can see that effortless feel and rhythmic power whether I'm on my game or off.

Against Blake, I play deeper, tougher, and more consistently. I like going to Blake's forehand on big points. That's how I beat him in Scottsdale last year, 7–5 in the third, and that's how I beat him yesterday. I've had an issue with James ever since our match in Vienna in 2002. I had just made my breakthrough in a tour event — getting to the semis of Tokyo, which is a million-dollar tournament — and had moved up to No. 55 in the world after having grinded my way out of challengers for the last two years.

I flew all the way from Tokyo to Vienna and played the next day against Blake in the first round. I won the first set, then Blake went up 3–0 in the second set, then I had to go to the bathroom, so I took a designated break. When I came back on court — at our next changeover, after I'd just won a game — James said something to me under his breath as we passed at the net.

"Nice gamesmanship there," he said. "You're trying to stall the match by going to the bathroom because I had the momentum. Nice try, buddy. We'll see what happens."

Before then, we'd been cordial to one another, but there was no real rapport. It wasn't good or bad. I'd beaten him in a Challenger the year before, then I'd beaten him again in Queens (London) in June 2002. So I'd beaten him twice already, and I think he thought, "I'm getting all this hype and I can't beat this guy. I better pull something."

I didn't say anything at the time. I was in shock. I hadn't heard trash talk since the juniors, where a guy actually tried to verbally intimidate me. Tennis isn't like basketball or hockey; there are no fights. The closest thing I ever saw to a fight was when Irena Spirlea bumped Venus Williams during a changeover at the U.S. Open. Rumor has it that Jeff Tarango punched Tom Gullikson in the locker room at Wimbledon for clapping for his opponent, Paul Goldstein. Gullikson was a coach for the USTA, and Tarango thought it was ridiculous that Gullikson would be biased.

But nothing like that had ever happened to me. I think Blake said what he did at the changeover because he didn't want to come across to the fans like he was being confrontational.

For the rest of the match, both of us were grunting loudly and trying to get the upper hand, celebrating after winners. We started showing more of what our true ambitions were. I was certainly more into the match. He ended up winning it, and I felt that he had thrown me off my game.

After the match, as we were walking off the court, I said, "Hey James, that was really an appropriate and professional thing you did. It really lived up to the image you try to portray of yourself."

"Hey, nobody ever questions the way that I operate," he said. "I get along with everybody on this tour. You're not the most liked guy out here. I've won the sportsmanship award. I'm known for that."

I said, "You know what James, you are known for that, and that's why I'm not going to further dignify your on-court commentaries with any more responses. The last time I checked, we were two pro tennis players, not a couple of juniors."

That was it. There was no swearing or "Let's get into it" talk. But I called him out on what I thought was unsportsmanlike of the "sportsman." A while later, Blake apologized to my coach, saying he was sorry the whole argument came to pass.

FEBRUARY 11

Cyril Saulnier warms up for his matches like an oven, a good 20 minutes of bouncing, running, and footwork drills, which he doesn't stop until the match begins. I think it's excessive, but to each his own. This is a real good opportunity to get the monkey off my back, playing against unknowns in the quarters of this tournament. Saulnier is ranked No. 60, but he starts out by not missing a ball, ripping forehands, backhands, serves, everything. My timing is off, and I get down two early breaks, then lose the first set 6–2.

I'm confused, ticked off, and I try to figure out his game. He's hitting big first serves, then using his backhand to go down the line for winners. His forehand is erratic, but powerful when he strikes it. There is neither wind nor sun to distract him from his demolition. I know he is a streaky player who mentally shifts like the sand on a beach. I need to be the wave that moves him into that irritable state.

I'm holding my serve, pressuring him to come up with big shots every point, but at four-all, 40–15 on my serve, I play a few careless, poorly executed points, and he breaks me. Cyril takes his flashy warm-up, No. 60-ranked game and polishes off the last game of the match like a Top 20 player. I'm struck down again. I sit in my chair awash in self-contempt, looking at my rackets and wanting to break each one of them against the umpire's stand.

It's losing matches like this that makes me think about my tennis future. The feeling of winning keeps me going. When I win, I feel so good. I feel omnipotent, there's an immortal aura. I'm happy with everything. If I've been in an argument with one of my friends or family, I feel the need to call them right away, because I suddenly know everything will work out. It's something to sit there and think, "I've just beaten a top player." It's the closest feeling to paradise that I've experienced. It's why Connors kept going, and Navratilova, too.

But losing is plain painful. Every loss takes a chunk out of me. I don't know what's left. In the grand scheme of things, I'm just playing a game. What does it mean at the end of the day? It's not war and peace, it's not world hunger.

It's just a game. I'm going to take today's match and learn from it. It's over, and now I have to regroup and go to Memphis. When it's all said and done, it's about how you lose, not that you lost.

I've always identified with David Banner, the alter ego of The Incredible Hulk. He's got this unique lifestyle that he leads that is distinct from everyone else. He goes into a town and he terrorizes it to find the bad guy. It's his job. At the end of the show, to this soft, lonely piano music, you see him walking away on the side of the road with his backpack on. That's exactly the way I feel after playing a tournament. David Banner, a.k.a. Vince Spadea, changes back into his street clothes and walks back onto the highway of tennis, searching for his next encounter, hoping one day he will find himself, his purpose, and his destination.

FEBRUARY 14
Memphis, Tennessee

Playing in Memphis is as homey a feeling as you're going to get on the pro tour. I get picked up at the airport and I start thinking of the King of Rock, Elvis. I've never actually had the pleasure of visiting Graceland to see where Elvis clipped his sideburns, but hey, I've got to move my hips, too. The tournament hotel is small and comfortable, and it's only a three-minute walk from the Racket Club of Memphis, one of the few tournaments to be played at a private club. It's unique and quite elegant, with both indoor and outdoor courts. I remember coming here once with my older sister, Luanne, when she was 14 and playing in the 18-and-under National Clay Court Championships.

Center court is not as big as the usual center stages of

tennis, but it's very intimate for the fan — only about 3,000 seats — and the court sits only inches away from the front row. It doesn't give the players much room to run down shots, so you have to come out blasting big serves and smacking groundies hard. The entire club is mobbed with members and fans constantly scuffling around, most dressed in their Sunday best. The ladies are adorably polished, and the men dapper in their business suits, Southern accents hanging in the air like perfume. It's easy to get intoxicated by all the Southern hospitality.

I sit on a couch in the Player's Lounge with a glass window looking out on the two side-courts where there are matches on. I'm waiting for my first-round match against Thomas Enqvist, the former Top 10 player from Sweden, to begin. Enqvist is an outstanding indoor player (he lost to Roddick last week in San Jose in three tough sets), and he knocked me out of this tournament last year, so I have a chance for redemption today. But it will be a tall task, since I'm sitting here holding my shoulder, which is full of pain and soreness. I don't know if by playing I will just make it worse, but I'm going for it. In the past, I've played through pain and it got better with anti-inflammatory medicine and ice.

Enqvist, 30, was a Top 10 player for four years, and he is one of the only players who can say he's played Agassi to a standstill, winning five matches and losing five over his career. In the last two years he has slipped badly — as most players do who continue into their late twenties — ending the seasons at Nos. 95 and 73, respectively. I have beaten Thomas twice and lost to him three times in personal pro battles. We also played each other in the juniors, dating back to 1996.

The match starts, and I go up a break right away. I'm serving well, the adrenalin easing my shoulder pain. Unleashing my shots all over the court — the injury has actually helped me to play more carefree and aggressive tennis — I put Thomas on the defensive (it's usually the other way around) and wallop him 6–2 in the first set.

Tennis is tricky. You can play a great first set and demolish your opponent, but there's no such thing as sitting on a lead and milking the clock. You have to go out and outplay him again in the second set. If he steps up his game, the pressure actually falls right back on your shoulders. I go up a break early in the second set, and believe I'm in control, but then I double-fault and drop my serve. Ughh, I hate when that happens, but I have my poker face on, and Enqvist doesn't know what I'm thinking. I focus in on the next point.

It's funny how my demeanor and patience vary from week to week. The tennis player is faced with an inner struggle not to get too high or too low, to stay on an even keel. It's a personal challenge to encourage yourself — to not get affected by lost or misplayed points — and to always stay charged, but relaxed. The reason why Swedish players — from Borg to Joachim Johannsson, the latest Swede star — have enjoyed so much success in the past 25 years is they have a great inner balance. When was the last time you saw a Swedish player throw his racket down in disgust?

At 5–6, Enqvist is serving to stay in the match. At 6-foot-3, he has a big serve, and I've done a good job throughout the match to cover it, block it, and take it early. With the score at deuce, I hit a bullet return-of-serve, connecting with my weight moving forward — like a Louisville Slugger meeting a Nolan Ryan fastball square. I see the seams of the ball unravel for a second as the fuzz grates off my Prince racket and the ball lands smack on Enqvist's line.

"Advantage Spadea," I hear the umpire holler. "Match point here I am," I tell myself. I go back to my corner for a few seconds' pause to think about what I want to do, and to make sure I'm ready. Enqvist serves big again and I hit a forehand return deep and true. He backhands it crosscourt, and I throw up a heavy ball with a lot of spin on it, down the line and out of his strike zone. Big guys don't like this kind of play, even indoors. Enqvist tries to take the ball early, but it's already too high and he hits it late, sailing the ball long.

My shoulders lower in a tremendous, relieved feeling similar to when you're sitting in the doctor's waiting room after taking tests, and he walks out and tells you that everything's OK, you're healthy. The pressure that lifts makes me instantly feel an excited, renewed zest for life. I'm walking off the court with a win over Thomas Enqvist, indoors, having played with a bum shoulder, and having avenged my loss from last year, and evened our personal series. It doesn't get much better than this.

FEBRUARY 16

My shoulder acts up over the next couple of days, and I go into my second-round match with Antony Dupuis feeling very achy. After I lose the first set and go down a break early in the second, I default the match knowing it's not worth risking more damage. I want to be able to defend my only tournament title in Scottsdale next week, so I will shut it down and not practice for the next few days, give my shoulder some much-needed rest.

It's too bad. Roddick, the No. 1 seed here, defaulted in the semis to Kenneth Carlsen, a 31-year-old Dane who I have beaten in straight sets both times I've played him. Agassi did not play in Memphis, opting to travel to the Middle East and play in Dubai next week. Tommy Haas, the No. 2 seed, was also defeated in the quarters. If I had continued to play at the level I'd shown against Enqvist, this might have been a good opportunity for me to win my second career title. In the end, Carlsen won his third career title, becoming the first player over 30 whose name isn't Andre Agassi to win a tournament since Rusedski won at Newport, Rhode Island, last year.

I had my chances in Delray Beach, San Jose, and Memphis to possibly win the title, and Scottsdale is my next big opportunity, because after that the Federers, Safins, Hewitts, and Nadals come to America to play in the Master Series events in Indian Wells, California, and Miami, before everyone heads to Europe for the clay-court season, starting with the Masters Monte Carlo. These last few tournaments have been 32-player draws, but at Indian Wells and Miami, two of the biggest tennis tournaments in the world, the draw is 96.

PART III
WILD WOMEN and SONG

FEBRUARY 20
Scottsdale, Arizona

This is where it all started for me. I beat Andres Gomez, in my first ATP tour event in Miami in 1993, and also played in the U.S. Open that year. But the Scottsdale qualifying tournament in February, 1993, before Miami and the Open, is where I made my regular tour pro debut. The following year, I played in the main draw here to kick off my first full pro season. I lost to Aaron Krickstein in Scottsdale that year, and until last year, when I beat Nicolas Kiefer to win the title, I had not won a single match here — losing to Philippoussis, Rios, and Richey Reneberg. This is my seventh time coming out here, and although I've flown over the Grand Canyon many times, I've never actually set foot in it.

I remember Brad Gilbert busting my butt out here in 1993. I was only 18, but he was giving me a hard time, telling me I was out of shape and needed to work harder. "I've been on the pro tour for 12 years and I still work like a maniac," he said. "You're just starting out and you're a lazy bum." Brad's from the Bay Area, and told me that for workouts, he sprinted back and forth across the Golden Gate Bridge.

I lost in the last round of the qualifying tournament to a guy named Doug Flach, the brother of Ken Flach, one-half of the Grand Slam-winning doubles team of Flach and Robert Seguso. I won the first set 7–6, then I lost the next two sets 0 and 2. Seguso was actually helping me out that week serving as my coach — and Gilbert was good friends with Seguso — and both of them accused me of tanking and being out of shape. I *was* out of shape, but I didn't tank. I just got tired.

So Gilbert told me, "Either reason is unacceptable. You've got a lot of work to do. For you to give up at all in the last round of the qualifiers means you should be running across the Golden Gate Bridge with me, training like you're going nuts."

The sponsor of the tournament in those days was a treadmill company, and they had three treadmills set up right on the tournament grounds. They were set up for display, not for real use, but at 10 p.m. that night, Gilbert and Seguso had me running on one of those treadmills, punishing me for my collapse. I was running on that treadmill for 50 minutes, just trucking.

Pete Sampras's older brother, Gus, is the tournament director here and seeing him got me thinking of the first time I ever saw Pete play a match live. I was 16 and playing in the U.S. Open Junior event — where I lost to Enqvist in the second round. After my match I ran into Louis Armstrong Stadium, past a waving usher, and right into the first row of Sampras's quarterfinal match against Lendl. Pete was going for his shots with the fearlessness of a bear in the wild. Lendl was trying to reach his ninth straight U.S. Open final. Pete won the first two sets and Lendl came back to win the next two.

Pete was 19 and throwing serves at Lendl like he was flinging rocks from a slingshot, not caring where they landed. He was double-faulting a lot, and this woman in the stands behind me cried out, "Pete, just get it in." He'd miss long by two or three inches, hitting 95–105 mph second serves. But in the fifth set, his serve started to click, and he went up two breaks and finished off Lendl with two aces.

Pete went on to beat John McEnroe in the semis, then crushed Agassi in the finals, beating him 6–4, 6–3, 6–2. I was also in the stadium for that match. On match point, Agassi served and Sampras hit a nothing return, but Agassi missed an inside-out forehand. It was kind of a semi-tank by Agassi. Joe Brandi, Sampras's coach, raised his hands and said, "I'm the coach of the U.S. Open champion."

Sampras had dropped Fischer after the 1989 U.S. Open. He had upset Wilander, who was seeded No. 2 or 3, in the first round that year, but then he lost to Jay Berger in straight sets in the round of 16. Fischer said that Berger was just better. He was the better competitor and he outplayed Pete. But Pete wouldn't accept it. Fischer said he didn't care that much when Sampras fired him, because by then his job was done. Sampras already had all the shots and Fischer said, "He just wanted a ball-feeder as a coach." I've heard Sampras just got tired of Fischer being so negative.

Fischer talked to me about how fearless Sampras was. I don't know if it was an innate quality he had, or he acquired it, but Sampras had it. He had it when he served, especially after he'd lost a big point, and in tiebreakers. I see it in Federer's eyes now. He just won the tournament in Rotterdam last week, and has now won 15 out of 16 matches he's played so far in 2005, losing only to Safin in five sets in the Australian Open semis.

I've asked Fischer who's better, Sampras or Federer, and he said Sampras. You have to respect his answer. Is he ever wrong about things? Yes, no one's perfect. But I think what he's saying is that Federer doesn't hit aces like Sampras. He doesn't quite volley and come in as much as Sampras did. He does hit his ground strokes a lot better, and moves better. But Fischer feels if you can hold serve every time like Sampras — Federer has a tendency to be broken — then you're the better player.

My favorite Sampras story is from when I got him angry before our quarterfinal match in Indianapolis in 1999. The first night I got to Indianapolis, one of the local television stations wanted one of the players to do an interview. The sports anchor asked me, "What's going to happen if you play Sampras in the quarterfinals?" I thought it was a silly question, so I gave it a silly answer. "Even though I'm shorter," I said, "he's going to run for the border."

A day before our match, Sampras walked by me on the practice court and said in this mocking tone, "Hey that was a pretty good interview you did the other night, Vince. I thought it was real good." My coach at the time, this character from South Florida named John Skelly, yelled at him, "Don't take everything so serious, Pete."

FEBRUARY 25

Playing James Blake in the quarterfinals of the 2005 Tennis Channel Open started out as a déjà vu experience. I'd played and beat him in the 2004 quarterfinal here at the Princess Resort, a feature night-session match. I was hoping for the same result as we began our 7 p.m. prime-time stadium court match.

I walk out the defending champion, while Blake walks out on the court after a disastrous year you wouldn't wish on your worst enemy. After a plague of injuries and family tragedy, James is courageously trying make this night and 2005 better times for him. I have beaten him the last four times in head-to-head ATP competition, so I feel confident yet insecure, not sure how many times in a row I can expect to beat a solid, dangerous player like Blake.

When they introduce us, I notice Blake receives the greater applause; he's clearly the crowd's choice. James has always been a crowd favorite — the personification of the likeable American. One fan in particular seems rambunctiously loud, obnoxious, and most likely intoxicated.

"Let's go James," he screeches out, "We're going to do it tonight. Beat him!" James turns around and looks into the crowd at the man. "Come on, James, you can win this. Right here, baby!" the guy yells out.

I've played a lot of matches, and witnessed biased or heckling behavior, but mostly it's done in moderation. This guy was beyond the pale and I decided to make the chair umpire aware of him.

"You wanna keep your eye on that guy," I say. "He's obviously not normal. If he gets out of hand, is there a security guard around?" The umpire tells me, "Yeah, I already told the tournament staff to keep an eye on him." I knew I wasn't being whiny or paranoid: when you've played in front of enough crowds, you can tell which spectators are fans and which are fanatics.

I've had fans who've abused me, and then once, a fan abused my opponent. When I was 20, I qualified for an ATP event in Palermo, Italy, by beating Moya. I'd made it to the quarters, and was playing a German named Oliver Gross, who I should have beaten. But this fan from Germany totally distracted me and drove me nuts. Every time I missed a shot, he blasted me. After the match I went up to him and we almost got into a fight.

The other time, I was playing a Challenger in Flushing Meadows in 1997, after I hurt my back and had gone 2 and 14 in my last 16 matches. I was playing my friend, Michael Joyce, and we split the first two sets. I had a doctor friend of mine in the stands, and I think he got drunk. He'd brought a thermos of wine and he started to go berserk, yelling, "Come on, Vince. Come on!" There's usually only a few people in the stands for Challenger matches so his voice really rang out. I was chuckling, but Joyce got mad and walked up to him and said, "You know, you're one of the most annoying guys I've ever met in my entire life." They started having this heated conversation, so I walked over and said to Joyce, "Play, you sissy." And I beat him.

Back to Scottsdale . . . as we finished our warm-up, 2,500 fans were ready for a good domestic battle between Blake and Spadea. The match starts strong and explosive. We're both geared up, going at each other shot for shot, trying to find the edge. I serve wide and Blake blisters a return, so I half-volley it at the baseline deep to get back into the point, and I try to direct my first few shots to his backhand. James likes to hit his forehand big — a lot bigger than I think he should — he lacks consistency and mis-judges his depths and pace. When it goes in, it's fierce, when it doesn't, it's a free point. His backhand can be solid but less potent, so I like to start my rally there and feel my shots before changing direction.

James moves well, scraps for every ball, but because he's so quick, he's often wild once he unleashes his shot. His

Vince, 2 years old, with his sisters (Luanne standing, Diana baby), in Chicago, IL

Vince, age 3, with his father and sisters, Luanne, 4, Diana, 2, in Wurtsburg, Germany

Vince, age 5, with his dad on Christmas in Boca Raton, FL

Vince, age 5, playing at Laver's racket club tournament, Delray, FL

Family portrait — Boca Raton, FL

Luanne Spadea, National
Champion, Girls 12s,
Wellington, FL

Vince and sister Luanne, ages 4 and 5, watch
Jimmy Connors play, Londwood, MA, 1977

Dad, the "opera singer"

At home with parents, Hilda and Vince Sr., 1992

Orange Bowl winner, Boys 18s

From left to right: Luanne, Diana, Hilda, Vince Sr., and Vince Jr.

Vince with sister Diana in Gstaad, Switzerland, 1995

Caribbean Satellite winner at 18 years old

After defeating Andre Agassi at the ATP Championship,
Cincinnati, OH, 1998

On the Champs-Elysées. French
Open, 1998. From left to right:
Diana, Vince, Luanne, Vince Sr.

Guest batter at the Baltimore
Orioles spring training site,
Ft. Lauderdale, FL, 2000

serve is adequate — a component I think he needs to improve, with more consistency and pace. He likes to come to net and use the element of surprise, making him a bigger threat. His volleys are sound, but not sharp. When I play James, I know I have to be solid, and then go on the offense quickly when he gives me an opening.

This is my strategy going in, but the mark of a great champion is someone who can adjust when Plan A doesn't work, and sometimes just battle. We hold serve for the first few games — I save a couple of break points in one service game — and then at 3–2 my favor, I break Blake's serve to go up 4–2. When I play James it's sometimes easier for both of us to break serve rather than hold, because we both have good returns. I focus on consolidating the break by serving into his body, which gives him less room to swing and jams his follow-through. Getting my first serve in is important — especially against a guy with a dangerous return — but I still have to hit it with velocity. I can't just steer it in.

"Yeah, let's go," I yell, after winning my service game to go up 5–2. I've silenced all the Blake fans, especially the boisterous guy, who I thought was going to play a bigger role in the match. When I'm in my best mental zone, I can't hear anything, no matter how loud it is — there could be 20 spectators in the stands or 20,000, and I wouldn't know the difference. This is done by tapping in to my full resources of will, desire, and concentration. But when I get distracted or I'm not competing well, it becomes a downhill spiral. I can hear the drop of a pin in the crowd and everything bothers me, including loud fans, bad line calls, ball kids, the wind, the sun, and my equipment.

I'm in the zone tonight, and after Blake holds, I serve for the first set at 5–3, only to be broken after having a set point and missing an easy backhand setup. There is nothing more annoying than to lose your serve when you're ready to take the first set and establish your momentum and confidence. The crowd roars over the turnaround, and I listen to the applause in frustration.

The key here is to be unaffected by failure, I tell myself. The best players let setbacks roll off their backs, and stay optimistic while looking for the next opening. If all of us were successful at our first try, anyone could march right up the rankings. But tennis is a sport that challenges and tests you many times in each match. I can either keep at it and find my winning formula again, or I can give up. My fate is in my own hands.

We both hold serve to force a tiebreak. I have already won two tie-breaks in this tournament, coming back in the first round to beat a young American, Bobby Reynolds, 1–6, 7–6, 7–6, after not having played for five days because of my shoulder ailment and a bout with the flu. I know I need to be sharp to win this tiebreak against Blake. "No loose errors with some offense should win it," I say to myself.

I move to a 6–3 advantage and I have three set points. James comes back firing, and I get a little tight and don't go for my shots. "Six-all," the umpire announces, and the gallery is in its glory, happy that they decided against going to the cinema tonight to watch this live gladiatorial battle.

I put my first serve in and get aggressive. I want to be the guy who makes the offensive shot, who dares to win in big matches and points. I hit a backhand, down-the-line winner and move up 7–6 for another set point. Blake serves two shaky serves and double-faults. I didn't have to hit a ball, but what a tough set to win, and it proves pivotal. I stay strong and up my level with aggressive play and great returning in the second set, and James falls victim to the "I'm still thinking about my missed opportunity in the first set" syndrome.

I break him three times to close out the match 6–1. I'm glad to win in straight sets, since it is cold and late and I'm playing in the semifinals tomorrow against a big Croatian, named Mario Ancic, who won earlier in the day and is now resting. This is just another night when I feel like I'm the happiest guy in the world. Not many things can replace the feeling of victory. I pack my bags and wave to the crowd, which includes the mayor of Scottsdale. I do my interviews and hurry back to my hotel, where room service and the television will be my company for the night as I plot out my strategy for tomorrow.

FEBRUARY 26

Playing Mario Ancic in the semifinals is another great opportunity for me. I've played him only once prior, a 2002 Brazil Open first-rounder in which I scored a third-set tiebreaker victory, after coming back from three match-points down. Two-and-a-half years later, Ancic is playing better — for one thing he's 20 years old now, and he's more physically developed. He has found a good chemistry with his current coach, Fredrik Rosengren, who was Richard Krajicek's former coach. Ancic is notably tall, around 6-foot-4 or -5, and is still quite wiry and gangly, but stronger than when he first joined the tour a few years back. His 2004 semifinal performance at Wimbledon proves that he is flourishing.

I think he still has a way to go. He obviously idolizes his Croat compatriot and predecessor Goran Ivanisevic, and has patterned his game to be a right-hand version of Goran. But his serve isn't quite the Goran monster (Goran had the best serve in the game, better than Sampras's or Roddick's), and his footwork and ground stroke stability are still in question.

His improving volleys are still not close to being at Krajicek's level. But he does seem focused and driven for a young player.

In tennis, it's hard to tell who will achieve greatness and who will be, in Andre Agassi's terminology, "a journeyman." There's a lot more to it than mechanics and physical ability. What is in a player's heart and head is more difficult to determine, and is often unfathomable. In the United States, it's the USTA's job to try to make this type of determination and help American junior players excel. In the generation just prior to mine, players like Sampras, Agassi, Courier, Chang, Todd Martin, and MalaVai Washington made the USTA look like geniuses.

But my generation was a different story. Even after I had that fantastic year when I was 14, and the USTA selected me for their national team, they were always looking for other players to move ahead of me. I was an overweight, big groundstroker, and they didn't know if I was going to make it. The USTA coaches — Brad Stine, Benny Sims, and Stan Smith — who traveled with us were all looking for the next Sampras. They liked 6-foot-7 Brian Dunn, 6-foot-3 David Witt, and Jonathan Leach, who is also a big guy and married to Lindsay Davenport now. The other players they touted were Brian Macphie, Will Bull — everyone thought he'd be the big lefty server — J.J. Jackson, and Michael Joyce.

I lost in the 1992 Kalamazoo Finals, the junior national championships, when I was 18, and Stan Smith sat me down at the U.S. Open that year and said, "I think you should go to college, Vince, because you haven't had the results to gain any sponsorship. Unless your family has a ton of money, I'd go to college and think about turning pro later. I went to college and it worked for me."

I told Stan I was passionate about turning pro, and then I

went out and won the Orange Bowl, the biggest international junior tournament. Then the following year, in April, I went to play the Caribbean Satellite. In those days, a Satellite was four weeks long. The single sponsor I got was Adidas and they weren't paying me a ton of money, so only my mother came with me. In the first round of the first tournament, I'm losing to this guy and I call out to my mother on a break, "Can you get the plane ticket home? I don't want to be here." I came back and won that match, and then won every match I played for the next four weeks: 20 straight matches, four tournaments, and 50 ATP points. After one Satellite, two weeks in Puerto Rico, and two weeks in Jamaica, I shot up from No. 1,000 to No. 300.

In 1994, my dad took over and we were both eager. We were like two hungry wolves trying to get out of the Boca projects. I won three Challengers and the Florida Satellite, moving from No. 300 to No. 70. In 1995, I played Kafelnikov on center court in the third round of the U.S. Open. It was a night match — I'd never played in Louis Armstrong, center court, before at the Open — and it was an intimidating, scary feeling. Kafelnikov was No. 7 in the world, but I took it out of him. My backhand was better and I aced him nine times.

Witt, from Ponte Vedra, Florida, played on the tour for four years and had a top ranking of No. 128, while Dunn, from Brandon, Florida, topped out at No. 166 after five years. Joyce made it to No. 64 in 1996, but then his career quickly spiraled downwards. Macphie became a good doubles player, but none of the other guys made it. The experience of making it, when no one else from my generation did, and still being out here is like having gone to law school where everyone sails through, but I'm the only guy who passes the bar and makes it with a premier firm, though I'm no Johnny Cochrane, either.

The other guys failed for various reasons: injuries, lack of a support team, and a lack of true desire to withstand the grind of winning and losing matches abroad, going out and doing what it takes to be a special pro. It's not just hitting balls and smacking big serves. It's being able to tolerate mentally the ups and downs of the tour, the living out of a suitcase, constantly going to and from airports and flying across the world every week to make a dollar.

I walk onto the court in Scottsdale looking to be a giant-killer once again. My strategy against Ancic is to be solid from the baseline and to move him around, because big guys aren't normally agile. I have to serve well so I can keep holding and wait for my one chance to break him. Against big servers like Ancic, you can't expect to walk through a match. The match might be decided by who wins the tiebreakers. I feel confident but not overconfident, trying to find that happy medium between certainty and humility.

Ancic serves the first game, and I have a break chance, but he hits a service winner. His serve is big and aggressive, but not dominating. His flat serve down the middle is solid, but his wide serves are nothing special. He doesn't follow it to the net for a volley, instead preferring to hit aggressive backcourt shots. Like so many younger players on tour today, his backhand is more solid than his forehand, which is dangerous yet inconsistent.

He holds serve, then I hold, and then everything goes wrong for me as I proceed to lose five straight games. I'm serving poorly, being impatient with my ground strokes, and I'm not thinking clearly. On top of all that, my footwork is sluggish. I fear having and pray that I don't have days like this, but it's happening. Ancic is playing strongly and I'm even losing the baseline rallies I usually dictate. I lose the first set 6–1.

This is embarrassing. I need to change my game plan, so I decide to move him side to side, forcing him to hit on the run and earn his points. It starts to work. He seems to get a little fatigued and I go up 3–0. Serving at 3–1, I play a couple of loose points, he hits a winner, and then I hit a pathetic drop shot that lands in the net on break point. At 4–all, I start misfiring on my first serves again and rush a few first-shot rally balls. Ancic breaks me and holds serve easily with a few 135 mph blasts and wins the match.

As I walk up to the net to shake his hand, I am shaking and deflated from playing so purposeless and disappointing a match. I had wanted to defend my title, or at least make it to the finals. I had been sick in bed with the flu days before the first round and felt weak, fatigued, and mentally drained from the pressures of defending my title and ranking points, but I can't blame my performance on that. It's just the normal anxiety that goes with competing.

I go back to my hotel room and take a shower with my head down and my right hand stretched out on the shower stall wall. I love this game, but right now I hate my life. If I didn't feel this way, I wouldn't be a competitor. I know sometime in the near future I'll return to being a rational and coherent person who's optimistic and grateful for the next challenge. I just got paid $15,000 for reaching the semis, and that will also temper my miserable feeling.

MARCH 1
Los Angeles

I've got a full week off before the Pacific Life Open Masters tournament starts in the desert of Indian Wells. The American Davis Cup team is playing Croatia this week just south of here in the new tennis center in Carson. Patrick McEnroe has put together a dream team of Agassi and Roddick and the Bryan brothers. Agassi has not played Davis Cup since the quarterfinal round of 2000. When he declined to play in the 2000 semifinals for John McEnroe, who was the captain back then, Spain trounced us 5–0.

I'm staying in Hollyweird with my sister and her longtime boyfriend, Eric Taino, who is also a pro tennis player. The first time I played him in Tokyo, he beat me, but I've since returned the favor twice. Before I get into writing about show business and celebrities, I want to talk a little about making money on the tour.

When you're a superstar in the game, there're lots of ways of making it. The tournament in Dubai, where Agassi just played and lost to Federer in straight sets in the semis (he also lost in straight sets to Federer in the quarters at the Australian Open), paid Andre millions just to show up. It's called an "appearance fee" and the top players in the game command one at every tournament they go to outside the Grand Slams and Masters Series events.

Last year, I made $700,000 in tournament prize winnings and a sizeable amount in endorsements. I've had a long-running deal with Prince, and I usually have a clothes and shoe sponsor, too. Certain companies do patch deals at Grand Slams where you wear the name of the company on your sleeve. I've done Dunkin' Donuts and Sharp at the U.S. Open, and Crown Casino when I played Agassi at the Australian Open. I get paid for wearing one, but the deal depends on whether it's for one match or the entire tournament, and there are bonuses if you advance into the later rounds or your match is televised.

At the 2003 NASDAQ, I made $135,000 for making the semis, but that money runs away quick. That was my ATM money for the next six months. The more money you make, the more money you spend. I like to buy shoes. I like clothes. (I sound like a girl, "I like shoes and clothes.")

Then there's this thing called taxes. A lot of countries take their own taxes out of your winnings. Germany will take 35 percent, and then I'll have to take that receipt and go to the IRS and say, "Listen, I've already paid 35 percent on this amount." The tournament will either cut you a check, or you can have the money wired to your bank account. I usually have it wired, because when I play consecutive tournaments I don't want to have to hold onto a bunch of checks for 30 grand, 15 grand, 5 grand, or 100 grand.

After I won the $135,000 in Miami, I took this Croatian model named Nevena out to a $300 lunch at the China Grill. Then I took her to Eckerds and bought her $65 worth of items. We hung out that afternoon, but then I didn't see her again. A few months later — out of the blue — I receive a phone call from her asking if I can pay for her phone bill. So money is easy come, easy go sometimes.

In 2000 and 2001, I actually lost money playing on the tour. I only made around $50–$60,000 playing mostly the Challenger circuit, and with the cost of airplanes, hotels, food, and coaching, I wasn't making any money. I stayed within the United States mostly because no one wants to travel the world to lose money.

The sport is so demanding on a marginal player's psyche and emotions, because there's so much pressure to win. Unless you're a superstar like Agassi — and I even hear Andre exhorting himself when he's off his game, saying, "God, don't miss that" — tennis players are paid to win. NBA, NFL and major league baseball players are already paid before they walk out on the court or field. We have to win to get paid. It's not only about money, it's about rankings and privileges, but none of that is predetermined when we walk on the court. I have to challenge myself to win as much as I can.

Ultimately, we are entertainers. The way to win fans over is to play great tennis: enthusiastic, positive tennis like Connors did. But it's much easier said than done. Sampras started getting more demonstrative and pumping his fist because everyone told him he looked like a slouch on the court, and his attitude change coincided with his two-year slump. It's dangerous when you ask a player to break his routine and his rituals to consciously think about how he's acting on the court or being perceived by the fans and the media.

The novelty and appeal of sports is that you can make a great living in an absolutely abstract, totally recreational activity. It holds such mystique for the average guy who goes to work at a regular job each day, but the tennis player takes a big risk in assuming that by practicing every day, he can then go out and make a living winning matches. It's a dare to be great. It's something so seemingly unreasonable to try to become a professional athlete, actor, or musician. You're basically entertaining people on a weekend. The average guy thinks, "I work all week, now you entertain me."

I don't think we're overpaid. The pressure to win is significant, the adversity is intense. We're well paid, but we're underpaid compared to pro golfers. The pro tennis players competing in the Challengers can say, "I've hit as many tennis balls as Andre Agassi, but I haven't made in my career what he spends in tips each week." But there are millions of actors taking your orders at restaurants, and they're not getting paid what Tom Cruise is getting paid. It's survival of the fittest out here.

A doctor can make perhaps $600,000 if he's a surgeon. He's dealing with a lot of pressure; he's got someone's life in his hands, so it's hard to argue that tennis players should be making as much or more money than doctors. But doctors can make money until they're 65. We can only make money until we're 35, if we're lucky. I think because of the excitement we bring to fans who appreciate our skills and grit, we're worth the money we make. People make a lot more money doing things that have a lot less to do with helping people out or entertaining them.

I've just invested some money in this new restaurant called Providence, in West Hollywood on Melrose just east of La Brea. It used to be Patina, a very high-end French place, and the new chef worked at the original Spago and Le Cirque. I'm a silent investor. The chef told me, "Listen, Vince, they're going to have a chef's table in the kitchen, and you can sit there and we'll make you grilled chicken with pasta." I know that 80 percent of restaurants go bankrupt after the first year, and 60 percent don't make it in the long run. But I didn't invest my life savings in it.

MARCH 3

I'm having a lot of fun out here. I went to a private party the other night and met Leonardo DiCaprio — he knew who I was — and Jack Nicholson. I got to shake Mick Jagger's hand. I met Lindsay Lohan a while back and she text-messages me a lot. She has a boyfriend, so we just keep in touch. I'm also good friends with the comedian Jon Lovitz. After I beat Agassi in Australia in 1999, I stayed out in Los Angeles at the famous Sunset Marquis Hotel. I went down to the bar and saw Lovitz, we started talking, and we were at it til 2 a.m. The bouncer had to kick us out. Lovitz was mimicking the serve and volley form that Alex Olmeda, a Peruvian who won Wimbledon beating Rod Laver, taught him.

Lovitz is a very passionate guy. When I hit the skids, and then started to make my comeback in 2001, I was living in L.A., and I ran into him again and he took me to meet Olmeda. He was about 65 at the time, and the pro at the Beverly Hills Hotel. I've taken a few lessons from Olmeda and now he and Lovitz are buddies of mine. Olmeda says, "Nowadays, the players all come over the ball and hit it with heavy spin. No one really steps into the ball and takes it early like Agassi, and players of the past."

Lovitz is always telling me how good tennis players have it compared to actors. If you're an actor, he says, you've got to wait until a director hires you. A tennis player can go to another tournament every week and turn his career around. When I'm in L.A., I watch him doing standup every Wednesday night at the Laugh Factory on Sunset. He makes me laugh. He told a joke the other night: "Why do they call it Tsunami Relief? The Tsunami doesn't need the money. Why would I give my money to a wave?"

My L.A. hangout is the Viper Room on Sunset. They have a live band performing original rock music every night. I call it my den, a good spot to escape. I saw Keanu Reeves playing electric bass guitar there in his band Dogstar one night this week. The other night I was sitting with a model girlfriend of mine in this restaurant on Melrose. It was 6 p.m. and there were only four people there, my girlfriend and me, and Spike Lee and his wife.

I walked up to Spike and said, "Hey Spike, how you doing, buddy? I met you last year." If I was Spike, I would be like, "Hey, put a sock in it," but he was friendly. I said, "I'm making it happen. I'm blowing up like Apollo 14. I'm 30, but I'm the story of hope. I made the Olympics last year. I'm no In-N-Out Burger."

Spike shook my hand, then he shook my girlfriend's hand and we talked about the Oscars. "See, our boy, Jamie Foxx did it," I said. Twenty minutes later, Serena Williams' agent Jill Smoller, as well as Rick Fox, the former Laker, and Jill's boss, some bigwig from William Morris, sat down with Spike. I told Jill of another rap I have for Serena, and the whole table was cracking up. I was going off the cuff, improvising. When we left, I called out to Spike, *Peace out. Holla. Brooklyn. Spadea, ain't afraid of ya. I got something to say to ya. Turn up your radio. I'm the next white hope. Because I'm not doing no dope. I'm still bloomin.*

It's true, too. I've never smoked marijuana or a cigarette, never experimented with any drugs in my life. I've never even been drunk. I've had a maximum of maybe a glass and a half of wine in a night, and I've never taken a shot of liquor. I don't need anything other than life, my personality, and other people. I've been to a couple of parties in L.A. where I've walked into the room at two in the morning and a guy says, "Hey, you got any coke?" I say, "No, but I got a Sprite." It doesn't even get a laugh at 2 a.m. I haven't taken ecstasy. I haven't even seen cocaine at a party. I believe in clean living and not pushing my limits by taking things that are notoriously bad for you.

At some of the parties I go to, the actors I meet want to play tennis with me. I played on David Spade's court with Kelsey Grammer of *Frasier*, and Billy Crystal, Jay Leno, and Donald Trump. Grammer and Leno can't play, but Crystal is okay. Trump is competitively adequate, meaning he's so competitive that he's adequate.

Indian Wells, California

I just got out to the desert and it's 80 degrees here when 125 miles east, in L.A., it was only in the sixties. My last day in Hollyweird, Stuttering John interviewed me for *The Tonight Show*. It's for a quirky thing they're doing, trying to find the person with the sexiest voice so they can put him on Sirius Satellite Radio. I skipped the audition, and I just started into a rap on how I'm the No. 3 American in tennis and a two-time Olympian. He told me it might be on the next Friday, but I don't know if he meant last Friday or this Friday. He wasn't too clear. He's Stuttering John, he's not a genius.

I admire show business and people who can perform. I like people who have a fearless nature, who are characters. My father was very theatrical, an opera singer. I don't like opera, though. There was a lot of opera played in my house when I was growing up, and I have an appreciation for it, but I prefer being a literary assassin, and rapping is really a poetic art. I can express myself in a unique style, creating catchy beats and tunes. There are rappers who have something profound to say. I love that rap is high, upbeat music. It's not so dramatic or emotional, but it gets my heart moving, my feet bumping, and my head bopping.

I like Jay-Z the best, and Timbaland, out of Virginia Beach. There's an East Coast rap that's different from the West Coast rap. Dr. Dre is West Coast, straight out of Compton, Williams sisters terrain. The West Coast rap is more vibey, bass, chilling — a lot of old school funk. East Coast is more freaky, crazy blast sounds. I like them both. I like the production of the West Coast and the rapping of the East Coast. Jay-Z, Nas, they're all from Brooklyn.

I'm like The Notorious B.I.G., I'm a writer first and a

performer second. The Notorious B.I.G. was one of the greatest writers, but he claimed he could never make stuff up off the cuff. Certain rappers can freestyle, and some can't. They're more like street poets. Rap is all about getting the upper hand. It originally came from the streets, where people berated each other instead of encouraging one another. But I like talented, positive rap, not bashing, degrading writing. Eminem is like that. He's passionate, fearless, and he has a good delivery. He didn't start out to become the Elvis of Rap, but the whole concept of him is cool.

I feel I have an authenticity in my rapping. I have an uninhibited talent for doing it in front of people. I rapped to Katie Couric on *The Today Show*, live from the Olympics in Athens. I'm not claiming I grew up in extreme poverty or that I've been shot at, but I don't think rap's about that, or how many guns you own or gangs you've been a part of. It's about expressing your thinking about what your lifestyle is all about. I like to think of myself as not white or black, but "off-white." I haven't heard too many other tennis players rapping. Roddick knows some rap. I heard him rapping Vanilla Ice. But I'll take him out. How's he going to hurt me? I've got more consistency, better flow, and realer stories.

It's good to see everyone hitting the courts practicing. Because there's a 96-player draw, you see a lot of players out here you don't see at the smaller tournaments. I saw Jan-Michael Gambill, once voted by *People Magazine* as one of the 50 most beautiful people in the world, along with MalaVai Washington and Patrick Rafter. Jan-Michael looks a little like a Ken doll. He's like an Adonis. He's had a drop-off recently, from the Top 50 to around No. 100. He's 27, the same age I was when I suffered my mid-to-late career, apathetic crisis. Maybe Jan-Michael's decline is because he travels with his dad all the time. Maybe it's because he just stopped improving, or he's more interested in video games or his Jaguars. The word is that he got his heart broken. Maybe he's doing real estate deals and doesn't care about tennis. I don't know.

I also saw Jeff Salzenstein playing the qualifiers. He is the guy I lost to in the 12-and-under Hard Court Championship in San Diego almost 20 years ago, the only American player my age still playing pro tennis. Jeff finally reached No. 100 in the rankings last year at Wimbledon, but he's been playing mostly Challengers for the last few years after recovering from injuries that sidetracked his career. He's not going to win Wimbledon, but he might qualify for the main draw and get to the third or fourth round if he has the drive and keeps improving. This sport does not dictate your destiny, you do. That's what we love about it. That's the underlying reason why players at the top and the bottom of the game come back year after year. Everyone's looking for their next breakthrough. Even Agassi still thinks he can do it. He's not here to sign autographs; he's here because he's trying to go further and win Indian Wells for the first time since 2001.

I practiced this morning with Donald Young, who turned pro at 15. Has any male that young ever turned pro before? Yes. Have there been better players than Young at 15? Yes. Nadal was better, and Hewitt qualified for the Australian Open at 15. Young's had a good start, but his future depends on what kind of guidance he gets going forward, and who his coach is going to be. I don't like the fact that his mother is coaching him. I don't know how he got this good in the first place, but I think his parents have this vision of him as the male Serena, and in my opinion, that's not going to happen unless he gets a top-notch coach.

Safin was practicing on the last court with his shirt off

showing the tattoo on his shoulder. He got upset and threw his racket, banging it and flinging it up against the fence. Finally, after a missed swinging volley, he smashed it and threw it over the fence. Then he sat down, took another racket out of his bag, and smashed it against the court. His coach, Peter Lundgren, took the smashed racket and held it in front of Safin's face, but Safin just pushed him away and walked off the court. After his win at the Australian Open, maybe Marat's feeling a lot of pressure again. I practiced with him right after he won the U.S. Open in 2000, and he was frustrated that he wasn't living up to everyone's expectations. He said, "Everybody tells me I should be No. 1. Maybe I'm not good enough." His coach at the time came by and asked, "You want to stretch after you play doubles this afternoon?" And Safin said, "Stretch after doubles? You're kidding."

Tommy Haas was also practicing on a nearby court. He's got long hair, and he wears those sleeveless shirts, but he's not the most flamboyant player. That's where the men's game has lost a lot of its appeal. The players no longer have any attitude on the court. Even Agassi used to have both the personality and the appearance going for him, but he's toned it down now to where he's become this completely efficient winning machine. If it wasn't for his earring, he'd blend in as another ordinary tennis player. I'm thinking of growing my hair really long, and dyeing it purple or some shocking color. As crazy as Dennis Rodman was, I know he wouldn't have gotten all the attention he did if he hadn't won five NBA championships. I need charisma, flash, and big-time results.

A lot of the Spanish guys were coming onto the courts at 6 p.m. for their second practice session when I was leaving the grounds. They have their siesta, and then they start battling again under the lights. The Spanish guys love the battle. They can go on forever. They believe in running, hitting strokes, improving all the time. I used to love the work ethic of this Spanish player named Felix Mantilla; he was the quintessential warrior. Some of the Czech guys, like Stepanek and Jiri Novak, practice a lot. Kafelnikov would practice nonstop. He lived to play tennis.

I also ran into Pancho Segura, the great Ecuadorian player who coached Connors for a while in the 1960s and '70s. Jack Kramer once said that Pancho's two-handed backhand was "the greatest single shot ever produced in tennis." Pancho told me that the worst night I ever had was when I played Chang in the third round at the 1996 U.S. Open when I was 22. He says I had Chang beat, and when I lost that match, it was the turning point of my career. I was serving for the match and I just got tight. I was the stronger physical player. "You've never been the same since, Vince," Pancho told me.

Pancho is, like, 84 years old now, and he can be quite dramatic. He was getting worked up just talking to me. He asked me why I hadn't learned to play the net yet after being a pro for 12 years. "You only come up to the net at the end of the match to shake hands," he said. "You're a nice guy. I like you, but you don't have a serve either." I guess he hasn't seen me play lately. I've been coming up to the net more and serving bigger.

I think a lot of people don't think I'm trying my hardest out there, because sometimes I look sort of blasé, like I'm going through the motions. But I remember when I was 14 and I had that Federer-Sampras thing going, where I was playing so carefree and smooth, but efficient. Playing that way allowed me to go out on a limb and achieve greatness, but when you start losing, you start looking lackadaisical or sluggish. I like the fact a guy like Roddick looks so intense. It's good to watch somebody who is so pumped up.

Ultimately, it's probably best to combine the two styles. McEnroe had that combination: his intensity showed after the point, but during the point, he had that smooth serve and effortless volley. He was part-Roddick and part-Federer. He wasn't as pretty as Federer with his ground strokes, but he had those legendary volleys.

I remember reading this article about Borg in the London *Guardian* where his coach, Lennart Bergelin, said, "I think Björn's greatest victory was not the way he came to master his ground strokes, but the change he underwent, with terrible determination, to tame his passionate spirit."

McEnroe and Borg had the best of both worlds going. I've got to find that quiet fire in me again.

MARCH 7

It's the first day of the Pacific Life Open, and I get a great feeling out here in Indian Wells. It's one of most beautiful settings for a tennis tournament in the world, with the backdrop of the mountains and the desert. It's also a sentimental place for me because I did so well here in 2003, winning seven matches, including two qualifiers, to get to the semifinals. At the time, I was ranked around No. 100 in the world. Now, I'm ranked No. 19 and I'm one of the seeded players. So coming back here is like a celebration of my tennis life.

It's also the first Masters Tournament of the season and the fifth biggest tournament in the world after the four Grand Slam events. I see it as a great opportunity to strive for things I've never accomplished, like reaching a Masters final. But with Federer dominating the tour (he won again in Dubai last week), Ljubicic coming in after beating the entire American team last week in the Davis Cup in Carson,

California, and Roddick and Agassi always a major threat, the going is very tough.

Right now, I'm eating lunch at the players' café on the tournament grounds after practicing this morning. The food here is as good as any restaurant near the tournament site. Since I've received a bye in the first round, I don't play my first match for two more days. I'll go back to the hotel after lunch and take care of some off-court business, then I'll return this afternoon to practice again.

I'm eating alone, and my coach is out scouting a match between a Czech player and a qualifier, the winner of which I will face on Wednesday. As I said earlier, I try not to bring the personal part of my life into my workplace. Rocky Marciano didn't talk to his wife for two to three weeks before a fight. I've never been married, nor had a girlfriend who was like a second half of me, and I've never brought a woman to a tournament with me. This is my competitor's den, and I don't believe I can get the same good 10 hours of sleep with a woman by my side as I can when I'm alone in a king-size bed. Angelo Dundee, Muhammad Ali's trainer, once said, "women are the scourge of an athlete's success," and I kind of take a boxing mentality when it comes to tennis and women.

At Miami last year, after I won a couple of matches, a woman left a note in my door at the Sheraton. It said, "Hey, this is Katherine. I really want to hang out with you. I'm in Room 604." I didn't know who she was. I didn't take her up on her offer, either. As I continued to win, people were calling me up left and right, and I was meeting girls in the hotel lobby and in the bar. They were just planted there, sitting around knowing they were going to see the players.

After the tournament, I went out in South Beach. I was supposed to meet these two girls I'd run into at the hotel, but they never showed up. I've been stood up a few times in my life. I hit home runs, I get kicked out of the game, I end up on deck. The game is ongoing. It's part of being a single man who likes to meet women.

So I got stood up this time, and I'm standing in this club alone and I meet this girl from Cuba. That's called redemption. That's like losing your chance on a break point and not worrying about it. You just start focusing on the next point and the next opportunity. Well, this was like that. I met this girl. I was more relaxed after getting stood up, so it didn't mean as much. She was like, "Call me Monday. I'm going away to the Keys for the weekend." So I called her up and we went out. We had a good time. It got a little crazy, but that's what you do when you're young. You get crazy and lazy sometimes. I know one day I'll get married, but until then: *it's time to have some fun, drinking rum, playing dumb, getting some, I'm not 21, but they think I am.*

We messed around some, but we didn't have sex. I got a little freaked out. I'm not a guy who likes to hook up with a girl and have sex with her on the first night. I have some moral character. I go to church. I'm a Catholic-born kid. Like Rocky, I wear the cross. There's got to be a meaning to all the craziness on this planet. I want something to look forward to.

Emotionally, sex is a complicated thing, especially for women. I think that I better my chances of having a friendship or a relationship with a woman when we don't get too crazy, too soon. Then I don't have to worry about the other repercussions either, like STDs, because I can't know when I first approach a girl — or she approaches me — what kind of a girl I'm meeting.

As a pro tennis player, I'm traveling to different countries, moving in and out of different cultures and situations, and it's amazing sometimes how many women want to be associated with me. Even if it's only so they can say to their friends, "I did this with Vince Spadea." It's like I'm a notch on their belt. I know that feeling, because I fall prey to that kind of thinking too when I meet up with actresses, models, and former Playboy Playmates. But I look at it like it's cheating. I can cheat and try to attain some kind of status by sleeping with a beautiful, famous woman. I know it's human nature, but I don't want to take advantage of women.

Two years ago, I met a girl on a stopover in the Dallas airport on my way to play this tournament. I started talking to her and we fooled around a little bit. She was from Tennessee, and said she was going to Palm Springs to meet up with her parents on vacation. I was in the qualifying tournament. I was on the upswing of my comeback, but my ranking still wasn't good enough to get right into the main draw of the tournament.

In the first round of the qualifiers, I beat Michael Joyce in three sets. A reporter wrote a story on me the next day in The *Los Angeles Times* entitled, "What Happened to Vince Spadea?" It had been more than three years since I'd been ranked in the Top 20. The next day I'm playing Magnus Norman in the last round of qualifiers, and this girl from the Dallas airport calls me up asking for tickets. I usually don't like to give tickets to girls who I don't know so well. I feel like it's too much of an obligation, and I don't have the time during a tournament for us to get to know each other better. So I told her I didn't have any tickets to give her.

The next day, I walk up to the net for the coin toss with Norman, and when I happen to look up into the stadium stands, I see this girl sitting right in my sightline. She had come with her parents, and it distracted me to see her right as the match was about to start. I ended up beating Norman, and her being there kind of helped me focus, because I was feeling nervous even before I'd seen her.

I called her up after the match and we went out that night. We started messing around together, but nothing major. She drove me back to my hotel, and the next day I beat Paradorn Srichaphan in the first round of the main draw. I got tickets for her for that match, and for the next couple of days. It's a tennis player's superstition that when you win matches with a girl in the stands watching you, you keep on inviting her back. She ended up staying until I got into the round of 16, but then she had to leave with her family. I thought, "Oh no, now I'm going to lose." But I ended up winning two more matches and made it into the semis.

The weirdest part about this story is that I had a day off after I beat Srichaphan in the first round, and she came over to my hotel and we started messing around again in my room. I thought, "I've got to watch my energy level, and my groin, and my shoulder." Hooking up with a girl can be like doing 100 pushups — it can take a lot out of you. So we messed around a little bit — again, nothing major — even though she let me know that she was willing to go much further.

Before she left, she said, "I want to fly to Miami next week and be with you during NASDAQ." I said, "Whoa! Well, you can't come to Miami because I've got . . ." She cut me off and said, "Don't bullshit me!"

I blew her off. She called me up a few times after that, and then the last time I talked to her, she told me she was pregnant. She said she'd gotten pregnant about two weeks before we met.

This is the type of situation where my sexual inhibitions really helped me. If I had had sex with that girl that night, I'm on the *Maury Povich Show* a few months later and Maury's grilling me to find out if I'm the dad of this girl's baby. I was messing with a girl who was already pregnant. So you really have to watch out.

There hasn't been a Wilt Chamberlain of tennis, but a number of big-name players have had their public troubles with women. A famously temperamental and amusing American tennis star used the grist of his first marriage to an Oscar-winning actress to fuel the flames of his book. A record-making Wimbledon champion's first marriage to a Romanian tennis player ended when he had a child out of wedlock with an underage girl. A booming German player claimed the Russian Mafia stole his sperm to blackmail him over a child he spawned with a Russian model. A tireless former number one champion supposedly wooed the maids at hotels. And I know one player today who gets to the airport an hour early for his flights so he can visit the massage parlors nearby.

I was with an infamous Chilean player in a bar in Indian Wells one year and he picked up three girls. We all went back to his hotel suite. He went into his room with one of the girls, and they weren't in there for more than five minutes when I heard her scream. She came out and all three girls started to run out of the suite. The girl who had gone into the room with the Chilean had tried to steal one of his rackets — I guess as a souvenir — and he grabbed it from her. I asked him what had happened, but he wouldn't tell me. He was a man of few words.

MARCH 8

I didn't watch any of the Davis Cup tie between Croatia and the U.S. team, but I heard that Ljubicic just destroyed Agassi, then teamed with Ancic to beat the Bryan brothers, and on the third day, beat Roddick in five sets, 6–2, in the fifth. After the match, Ljubicic made some unflattering remarks about Roddick's game, saying, "Once you get his serve back, he's easy to play, because his game is predictable." There's been bad blood between Ljubicic and Roddick since Roddick beat him at the 2003 U.S. Open and Ljubicic trashed him in the press conference after the match.

Basically, Ljubicic is a bit nerdy and tries to overcome that nerdiness by playing it cool, like a lot of other tennis guys out there, including myself. He thinks he's the best player in the world (as do we all), and in any given week, he sometimes is. This past weekend served to prove this point. Hewitt and Ljubicic match up well against Roddick. They stay way back behind the baseline to return his serve. They know Roddick's not going to serve and volley. He's not a confident volleyer; his volleys are barely serviceable. Gilbert was trying to get Roddick to serve and volley more.

I think Roddick's game has slipped a little since he fired Gilbert as his coach. I heard that Roddick's dad didn't want to pay Gilbert the money he wanted, but I've also heard that Gilbert's strong personality, and the fact he talks a lot and is opinionated, rubbed Andy the wrong way. What Gilbert is particularly good at detecting is what's wrong in a guy's game and adjusting it. He doesn't change technique too much, but I definitely think he adjusts the way his players hit their spin so that their trajectory and percentages get better.

He helped Roddick's forehand. It changed over the course of the year and a half he worked with Gilbert. But now it's off track a little bit. He used to have this big elbow, loopy-type heavy forehand, almost like a clay-court forehand. Gilbert got him to be more compact, so he started hitting a big, flat forehand on the winnable shots. On the other shots, he'd still have him hit heavy, but with a little more authority.

When I played Andy, I could feel and see the difference.

I practiced with Roddick the last few years he was with Tarik Benhabiles. Roddick used to serve flat all the time and try to break records. Now he serves flat two-thirds of the time. Gilbert told him, "Hey, at 40–30, instead of hitting a flat serve out wide at 140 mph and having a 50 percent chance of making it — if that — you want to hit a 124 mph serve with slightly more spin. A 124 mph serve out wide is going to be an ace anyway, or it's going to be virtually unreturnable."

Gilbert could see the change was needed, because he knows the game and he was watching Roddick carefully. Roddick couldn't have changed it on his own, because he can't feel that slight adjustment. It's just a bit of a nuance for him to hit the 124 mph rather than the 140 mph, but it made a big difference in his consistency. But now Roddick's getting a little sloppy again with his service technique. He's pulling his head down and not really reaching up fully for his serve. I've never seen him this frustrated with his serve.

Gilbert had him moving a little better, making sure he was quick to the ball. I remember practicing with Roddick one time when Gilbert was coaching him. We played two tough sets, a one-hour-and-45-minute practice. I was winded, and Andy and I were drinking some Gatorade on the side. Gilbert said to Andy, "Get up right now. We're going to do suicide lines under a certain time." Every sprint, he'd start by saying, "Let's go. Let's go. Let's go." All these people were watching, but he didn't care. You could see how that attention to detail — Gilbert tightening the screws, even at that level — made a difference. Roddick hasn't lost much, but that little bit he's lost has been big.

Roddick has a lot of pressure on him. He's the only American player who's the real deal right now. Fish is heralded, but he's overhyped. Ginepri and Blake are playing poorly. Dent definitely has potential, but he won't get better unless he works harder. He has a soft mind and a soft body. But he serves big, and has good volleys and improved ground strokes. Everyone said Sampras was lazy and lacked some head, but you can't compare Dent with Sampras. Roddick is a tough son of a gun, and Dent is happy-go-lucky. American coaches are hoping Roddick can inspire Dent and Fish and the rest of his generation the way Chang did by winning the French Open, spurring on Courier, Sampras, and Agassi.

My childhood friend from Boca, Richard Laver, is out here to see me play. He lives in the area, but we grew up playing together at his father's tennis academy in Delray Beach. His father was Ian Laver, Rod Laver's brother, and he let me play for free. I traveled with Ian and Richard to a lot of the national tournaments when we were both 11, because my father couldn't afford to go. Ian watched over me.

I was supposed to go to San Diego with them for the boys' 12-year-old National Championships, but at the last minute, my father felt it was too far and too expensive to go for a tournament I wasn't favored to win. So Ian and Richard took a Delta flight and they were supposed to connect in Dallas on their way to San Diego. But the plane crashed and Ian was killed. Richard, sitting in the seat next to his father, miraculously survived. Afterwards, he had third-degree burns on parts of his body and a bad knee problem. Mentally, he was out of it for a long time.

When I was having my career crisis a few years back, Richard and I were in this bar called Gatsby's in Boca, and he said, "Vince, remember this moment, right now. Because no one around us — all these tennis players — wants to know you right now because you've fallen so far. When you climb all the way back up, remember they were never there for you when you were down. Never forget where you came from as a kid, and how you can fight back again. We call you the 'Last Survivor' for a reason. Out of thousands and thousands of players, you're the only one still left."

I fired my agent today, Ken Myerson of SFX. I told him, "Hey, thanks a lot for believing in me and doing the best you could, but I'm going to move in a different direction." He didn't take it very well. It got slightly heated at the end on both sides, and I ended the conversation. I'm a professional. What's not good is if I don't tell him I'm signing with a new agent and he hears about it. At least there's closure now.

I told him I felt I was being underpromoted. He tried to tell me I was disillusioned and being brainwashed by other agents. We had a difference of opinion. I told him, "I am a person who is on a mission and going somewhere. And I don't feel that you really believe that, and I need someone in my corner who does."

Before I retire from tennis, I want to be in a position to shock the world. I felt Ken believed in so many other players more, and I resented that. Whatever young player SFX signed — Brian Vahaly, Robert Kendrick, Alex Kim, who's not playing anymore — that's who they put their time and attention into. Obviously, they were much more high on Roddick, Mardy Fish, and Paradorn Srichaphan. I deserve more than just being put into a stable of players. I have merit based on where I'm ranked and the longevity of my career. The art of marketing is maximizing your opportunities.

I have to look for a new agent. Obviously, there's IMG, Octagon, and Jill Smoller of William Morris. I've entertained Lee Steinberg and Jeff Schwartz, too. I've got to pursue every opportunity that I can get. I've interviewed a few already; I'll contact more after the tournament.

In 2000, when I dropped all the way down in the rankings, no agencies were interested in me. I had no clothing deals. I was calling the 800 numbers of sporting goods companies saying, "Can you get me some free T-shirts?" Then I got more inventive and served as my own agent, using a fictitious name. I'd call up some company and say, "Hi, am I talking to the head of marketing? Yeah, hi, my name is Drew Goldberg. I'm an agent. I have my own firm down here in South Florida and I'm representing Vince Spadea. I don't know if you know his name, but he's one of the hottest up-and-coming players in pro tennis. He's making a comeback you cannot even fathom. He's got everything it takes. People like you are going to miss the boat if you're not ready to jump on and . . . listen, you want to make things happen? We're doing whatever it takes to make it happen and we want to know if you want to jump onboard. What's it going to take?"

I ended up getting myself free sneakers from Diadora and K-Swiss.

MARCH 9

I walked out onto the court this afternoon to play Jan Hernych, a Czech player ranked No. 75. The courts are painted purple here to make the ball more visible on television, and the heat is so intense that the ball boys and girls held an umbrella over my head when I sat down in my chair after the warm-up. I've been battling bronchitis, and I feel under the weather and a little out of sync and edgy.

I get broken in each of my first two service games and I start to come unglued. The clothing company that was sending me my clothes and hats didn't send the latest shipment, so I'm wearing this newsboy hat I bought for $5 at Wal-Mart. I hit a ball that lands squarely on the line, but the linesman calls it out. I ask the umpire to overrule, but he says he won't overrule the linesman's call because it's on the line furthest away from him.

The linesmen in pro tennis get paid $105 a day, and they have to pay for their own travel. There is a group of seven on court in a match, rotating one hour on and one hour off with other groups of linesmen. Some are very good, and others aren't, but what can you expect when major league umpires and NBA refs make hundreds of thousands of dollars, and these guys are doing this as a hobby? The linesmen receive ratings from the umpires. If a linesman's rating drops below a certain level — they use a two-year rolling average — then they can't work on the ATP tour. They are not full-time employees of the ATP, the way most of the umpires are.

I'm out of sorts. One of the ball boys drops the ball as he is trying to bounce it to me and I get impatient. A fan yells out, "C'mon, Vince." The ball kids only bother me when they are inexperienced and they screw up by dropping the ball a lot, causing delays in the game. But I don't like to give young kids a hard time. I used to be a ball boy myself. I know it can be nerve-racking, especially when it's hot. When I played the Challengers, the ball people were sometimes between 60 and 70 years old, and the matches would last between three and four hours because of all the delays.

The best ball boys are in France and at Wimbledon, where they are trained extensively. They have these little marches and patterns that they follow to run on and off the court. They even show you the ball before they bounce it to you. Pro players like to have three balls thrown to us before each serve so we can see which ball is the least puffed and fuzzy. You want a ball that will keep its velocity. I like the most-skinned ball. All we're doing is measuring the shapes of the balls.

I lose the first set 6–2. I'm mouthing to my coach, "What

am I supposed to do?" He had told me that I should play Hernych's forehand — that it's the weaker of his two sides — but today he's killing the ball with his forehand. I play better when I get a little angry. I start thinking, "I've got to get going here. I have to make it happen, otherwise this guy is going to run away from me." I like to pump my fists a bit and get my neck muscles straining. If I get too juiced up, though, I use too many unnecessary muscles, and that can hurt me.

I start to figure out his game, working him over with my backhand, and I take the second set 6–1. Hernych, to his credit, picks up his game in the third set, but my return of serve — the best part of my game — is crackling, and I break him to take a 5–4 lead. The match is on my racket; I can serve it out. But I get tight and Hernych breaks me back. The match will be decided in a third-set tiebreaker.

Again, I jump ahead and take a 6–5 lead. I serve to Hernych's forehand on match point, and he nails it deep into the corner. I get the rally back to where we are going backhand-to-backhand crosscourt, as I have been breaking him down in these types of rallies. On a short ball, I aggressively hit my approach and come up to net. He mishits a passing shot, but at the last moment, I decide it might go in so I reach up and hit a backhand volley down the line. Somehow, he extends his 6-foot-4 frame and pokes a forehand volley by me. The next point he aces me, and then I double-fault the match away.

I wasn't thinking, "Don't double-fault." I was trying to get the ball out wide to his backhand so I could open up the court, but I was still a little distracted from what had happened when I had served for the match two points back. I didn't feel confident. It wasn't like a total choke of a serve; I hit it fairly aggressively with some spin, so people wouldn't accuse me of hitting too passively. But he attacks it and hits a winner, making me look like a fool for hitting a cream-puff second serve.

As I'm walking back to the locker room, Robert Lansdorp, another famous Los Angeles tennis teaching pro, comes up to me and says, "Vince, you've got to win serving for the match at 5–4 in the third set."

Maybe I got a little uptight on match point. Maybe I didn't execute as well as I could have. I usually live for those moments. I work on all my shots in practice so I can perform them in those critical moments. I'm disappointed, but I need to get my health back and my game sharper so I'll make some of those easy shots I missed today. I've got to keep my spirits up, that's the key for me. It's a long year.

MARCH 17

I'm back in Boca getting ready for the NASDAQ, which starts in four days. But I won't play my first match for at least another week. I heard Cliff Drysdale of ESPN say on the television the other day from Indian Wells, "Can Spadea get to the Top 10? I doubt it." I love when people say I can't do something. It makes me want to do it even more. If it weren't for people like Drysdale, I probably wouldn't be where I am today. I don't want to measure my success by the approval of other people, but at the same time, their comments often work to get me fired up. A lot of successful people use the opinions of negative people as springboards to great achievement. Attitude is everything.

To make it at this level, I have to be ultra-focused, 18-hours-a-day focused. Unfortunately, I've been bogged down by some illnesses and injuries, and have turned my attention to other interests outside of tennis. Now I'm back, looking for that edge to get stronger, fitter, and faster. I'm always going to be in the mix when my game is on.

One of those outside interests was trying to get on the television show, *The Bachelor*. The producer, Lacy Pemberton, had come down to the 2003 U.S. Open, and interviewed me, Blake, and Gambill. I went out to L.A. and met with her again, where she asked me what kind of girls I was interested in and if I like cameras. Then they took a Polaroid of me. I got a little celebrity with the other guys on tour. They all thought I was going to do it. But I would have had to take a month off, and I couldn't commit. Now the ratings for the show are so bad, they're thinking of dropping it.

Another reason why I didn't want to do *The Bachelor* was that they wanted you to get married to the woman you choose. I didn't feel I could do that. I'm 30 and single, but I stay away somewhat from dating and relationship commitments, because I'm not looking to stabilize my personal life. My career is my real priority. Plus it's very difficult to keep a relationship going on tour. I think it's a great tribute to the people who actually make it happen, because they're doing more than the average couple. The odds are not in any tennis pro's favor when it comes to making a relationship work.

I'm all for emailing, keeping in touch, and staying friends with the girls that I hook up with. I'm not afraid of commitment, but sometimes I get frustrated with them. They're always talking about finding a soulmate and believing in fate. And then you leave town for a week or two — you turn your back on them — and when you come home, they're off with somebody else. A lot of the time, these girls' boyfriends go to the same school as them, or work at the same restaurant. It sounds more like convenience than fate.

I have a couple of 19-year-old girls who like to hang with me and watch movies, and then I have a girlfriend who's about 30 and ready to settle down. She's very attractive and works in real estate, but every time I go out with a girl over 25, it's like an episode of *Oprah*. I have to ask if they see themselves married and how many babies they want. Do I know where I want to be five years from now? Actually, I don't know where I want to be five minutes from now.

My type is someone who's about 5'11", blonde, blue eyes, 38–24–34, the daughter of Bill Gates, likes money, and is a graduate of Harvard. But besides that, I don't ask that much. She also has to have a very strong moral character, no personal crises or anything. At the the same time, she has to have very low miles on her gas tank, if you know what I mean. Seriously, I like a girl anywhere between 5'5" and 5'10", lighter hair perferred, who has a good smile. She has to be fit, doesn't smoke, drink much or do drugs. I like someone who has a good moral base, likes to go to church, a good family person. She has to be outgoing — stoic yet outgoing at the same time. I'd like a girl who will be faithful, enjoys fashion, and is goal-oriented. That's a hard combination to find.

A lot of girls don't comprehend what being a pro tennis player is like, or they come from a rich family and they do know what professional tennis is like, but they couldn't care less. All they care about is where they're going to buy their next Chanel bag. Then I have to explain what I do and, in essence, prove myself to some girl who is studying psychology in college.

A few times, I've gone out with multiple girls in one day. I call it "slotting." Once I did it in Switzerland, another time in London and once in L.A. too. Three and a half dates is the most, and the half was for like a quick coffee. Sometimes, time becomes an issue, and I have to get out of a date early to meet the next girl. Then, maybe, I'll say, "I got myself in a situation for whatever reason. I thought we could go out, but now I can't. But let me rectify things before I get in any deeper, what are you doing tomorrow?" If it gets really sticky, I tell a girl that I was in a relationship for a long time, but I thought I would be better off being single. "It's been great," I'll say, "it's been wild, but lonely too, and I knew I should hook up with you from the moment I met you, but I didn't. The reason is I was wary of you because you trigger some real feelings inside me." No, I don't go that far, except when I'm screwing around at a bar and I sense the girl knows it's just a rap I'm laying on her. It's funny because I'm saying these deep things out of nowhere.

I like girls who are not into the tennis scene. Maybe they played in high school or college. The female players on tour are so focused on their careers, it doesn't offer them many options for a long-term relationship. There was Connors and Evert, Hewitt and Clijsters. Justin Gimelstob is dating Corina Morariu, who is from Boca and used to be Lindsay Davenport's doubles partner. Martina Hingis dated a lot of male players; I guess you could say she was a serial tennis dater. I certainly don't want to do that, but I'm not like, "You're a tennis player. I don't like you." I had Jennifer Capriati's phone number. Several of the Russian girls on tour are quite attractive, and while Sharapova is among the group of Russian starlet beauties, she's not really my type.

Just an aside here, Kournikova revolutionized the interest in women's tennis by wearing skimpy outfits and being blessed with great genetics. She has a great body and has made a lot of money by showing it on the tennis court. I haven't seen too many women players going over the limit in this regard. If they don't have the body, they don't try to show it. And if they do have the body, I think they should show it. Female players revealing more of their bodies have actually helped the women's tour.

Maria Kirilenko has got a young, amazing face. Nicole Vaidisova is cute. Then there's one girl that I don't even know her name, but she's fabulous. I think she's Czech.

Boy, I'm confused. I'm going to have to check The Da Vince Code again.

MARCH 27
Miami, Florida

NASDAQ 100, second-round match against Ljubicic. It's five-all in the third set, 15-30 to my advantage, swirling winds, thousands of Floridians on this Easter Sunday sitting on their cushions to pull for their homeboy, Spadea. Ljubicic serves big, I return deep, and we start a heavy-grind rally of forehand and backhand, alternating exchanges. I feel tentative owing to a slight insecurity of measuring my ground strokes due to an ever-changing, ominous gust. Or maybe it's just the situation. I know that if I win this point, I will have double break-point to serve out the match against one of the hottest players on tour, the conqueror of our American Dream Team in 2005 in three successive days on foreign soil, a feat unlikely to be repeated for quite some time. Ljubicic will be able to sit in his rocking chair 40 years from now, reminiscing to his grandchildren, "Goran was our country's best ever, but how many people can say that they single-handedly beat the U.S. Davis Cup team twice."

"Thirty-all," the chair umpire announces after I net a forehand crosscourt. It's a crushing blow to my confidence — not so much that the point is lost, but by how I lost it, with an overly cautious forehand shot that didn't clear the net. I lose the game, hold serve carefully, and we go into the tiebreak. I'm on thin ice if I continue to play "not to lose" tennis against a player who has beaten everyone he's faced this year with the exception of Roger Federer. But I continue to play defensive tennis and go down 7 points to 3 in the breaker, losing the match.

Ivan serves big, but not huge, yet he bullied me with his serve in the breaker. His big, heavy, winding, swooping strokes are consistent but not overpowering, as he stands five to eight feet behind the baseline trying to egg me on to overhit or hit a short ball he can punish. I kept up a good fight, but fell short by making marginal tactical mistakes, misjudging my power zone and when to make my final blow. I finally lost the match, on a pivotal double-fault — sound familiar? — that put a damper on my courageous effort to reverse the Davis Cup hex.

Luby's backhand is his real weapon. When he has time to set it up, he crushes it, but it's my feeling that if someone can rush him and hit steadily to his lefty wing, he can be beaten. I felt close to beating him. My game is improving, and with continued practice, I'm eager to repeat my close third-set battles and change their outcomes.

The minor tactical errors I made today were hitting too many balls to Luby's backhand. When I beat him twice in the past, I hit to his forehand more — on about a seven to three ratio. His forehand breaks down more often, especially on critical points. Another error was not taking short balls and coming in to the net, pressuring him to hit passing shots, especially on a windy day, where it's more difficult to pinpoint passes with me at the net.

Another mistake I made was not getting my return in play off his serve, especially his first serve. The more you make a big server play, the more annoying it is for him, because he is used to hitting aces and service winners. Any ball I could reach and put a racket on I should have hit deep and steady. Instead, I went for broke too many times, especially with the wind creating less of a margin for error. My return is my greatest asset, so finding a medium between aggressive hits and getting the ball in play is a challenge, and one I didn't rise to in this match.

Power zones are the areas where a player sees and feels the ball as big as a grapefruit, like a pinata waiting to be punished. In baseball, it is called the wheelhouse, and in tennis it's very similar — any ball in the shoulder-to-knees area is in the zone where all my weight, backswing, and confidence are maximized. In tennis, there are different spins and depths placed on the ball which change how it arrives on your side of the court. There are low slices, heavy high-arcing shots, penetrating topspins, and flat, deep hits, and I have to decide in a second on any given ball whether to hit it back safe with top spin, drive it into a corner for a running ground-stroke winner, hit a drop shot, approach shot, or if my opponent comes up to net, a passing shot, or an offensive or defensive lob. Optimally, I wait for a ball that lands and sits helplessly in my power zone to hit an outright winner.

I had many opportunities to put a stranglehold on Luby and seize this match, and yet I was content to steer my shots or grind, waiting for him to miss. It wasn't the right way to send a message to a confident Croat. This is a game where the top ball-strikers, and players with fearless mindsets, dominate. Hopefully, after a few adjustments, I'll be the one waving to the crowd in triumph next time. But for now, Ljubicic gets the respect. Roddick said back at Indian Wells after he "stayed around" to beat Fernando Verdasco of Spain, 7–6 in the third set, "The biggest thing that separates the players in the Top 10 from the guys 40 to 50 in the world, is that we find a way to win even if we don't have our best stuff." I didn't have my best stuff today, but I still should have won.

MARCH 29

Do tennis players party? Or do they sit in their rooms at 8:30 p.m., meditating, visualizing, drinking Gatorade, rehearsing their victory speeches and practicing their waves, smile, and forehand in the mirror? Well, some might do a little of that, who really knows? But the nightlife on the tennis tour can be as good as any. I'm not the best judge of partying, as it's not my forte, but I get out every now and again to see which night owls rule each town.

I'm staying in a hotel in South Beach, and I head out at about eight. I'm meeting a couple of girls I met a few nights earlier for dinner and drinks with my buddy John. I'm interested in one of the two — both are beautiful South American girls who live in Miami. We meet at the Shore Club, a hip, trendy hotel famous for having the wealthy and celebs stay and chill out by the pool. We eat at one of the two restaurants inside. Dinner is fun, with energetic conversation, great food, atmosphere, and music pumping. It's always nice to live the life occasionally. Growing up, I always had to watch my budget, look at the prices on the menu, order from the appetizer section, choose side dishes — the tap water with lemon, forget the entrees. Tennis has given me the opportunity to have a good time with friends in nice, classy places and not have to worry about the mathematics of the bill.

After dinner, we go to a party celebrating Jennifer

Capriati's 29th birthday. The beauties had previously arranged plans, so they couldn't join us — which kind of hurts as the momentum was rising — but I get over it. I'm in a land of flawless female creatures, physical miracles from head to toe. It's the Astor Hotel, another young, groovy nightspot. Jennifer is recovering from a recent surgery, and is in town because her mother, Denise, lives in Palm Beach.

Jennifer told me to call her if I had any problem getting into the VIP velvet-rope event. I told her I'd be fine, as I'm a pro at getting into glitzy affairs. I walk to the front looking to give my "Hi, I'm Vince Spadea" speech, but apparently there is no list after 11:30 anyway, so the bouncer just signals us in. I notice Jennifer's younger brother, Stephen, a law student in New York and a kid I grew up with running obstacle courses at tennis academies.

"Hooray, Vince is in the house," he says as a greeting.

"Hey great," I say. "How you doing, party dude?"

We venture downstairs into the core of the fiesta. Music is blaring, crowds of people are shuffling and rubbing against each other. I can't move, but I manage to edge away from a woman with a cigarette and a drink in her hand, who, at the same moment, almost burns me and spills her drink on my smooth shirt. The view is classic: Tom Gullikson is boogey-ing, Iva Majoli is laughing and being cheerful — coming out of the relative obscurity she's been in since she won the French Open back in what seems like ages ago — and Robert Seguso, even more of a missing figure in tennis, is hanging out without his ambitious wife, Carling, who's back home tending to their Brady Bunch brood of kids.

Tommy Haas is here with some friends. It's nice to see another competitor letting his guard down and having a good time. I have mixed feelings when I'm out late, partying like a pop star, because while I enjoy the release, I don't want to lose my edge over my opponents. So it's good to know other players have some fun, too, without worrying about losing their confidence. I assume they're going out, but it's always reassuring to see it with my own eyes.

It seems like the competition never ends. Who's the better dresser, better drinker, better dancer? Who's got the hotter girl on his arm?

"Who's that girl with Tommy?" I ask my buddy.

"I think it's his ex-girlfriend," he says. "She lost weight."

We all have to know each other's business. It's an intrinsic part of a pro tennis player's psyche.

"Hey, Spadea ain't afraid of ya," Haas's raised, sarcastic German-accented voice says.

"Hey Tommy, you're looking tired, brother. Don't go to sleep too late tonight," I say. As I walk by his ponytail, I continue to people-watch, seeking the birthday girl herself. I finally spot her in the back, and I have this flashback of the bubbly 14-year-old sensation she once was. Her ingenious tennis precocity and smiling innocence was a throwback to the classic Floridian femme fatale, Chris Evert. Now fast-forwarded 15 years, three Grand Slam titles, and an Olympic gold medal later, Jen is looking cute and dominating the dance floor.

I walk over and give her a hug, and say, "Happy Birthday, Jen. You're looking great, confident and radiant, and what a dress. Thanks for inviting me." With the music banging like a live concert speaker, I might as well have said, "Blah blah blah," but Jen is warm and appreciative. She tries to pull me out onto the dance floor, but I motion at my knee injury and let her continue her festive partying. I'm ready to head out. We taxi back to the hotel, where I see Safin walking out the door.

"Marat, what's happening, dog?" I say. Marat is with his

Russian girlfriend, looking cool as always in his leather jacket and jeans.

When I walk into the lobby at four in the morning, it's deserted — not even the hotel clerk is behind the desk. I hear the elevator bell ring, and as the door opens, out steps Paradorn Srichaphan and his trainer, dressed in street clothes.

"Hey, what are you doing up so early or late — depends which way you're going?" I say.

"I'm leaving for the airport. My flight is at 6 a.m. What about you Vince?"

I stumble and tell him (here's my "competitor's edge" ego surfacing), "I'm going to the airport, too. I just forgot something in the room." But then I smile and say, "I'm just kidding. It was my friend's birthday party and you missed out, Paradorn. We had a great time."

He laughs and we wave each other goodbye until the next tournament and the next match.

As I lie down, ready to doze off for a good 11 hours, my inner voice awakens me, screaming, "Oh no, I have to check out of the hotel by noon." There goes my beauty sleep.

APRIL 6
New York City

I decide to take a trip to Manhattan for two days before flying to Monte Carlo to start the European clay-court season. I talked to Jim Courier at the NASDAQ and he told me to call him — Jim lives in Manhattan now — and we could hit some balls. I fly into JFK airport, arriving on a morning flight. As soon as the plane hits the runway, I take out my cell phone and call Tennisport, an indoor-outdoor tennis club in

Queens where Courier and this guy named John McEnroe practice to stay in shape.

Courier told me the day before that he had to go out of town for business, but I could hit with the club's pro, Alex Asta, a Challenger player a few years back. So I talked to Alex and we agreed to play an hour later. I get my four bags at the baggage claim (my backpack, racket bag, and two duffel bags — I'm going to Europe for two months so I packed a lot of clothes). On international flights it's annoying to carry so many bags because the customs officers always put you on the screening line and ask a million questions, like, "Why do you have so many tennis clothes? Are you selling them?" I always reply, "No, I'm a pro tennis player and I sweat a lot."

I hop into one of the famous yellow NYC cabs and tell the guy how to get to Tennisport. I change clothes quickly and we have a good workout. I jump another cab to the Paramount Hotel in Times Square. The driver drops me off on Broadway and 46th Street, and throws my bags on the busy sidewalk with people scurrying all around. As I go to pick up my first bag, a young teenage girl approaches me and asks, "Can I have a picture taken with you?" I turn around and figure she wants me to take a picture of her in Times Square, but then her mother walks up and says, "You're Vince Spadea, right?" I say "Yeah, that's right. Wow, that's cool you recognize me. Let's take a picture."

I check into the hotel and call Paola, a Brazilian-American model I know from Florida, who is living and working on and off in New York. Paola and I are just friends so far, but who knows what lies in the future. She's 19, and a girl who defies the word "flaw." She's brunette, a 5-foot-8 beauty with brains. Uncharacteristically for a model, she has a voluptuous rump region, too. We get together and have lunch, then go for a little shopping and storytelling. I get out of the taxi, pay the man, jump out into traffic, cross the street, and put my hands in my pocket to feel my wallet, and it's not there.

"Paola, I just lost my wallet in that cab!" I say. It's gone forever, and I'm left with no money or credit cards and I'm leaving for Europe tomorrow. I apologize to Paola and tell her she may as well go home, as I'm going to be busy stressing. Then I beg the subway clerk to let me on for free because I'm macaroni-and-cheese broke. He relents and I arrive at my hotel to make phone calls to cancel all my cards. What a nightmare!

Later, I call Alex Asta and set up my tennis practice for early tomorrow. "Hey Vince," Alex says, "I'm going to hit with John McEnroe tomorrow. Why don't you two just hit instead?" I say that sounds like a great plan. My brother-in-law, married to my sister Luanne (they live together in the city with their young son and daughter), comes to my hotel and gives me plenty of cash for expenses. So the following morning, I cab it out to Tennisport for the big practice with Mr. Manhattan.

I arrive a few minutes early to stretch, and not long after that the main entrance opens and a salt-grey-haired man walks in the door with a bag of tennis rackets in a backpack. He looks like an older man ready to go to school, only with rackets rather than books in his pack. He greets me with a confident smirk, shaking hands in a manly arm-wrestling grip, like we've known each other for a while and been through some great experiences together. Which is not the case. I played for John when he was the captain of the 2000 American Davis Cup team and I've talked to him on a few other occasions. John is cool, frank, intelligent, and opinionated, and yet he still comes off as generous and warm.

"What brings you to New York? A rap video?" he asks sarcastically, as he likes to tease me about my rapping interests.

I tell him I'm here to hit with him and he says, "You want to hit a few balls and grind? I'll move you around and give you a good workout."

I grin and say, "Sure man, bring it on. I'm going to hit the ball heavy today. It's the clay court season." He laughs and moves off to the locker room for a few minutes.

We start off hitting down the middle, but hitting in any fashion with John is intense. He goes for every ball, even if I hit the ball outside the lines. He's digging, coming to the net, starting a new rally from any part of the court, hardly taking any breaks. It's nonstop hitting. He goes for a forehand, down-the-line winner and misses long. "No! Make that shot!" he bellows. But he says it with a smirk, almost as if he's mocking his own famous reputation for being a perfectionist.

A few shots later, he misses another and says, "Can someone tell me what I did wrong on that shot?" His comment is directed at the eight or so people who have gathered in the bleachers to watch us hit. They chuckle, but no one responds, as they assume correctly that it's really a rhetorical question.

I can still see the competitiveness in his eyes. His footwork has slowed, but his will hasn't. His shots still have pace, depth, and consistency. His volleys are crisp, effortless, and efficient, though he misses more than he used to. Still, his reflexes are second to none. I'm hitting fierce, heavy-spinning ground strokes in a grunting, tireless mode and he could have a pina colada in one hand as he responds to my shots at his body without a flinch. His volleys cut into the court with minimal bounce, and hurry away from me as if I'm trying to run them down on a treadmill.

His serve is as accurate and consistent as ever. His classic stance, with his back facing me as he manipulates his left arm and slices his serve out wider and wider into the service box, gives me a déjà vu feeling I'm watching the videotape of his brilliant 1980 Wimbledon finals match against Borg. John floats in to the net, smiling as he swats my ducklike return away with an angled volley that paints the lines. Thirteen years after his last year on tour, I still can't get a lob over his racket — McEnroe was famous for his lightning first step going back for his overhead. His conditioning is at a high level, especially for a man of 46. His running out wide for balls isn't vintage anymore, but something's got to give.

He's generous and helpful with tips as we play, complimenting me — "nice shot" — on my winners. On our water breaks we talk about tennis in general. "How many majors will Federer win?" I ask. "Will he beat Sampras's record of 14?"

Mac responds, "If he stays healthy, he can win 10, maybe 11." Interesting, Johnny Mac doesn't think Federer can break the record, but he does think highly of him. "Ten ain't too shabby if he stays healthy," he says again.

I ask him about his television talk show that debuted in July, 2004 but was cancelled at the beginning of 2005. He says the problem was that he was used to being interviewed, but he wasn't used to interviewing other people. He says he was just getting the hang of it when they pulled the plug.

"Maybe I should have had you rapping on the show," he says.

"You know, that would have changed your ratings, John."

Actually, his producer was at the 2004 U.S. Open, and I asked my agent to try to get me on the show, but his producer said they were only looking for semifinalists or better. *That was low, and guess what? Now there's no more show. Because John wasn't the CEO of flow. I've got more dough. My name's Edgar Allan Poe.*

"Hey John," I ask him in all seriousness, "how can I

develop a big weapon at the age of 30?"

He doesn't hesitate. "You're better off honing what you have. Consistency is rare in today's game. But go ahead, try to prove me wrong. You already did by coming back from your losing streak and making your great comeback. The youngsters can learn from that." It's uplifting to hear such praise coming from such a legend.

After about 45 minutes of hitting, he says, "Let's play a game to 21, alternating five serves each." We played points and Mac invites Alex to join him, playing alternate points against me. After I win a point on John's error, he gives us a classic Mac flashback by striking a ball into the fence in a fury and saying, "Come on, that's ridiculous."

As the game gets more intense, and he becomes more involved and competitive, John viciously hits a ball into the stands after losing a point. I turn away like I'm not involved, walking around looking for a ball to pick up. I don't ask why he's getting so upset. What am I going to say? "Why are you hitting a ball into the stands and throwing your racket, John? You're 46 years old, brother. What's the deal? C'mon, get with the program now. Go back home, you've got kids to feed. You cannot be serious, John."

That's not the right approach — and besides, while I can write it now for humor's sake, I would never have the guts to say it to him face to face.

It's all good in the end. He smiles joyfully, and we thank each other for the workout. John doesn't let his anger affect the overall tempo of the day, it's just that in the heat of play-ing the points he loses it a little. But as we close our racket bags, he's an uplifting, jovial guy who looks like he really and truly enjoyed himself, no matter the result of the games. (I won the first 21-point game, but he and Alex edged me out in the second, 21–19.)

I was off to the city a wiser man, after sharing a priceless experience with a legend I can remember fondly and learn from. If I had to choose between having my wallet back or having the chance to hit with John McEnroe, I'd choose the latter anytime. There was good news about my lost wallet, too. A guy named Mark found it and discovered a receipt in it from the Dean & DeLuca in the hotel. He returned it, with all the cash and credit cards still inside.

APRIL 11
Monte Carlo, Monaco

I'm in the Las Vegas of Europe, that's what they call Monte Carlo here. It's got the glitz, the glamour, the nameless, and the shameless. But it's very gloomy outside and I'm bored. I stay in the hotel the whole time, except for when I go out with my coach to practice on the slow, red clay courts. Rene Gomez, another Bollettieri disciple, has taken over for Greg Hill. I'm paying him $1,500 a week and paying all his expenses.

I play the fourth match of the day on Court 9 against my nemesis, Radek Stepanek. He is one of the least-fun guys for me to play. He's always tying his shoes, stepping back as I'm ready to serve, taking a bathroom break, or a trainer's break when he's not really hurt. He's a weasel. But Nadal did that to me in Spain last year, and Chang used to bounce the ball as he got ready to serve, and then right before he went into his motion, he'd look up into the crowd as if someone was disturbing him. I'd look over to where he was looking, and when I'd turn back, he would be serving the ball. It looked like an idiosyncrasy, but it was actually an offense. Look, I'm sure I do things that bother these guys, too.

Vince with his parents at the 2000 Olympics in Sydney, Australia

Vince signs autographs at an ATP tournament

Vince with his friend Dr. Fareed, a Davis Cup physician

U.S. Team at dinner in Dusseldorf, Germany. From left to right: Vince, Alex O'Brien, Paul Ankaeome, Pete Sampras, Bridgette Wilson, Jared Pahuer

Sisters' law school graduation from Northwestern University, Chicago, IL, 2001. From left to right: Vince, Diana, Hilda, Vince Sr., Luanne

Davis Cup practice in Santander, Spain, with John McEnroe

Vince with niece Elle, age 2, and nephew Alec, age 3, in New York City, NY

I take some Advil because my shoulder is bothering me. I don't like to watch the matches going on before mine. I go to the trainer's room to get a massage, but tennis players are like vultures when free massages are being offered. Doubles players — who don't start playing until later in the week — sign up for three a day. Some of these guys live in the massage room.

I don't get on until 6:30 p.m. They switch our match from Court 9 to 11, which is higher up on the hill. It's cloudy and getting dark, and there are no lights above the court. I say to the umpire, "Listen, technically you're not supposed to start a match you can't finish." He calls the supervisor, who tells him to start play. Nadal has just gone on the center court against Monfils, but the center court is at sea level, with much better visibility. We're up three to four stories. I could lean over and see Nadal playing, but only with a strong pair of binoculars. Our court is set up against a huge wall, making it even darker. It doesn't seem right.

I lose the first set 6–0 and I start to panic. I don't feel good, but I'm still trying to grind. I think about how I beat David Sanchez 0 and 0 in my first match of the year. Sharapova lost to Davenport at the NASDAQ two weeks ago 0 and 0. I win the first game of the second set, then break him and I'm up and running. I go up 3–0, but then I get broken.

It's getting really dark now and I get flustered. I can't lift my shoulder. At 5–4, I say to the umpire, "If I win this set, we're not going to be able to finish the match." I lose my serve, and my confidence. Stepanek beats me 7–5 and wins the match.

Boca Raton, Florida

I'm back in Boca, rehabbing my shoulder at a local physical therapist, while the tour has moved on to Barcelona and Munich. I will probably miss next week, when the Masters Series tournament in Rome is played, and return for the Masters Series event in Hamburg. Two weeks later is the jewel of the clay court season, Roland Garros, the French Open, and I hope to be back in full form by then.

I went to see the Miami Dolphins team doctor and after examining my shoulder, without having to take an MRI, he told me that I have tendonitis of the right shoulder. I had the same injury in 1999, and I came back to my best year on tour. Even though the pain now is most severe in my shoulder, it actually starts in my back. But because it affects my nerves, it creates a tingling and numbness all the way to my fingertips. The night I lost to Ljubicic in Miami, I couldn't sleep because of the pain in my shoulder.

I'm pleased that I'm taking the time off now to do something about it. It also gives me the time to work more with my sports psychologist, Dr. John Murray, here in Boca. It's hard to put into words the benefits I've derived from mental coaching, since the practice is both a science and an art, but it has helped me in staying calm on the court and embrace the competitive challenge. Everybody panics at one point or another when playing pro tennis, so Dr. Murray and I talk about the importance of keeping the focus on "performance," when I'm playing — staying in the moment, rather than thinking about my ranking or my career goals. Our sessions reinforce that I need to stay focused on one point at a time, with no excuses. To help achieve this, Dr. Murray and I created a variety of "mindsets" that I focus on before tournaments or matches. Before one match he had me memorize the following three phrases to reinforce the message in our session: "Stay extremely excited" (for energy and passion); "Perform my best" (to stop worrying about ranking or outcome); and "Never give up" (in those grueling three- and five-set matches).

I started working with Dr. Murray just after I endured the longest losing streak in tennis history. I felt I needed to start from scratch, let go of my fear, and take very small steps in eventually reversing my downward course. Anybody can win one point or one match, but if you think about how long it may take to move from No. 270 to the Top 20 again, you'll never make it back.

At my lowest point, I fed off Dr. Murray's enthusiasm, and he helped me realize that there was nothing I enjoyed more than the challenge of a competitive match. Through our daily sessions, I became more organized in my practices and daily routines and Dr. Murray emphasized that my pur- suit of excellence needed to be greater than my pursuit of a winning outcome. The latter is impossible to control. I felt a release of pressure and I began to thrive on the long and gru- eling matches again. Eventually my talent reemerged and I saw a marked improvement in my confidence, focus, pas- sion, and desire to reach the top again. Today, I signed a contract with Dr. Murray to get to sleep at a reasonable hour. I have been going to bed late and that has affected my performance on the court.

As for the rehab of the shoulder, I'm resigned to it. What else can I do? You can't play on tour with a bum shoulder. I've got to get my shoulder strong again, and then get back out and play again because my ranking has already slipped down into the 40s.

I do not even think about retirement. I'm far from that

point. I do not have so much money or many career opportunities outside tennis to pursue after I do retire. Maybe I'll be a tennis commentator on television, maybe I'll try music or acting. But whatever I do, I want to be legit. I want to pursue my new career with passion, not in a harebrained, Paris Hilton–style.

When I do retire from tennis, I think I'll be emotionally unfulfilled. I'm going to feel drained, pathetic. I'll have to transition quickly into something creative to wipe that feeling away. Whatever I do, it's not going to be a redundant desk job. It's going to be something interesting.

Look at Jim Courier. Last night, he took a wildcard in Houston to play doubles with Agassi. They lost, but it's good that he came back and played. It shows his competitive spirit never died. Retiring from pro tennis is like having someone close to you die. Coming back and competing again is like trying to bring that person back to life. Courier probably got tired of walking down the streets in SoHo and only having three out of a thousand say, "Hey, Jim Courier, what's up?" Five years after retirement, he stepped back onto a court to play a pro match again and probably 5,000 people in the stands were rejoicing that they got to see him play again.

APRIL 27

I got up at 8:45 this morning, showered, left the house and went to the Starbucks on Glades Road. There're like five Starbucks in Boca Raton. Starbucks is like the couch outside my home for me. I'm not a big coffee drinker, but I'm a big Starbucks fan. I like the lifestyle. This Starbucks has the best female traffic in Boca between seven and 11 in the morning. I drink my coffee and girl-watch.

I usually get a Caramel Macchiato with no-fat milk. Sometimes decaf, but I like the caffeine in a nice, warm drink with a little sweet caramel. I get the yogurt and the orange juice, too. Or I get the chocolate milk. I need the dairy, fruit, and fiber, and for the carbs, I get a bagel or a muffin. It's all part of my nutritional plan.

I've gone to Starbucks in Tokyo, London, and a few times in Spain. Roddick went to a Starbucks on a daily basis at one tournament. He would go every morning like he was going to church. But he wasn't there to hang out like I am. I go mostly for the festivities. I meet new people. I get that from my father; he loves to meet and entertain people.

Roddick knows how I like to hang out at Starbucks and malls. He once said, "If Vince is in the finals of a tournament on a Saturday night, on Saturday afternoon, you'll find him in the mall." I told him the only reason he knew that is because he's always walking around malls, too. It takes a mall rat to know a mall rat.

I saw a program on TV with a financial advisor who said if everyone saved the money they spent at Starbucks, and they actually invested it, it would be amazing how much money they would make. So sometimes I just sit in Starbucks and have ice water.

After Starbucks, I drove over to the Gold's Gym in Boca where Chris Carter, the former wide receiver for the Minnesota Vikings, has his F.A.S.T. center (which stands for Functional Agility Speed Training). I've been working out with the trainers here for a few years. The idea is to get faster, fitter, stronger, and become inspired and challenged by the trainers and athletes working out here. It's a real sweatbox; it's not a country club. It's tougher to work hard in an environment that is not gritty. If you're tired and feeling sick in the hood, it's a lot easier to get through the struggle of working out than it is if you're running sprints in Mizner Park. The F.A.S.T. gym is like the one Rocky worked out at in Philadelphia. The real Rocky, Rocky Marciano, used to go into hiding for three months before a fight. Sacrifices have to be made.

I live out of my car here like I do in L.A. I leave the house at eight or nine in the morning and come back at 11 or 11:30 each night. When I come in my dad asks, "Where have you been?" I usually say, "I'm 30 years old. I went out to the store." My parents would lose sleep if I was 65.

My car is like my apartment on wheels. If I need to tap into something right away, say it's cold outside and I need long pants or a hat, I have everything I need in the backseat of my car. A $400 Coogi sweater I just throw around. My Hugo Boss Davis Cup warm-up top; on the sleeve it says, "2005 Davis Cup, Spain vs. USA." I have it all back there. There's a gift from the U.S. Open; they give every player a baseball jersey from his home state team, so I have a Florida Marlins shirt with "Spadea" on the back. I even have Fig Newtons; my nutritionist wants me to get 300 calories into my body within 20 minutes after every workout. And of course, I have Advil.

The clothes and hats allow me to morph into different personalities. I'm big into having multiple alter egos. Am I feeling like Vincenzo today or am I feeling a little quirky? Do I want to be in a fight club? Do I want the conservative, frat-boy look? Do I want the distinguished, cool New Yorker look where I can go clubbing and out to a nice, fine restaurant? Mardy Fish said that I'm the worst dressed guy on tour because I always wear sweat pants and a jean jacket. But he hasn't seen my full wardrobe.

I definitely believe in being organized and neat, but I think people can relate with not having the most perfect-looking backseat, closet, or bedroom. I'm not afraid to reveal it. I think part of the reason why I get along with a lot of different types of people is because I say and do things that they think and do themselves, but while they might feel embarrassed by their actions, I'm comfortable with it.

I once walked up and introduced myself to the famous Maxim model Victoria Silvstedt, while she was having lunch in South Beach with her mother and sister. She probably thought I was a stalker, but it didn't stop me. I'm fearless. I started up a conversation with her. I said, "I know you like tennis." She asked me if I knew Tommy Haas. Every woman I meet who knows I'm a tennis player asks me if I know either Tommy Haas or Andy Roddick. I changed the subject and we talked about how I had just traveled to Spain to play Davis Cup.

My publicist in L.A. just called and said she wants to set me up on a date with a former Playboy Playmate named Dalene Curtis. I'm game. I told her, *"Tell the Playmate, it could be fate, I'm feeling irate."* I just like talking and meeting women, all kinds. "You come from a trailer park? You're an insomniac? OK, I'm interested."

APRIL 28

I told you that I'm big into different personalities and alter egos. I have these different business cards that I give out once in a while for kicks. One says I'm a movie producer and another, closer to home, reads:

Passion and Confidence
Vincent Spadea, Tennis Pro
All Ages, All Levels, Technique Specialist, Motivator,
Guaranteed Improvement
Florida, California

And then it has my number listed. I only give it out to friends.

MAY 7
Hamburg, Germany

I'm about to go to bed, it's almost midnight, and I've had a long day. I haven't been able to get to sleep by 10 o'clock, like I'm trying to do, adhering to my new resolution. The qualifying rounds started here today. I got up in the morning at 9:30 and ran down for some breakfast. I sat down with Sebastien Grosjean and Paradorn Srichapan. We were all just chilling. The breakfast was up on the 8th floor of the hotel, in a conference room just for the players. The hotel is awesome. It's a Royale Meridian and the rooms are enormous. There are great big comfortable beds with ten pillows, really soft and spongy. It's arguably the best hotel on tour. I really am enjoying just sleeping and chilling.

After breakfast, I ran downstairs and met my coach, Rene Gomez, and we ran over to the tennis courts. It's extremely cold and rainy. I have to wear two shirts just to practice. It's in the 50s and it's ugly, raining, and bitter. But I'm honing my game. I've missed the last month rehabbing tendonitis in my right hitting shoulder. I've missed the bulk of the clay-court season in Barcelona, Estoril, Portugal, and Munich, and the Masters Series Italian Open last week.

I hit with a guy who I don't even know. He's a German player who hits the ball pretty well. It's crazy, you can just pick up a guy to practice with out here — who looks like he just dropped off the back of a truck — and he hits the ball great. That's pro tennis for you. Whether someone's ranked

No. 1 or No. 301 in the world, everyone out here can hit the ball great.

We shared a court with Joachim Johansson and Tim Henman. I hit on the same side of the court as Henman. He's up to his old pranks and sarcastic ways. He asked me why I pulled out of the Italian Open last week, and made a few dry remarks when I told him. But he's a nice, fun guy, always trying to bring a little light, British humor wherever he goes. I asked my hitting partner if one of my forehands was in during a practice point, and Henman said, "C'mon, Vince. Why don't you question that call? You haven't missed that shot since '86." I guess that was his way of giving me a compliment. All I wanted to know was if it was in or out.

I practiced for an hour and went back to the players' lounge and had some lunch, stretched out a little bit, and changed clothes and had a shower. I sat next to Juan Carlos Ferrero, who was sitting next to some other Spanish players and his coach. It was amazing, he was eating his lunch — penne and marinara sauce — and getting ready for his qualifying match. Here's a former German and French Open champion, No. 1 in the world in 2003, a clay-court specialist, and he's back playing the qualifiers. It's scary, but it's pro tennis. If you get injured, lose your inspiration, go into a funk, or go on a losing streak, your ranking drops very quickly. And then you find yourself sitting in the German Open cafeteria eating penne pasta about to play in a qualifying match.

One of the players' girlfriends was doing her homework. All of these girls are between 19 and 25, and most of them have their own careers or term papers to work on. I get a little scared when I see the real world intruding on our sanctuary. I can't remember the last time I finished a book. She had a ton of textbooks surrounding her and she looked very studious.

The buffet line had plenty of choices: pasta, luncheon meats, and big desserts. The Europeans take pride in their cuisine, but German food is not my favorite. Still, they do it right in these big Super-9 Masters Series tournaments, hiring the best chefs. Ljubicic was sitting with Ancic's coach. It was weird to see a player sitting with another player's coach, but I guess they're all from the same country. Roddick's coach, Dean Goldfine, was there having lunch, but Roddick was nowhere to be seen.

Later, I went downtown with my coach and did some shopping. I bought a little polo shirt made by Echo, which is in fashion now. I needed to get my mind off tennis for a little bit before my next practice at five. I practiced with Nikolay Davydenko, and got a good hour in. It was another cold windy afternoon, raining off and on. I practiced next to Rainer Schüttler, who was being drilled by his coach. He was feeding balls relentlessly, moving Schüttler side to side. Everyone has different ways of preparing. He's got his repetition, and I'm playing my points in a set against Davydenko.

The locker room is very dirty. There's red clay all over the floor, tracked in from the players' sneakers. You can't walk around with bare feet. It's a little too untidy in my opinion, probably one of the worst locker rooms on tour. The stadium court is very nice, though, with great sight lines from every seat. There are also two grandstand courts that are very intimate. Vendors are everywhere, selling bratwurst and Deutsches bier, the German beer, and German pretzels, and everyone except for the tennis players is walking around looking very German.

I had five huge boxes of Le Coq Sportif clothes waiting for me at the hotel. There were so many beautiful, immaculate tennis outfits it was a little absurd. It's probably the best gift I've ever gotten from a clothing sponsor. It was so much abundance it was almost overboard, because on the road it's hard to travel with five boxes. There are different styles, different sizes, different colors of warm-up suits, T-shirts, collared shirts, socks, headbands, bandanas, probably 15 to 20 pairs of shoes total, 80 shirts, 50 shorts, 50 hats. Absurd, but I'm very grateful and appreciative. It's exciting, like a second birthday or Christmas present, getting all these clothes for free. If they pay you to wear their stuff, it's even more of a bonus. Sometimes it's so awesome to be a pro tennis player.

I went down to the gym to loosen up my legs by riding on the stationary bike, then I got a good stretch in. I was watching the television and they were showing the finals of a world poker tournament from Monte Carlo. Yevgeny Kafelnikov, who retired about a year or so ago from the tour — the great Russian champion who won the French and Australian Opens, and who I grew up playing against because we're both 30 — was in the final on EuroSport Television. I'm sitting there watching it in the gym in Hamburg. It was shocking to see in the span of a couple of years a guy go from being one of the best tennis players in the world to being a top poker player, but Yevgeny's a competitive guy who excels at whatever he does.

I had a quiet dinner in the hotel bar, spaghetti with basil sauce and a little turkey on the side. I went onto the Internet and checked out some scores. I saw Nadal was in the finals in Italy for his third straight Masters Series. It's scary. He's going to be in the Top 5 in the world now. And Coria, the guy I play in Hamburg this week, is in the finals against Nadal. It's good to see Coria's legs are going to get a little tired playing in the finals against Nadal. Maybe he'll be a little bit stiff and sluggish when I play him. He's obviously a great player, and a tough draw, but I'm looking forward to it. It's an upset in the making.

MAY 8

Happy Mother's Day. I called my mom just now. I'm tired, it's 11 o'clock, getting close to my bedtime. Today was pretty straightforward. I had breakfast alone. Hey, there's Vince sitting with all his friends on the tour. My coach wasn't around, so I just opted for a lonely breakfast. It was my typical cereal, yogurt, toast, jam, and one scrambled egg.

Eating in these pro tennis dining halls is kind of interesting. At each table you have players from different countries. There's the Czech table with Jiri Novak, Stepanek, his coach, and a doubles player named Friedl. Then there's the Argentineans. I didn't see any Americans like Roddick, Ginepri, or Kevin Kim, but maybe they just don't eat breakfast. The French players all sit together. It's a congregation of countries, almost like you're playing in a team competition. Mostly, it is a habit and association built on language and friendship.

I practiced at 11 with Oliver Rochus, an outstanding 5-foot-5 player from Belgium, a big-time overachiever for his height. Everyone talks about how great the big, tall monsters are in tennis, but here's a guy who's succeeding despite his size disadvantage. What he has in touch, speed, and spirit makes up for his lack of mass. Thirty minutes into the practice, a downpour started and everyone ran off the courts except for Rochus and me. We kept playing for another 10 minutes. It wasn't the smartest move. I started getting frost-bitten, but we felt like hitting more on that good, gritty, muddy clay surface. It was inspiring, but slippery and mucky tennis.

After showering and eating lunch, I ran upstairs to the players' lounge and there were two girls sitting behind counters giving out Gummy Bears — the famous German Gummy Bears — you can't go wrong eating those. I'm reading Phil Jackson's book, *Sacred Hoops*, and I jumped on the Internet and read some tennis and NBA scores. I like to stay in touch with U.S. sports scores. It keeps me feeling close to home.

I feel like a tennis slave here, waiting for my next practice. I'm just waiting to play my match on Tuesday. I hit with Grosjean, a fellow Boca Raton resident, sharing the court with Thomas Johansson and Karol Beck from Slovakia. There was no rain, but no sunshine either, and it was very cold.

I took a nap from 5 to 5:30, jumped into the Jacuzzi, and then went into the gym to do some stretching before my massage. I saw Roddick there cycling furiously with his iPod on, a cellphone in his left hand, like he was waiting for a big call. I joked with him about it. There was an umpire on the bike next to him, and an ATP trainer on the floor doing his exercises.

Dinner was pasta and turkey. I've had the same food for the last four nights. I'm a simple, unadventurous eater. I like to know what's in my body. If I get really tired of it, I change, but it takes a really long time for me to get tired of my food, especially if it tastes pretty good.

MAY 9

Another good day. Got up at nine and had a practice from ten to eleven with Kevin Kim, a fellow American. I rushed my breakfast. Normally, I like to eat one or two hours before I practice or play. The weather was cold, inclement as usual. You'd be surprised how fast days go by eating three meals, practicing and stretching, practicing and stretching, and then coming back to the hotel to chill out before I go to bed.

I'm feeling the ball well, but I'm not hitting with much spin. Normally, I want to hit a heavy ball with a lot of spin on clay. The more spin you put on the ball, the less risk you're taking. There's a better chance for the ball to go in. When the ball hits deep and bites, it bounces with more force upwards and into the opponent, and usually out of his strike zone. It's a higher percentage play than hitting the ball flat, and if you do it many times over, it eventually can wear your opponent down. Obviously, a blast that goes in is ultimately the best shot, but you're not going to be able to hit that shot consistently over an entire match.

With my shoulder problems, hitting topspin puts more pressure on the joint. It's a different backswing and hit, and I'm using different muscles to contort and twist into the ball. I'm trying to ease into it day by day, because I haven't been practicing that much. With the cold conditions, I never want to rush into hitting big topspin.

This is my job. At the end of the day, it can sometimes seem to other people redundant and repetitive — like a *Groundhog Day* situation — but that's not the way I look at it. I look at every new day as a new challenge to prove I'm a better tennis player than I was yesterday. A lot of days I achieve that goal. I'm just doing my thing; I'm on a mission.

I saw Gustavo Kuerten at lunch. Kuerten goes through these spells where he never shaves or gets a haricut. He looks very barbaric: scruffy, disheveled, unkempt, and untidy. I think he does it on purpose, especially during the clay-court season, when he seems even scruffier and wild-looking. I think it helps him get into the warrior mentality — being an animal out there — grunting and grinding and powering through guys in his matches. He feels rough and tough and whacked-out. I'm starting to grow my hair longer to see if some of that wild man feeling comes out in me, too.

I saw Federer getting ready for his match today. His trainer was in the locker room getting Roger's drinks ready — he has a special powdered drink, his energy drinks. I saw Roddick getting ready for a match he lost to Nicolas Massu, the Olympic gold-medal winner, in a close hard-fought match. Roddick will probably jet home in a private plane now because I can't imagine he's going to stay in Europe for two weeks until the French Open begins.

I practiced again at 3 o'clock with Feliciano Lopez of Spain and Paul-Henri Mathieu of France. It was a down-to-business practice. Lopez is a big lefty with long hair. He seems self-involved, the type of guy who never met a mirror he didn't love. He's one of those Don Juans from Spain; a real passionate guy. I did my biking and stretching in the gym, then went grocery shopping to get my liters of water (to keep hydrated in the room), and my strawberry yogurt, some gum to keep me relaxed, and some more Gummy Bears. I'm beginning to like this stuff.

I went back to my room and organized my clothes for my match with Coria tomorrow. I don't know what to think about this match. I'm just going to be confident, go for my shots, rise to the occasion, and play like a champion. I'm going to be courageous and fight to the end, win or lose. I will not lose. I will not lose.

MAY 10

I lost my match to Coria. Coming back from a month off and playing a guy who is playing phenomenal tennis, I felt like I was facing Greg Maddux in his prime and I was taking my first at-bat in months. It was not a good situation. I lost 6–0, 6–2, but I actually played well in the second set. I was up love–40 on his serve to get back to three-all and I could've turned things around, you never know. I'm a warrior, right? Well, so much for the optimism. I didn't make it happen, and now it's over, all said and done.

My coach took me out on a practice court after the match and we worked out for an hour until I couldn't breathe or even blink. I'm just trying to get my conditioning back, my strokes back in shape, because I'm very rusty. I'm going to practice as much as I can this week. It's cold and bitter, but it's what I've got to do. Sometimes you have to do things in life that you don't want to do.

I went back to the hotel and had some dinner. I had a few drinks with a couple of girls, but I'm calling it a night early. I'm tired. I've got to get some bed rest. My body and legs feel weary. I've got to get focused; I can't be messing around anymore. I've got to get back to tennis business. Today was a very poor day on a results basis, but it was a wake-up call. I've got to look at it from the bright side. Losing this match will help me in the long run. That's who I am, Mr. Bright Side.

I believe that there is always a great tomorrow. Whether you win, lose, or draw, you always have to challenge yourself and look for improvements. It is very important to be optimistic, to know that you can really have an impact on yourself, so you know you can get better and do better, even when you've just won a tournament. They say U.S. Open winner Ben Hogan was out practicing on the driving range 20 minutes after the trophy ceremony. Playing pro tennis is a relentless pursuit to challenge yourself to be better. I think that's why I'm optimistic. Whether I'm winning or losing, I love what I'm doing, and am passionate, and that makes me happy and positive.

MAY 11

I'm still in Hamburg. I didn't practice today until 5 p.m. You learn to cherish days like this when you've been on the tour as long as I have. I woke up at 11 and just chilled out in my bed until 12, getting all the rest that I could. All the rigors, stresses, and physical ailments from training and playing hard and the jet lag from traveling makes sleeping really important.

I practiced from 5 to 6:30 very intensely. Side-to-side drilling for about an hour, then I did some volleys, overheads, and serves. I ran over to the gym afterwards and worked out. I saw Kuerten in there, after getting destroyed in his match, 6–3, 6–0, by Tommy Robredo of Spain. He was running on the treadmill really hard. It looked like he was punishing himself the way I did yesterday after losing.

Some of us just punish ourselves after we lose a match. We don't go out and have a beer — some do — but most of us feel masochistic and work even harder. The tennis player's mentality is funny. We think, "Hey, I didn't work hard enough in that match. Well, guess what? I'm going to go out and inflict a lot of pain on myself so that the next time I feel like performing this badly, I'll remember how I'm torturing myself now, and think twice about playing that way again."

MAY 14
Dusseldorf, Germany

The World Team Cup competition starts tomorrow, with the U.S. versus Germany. It's a competition between the eight teams who qualify with the two best singles players rankings from the same country. The U.S. qualified with Agassi and Roddick, but since neither guy wanted to play in the event, the ATP went down the list and picked me because I was the third-ranked American last year. I automatically became captain, and chose Dent to play alongside me in singles, but when he bagged it, Jeff Morrison became the second singles player. It's a Davis Cup setup, with two singles players and a doubles team in a round-robin format. I picked the Bryan twins, naturally, as the doubles team. Eat your heart out, Pat McEnroe.

MAY 15

Tommy Haas has a hot-and-cold personality to fit his hot-and-cold tennis game. Coming into today's match, I have a losing record against him of 1–3. He beat me in the biggest match we've played, a straight-setter in the quarterfinals of the 1999 Australian Open. In fact, the only match I won against him was his first match after shoulder surgery in San Jose back in 2004.

Today, I went down again, a straightforward 6–2, 6–4 loss. My game was gloomier than the skies, which rained throughout the morning. We went on the court with no warm-up, my body was colder than the North Pacific, my legs chillier than Alaskan crab legs waiting to be dipped into tartar sauce and consumed by a hungry German. Haas had a partisan crowd behind him, chanting after every point their golden boy won.

Tommy can often be sullen and seem not to care on the court, but when he plays in Germany, he plays with a lot of pride. He puts a lot of pressure on his opponent when he's on, striking the ball well and running fast. His backhand is his signature shot, but he hits with heavy spin off both sides, and then flattens the ball out with pace when he takes a short ball.

Today he was focused and strong willed, measuring every shot, playing patiently when he needed to, but hitting decisive winners when he saw the smallest openings. He served powerfully, and even came up to the net at times, something he usually doesn't do often. I, on the other hand, played like a little kid lost, looking around for help, carelessly hitting balls out, making a mess of my debut match here in Dusseldorf. There were moments in the second set where I dictated and played enthused tennis, but they were too few and far between. I didn't have a break point the whole match — a nightmare statistic for me, because of my supposed great return of serve. My shots made the balls look like they were full of helium as they sailed above and beyond the baseline with no direction. I was about as relaxed as a TV reporter in the eye of a hurricane, just looking for a moment of stability.

Bottom line is, he kicked my butt today. Time to shake it off and get ready for tomorrow. When you've played the game as long I have, you learn not to fret as much after a loss. Nobody wins all the time, but at the same time, I need to make changes to my game soon. I'm tired of being a punching bag for dominant players. I've got to turn myself around — starting tonight.

MAY 16

I just did one of the craziest things I've ever done when it comes to tennis. After 20 years playing with the same racket, the Prince Graphite 110, I switched to the innovative technology of the Prince 03. Yeah, it's the middle of a big team competition, yeah, it's five days before the French Open, but here I am trying out new equipment. I'm tinkering with my game too much.

I got spanked like a redheaded stepchild yesterday in my match against Tommy Haas. I figured if all these young, big, strong players are clubbing balls with their thick, wide-bodied, aerodynamic sticks, I needed to be on a level playing field with everybody else. Nobody uses my racket on tour anymore. So I made the switch and practiced vigorously with this new racket, working on putting balls away aggressively at the net with overheads and swinging volleys. I lost so many points playing against Haas by not being able to put away the last ball.

Putting the ball away is a vital element for me to develop to bring my level up a notch. I play good defense, but when I set up the point for a winner, I don't dominate and torpedo the ball into a corner like Federer or even Henman. I worked with Gomez for another hour and a half after my match, and then my shoulder was sore again. It seems like I'm married to this throbbing ache. It never goes away, except during the 15 minutes I ice it down. I lose sleep and pop anti-inflammatory pills like they're M&Ms. It's not the best thing for my liver, but it's my only option right now.

Mike Bryan is only 26 and he told me his shoulder is killing him, too. He just switched the strings on his racket to the most popular string on tour now. It's supposed to give you more spin and durability — plus power and consistency — but it's a tough material that makes your arm work harder than it does playing with the popular gut or synthetic strings. I string my racket at 75 pounds tension — one of the tightest on tour — but Borg used to string his rackets at 80 pounds, and his were made of wood.

Mike points to the top of his shoulder and says, "It hurts right here, Vince. Is that where your shoulder hurts?"

I say, "Yeah, mine's in a similar spot. It's out of control, man." I showed him some key exercises he needed to work on. That's the benefit of being 30, when people ask your advice you can actually help them out some of the time. We headed back to the hotel with the team, the guys talking about video games the whole way back while I opted for my headphones and my rap music.

MAY 18

Another day off in Dusseldorf and I'm starting to go a little stir-crazy. The weather in Germany makes me feel so lethargic, like I'm depressed. I find myself anxiously waiting for the three meals of the day to break the monotony. What's happened to my unquenchable energy? Is it my age? Is it the weather? I'm not sure, but I don't want to dwell on it.

I practiced today with my teammate Jeff Morrison. I had problems beating Jeff, which concerns me, considering he's not a clay-court specialist. When I struggle in practice, I just think about how Sampras never seemed to care about how he performed in practice. I remember beating him in a practice match before he won the 1995 Davis Cup and thinking, "Geez, Pete's game is going downhill."

On this boring day with no action, I find myself thinking of God. I've always tried to pursue a clean and pious lifestyle and be a good person. On tour, you have a lot of free time to reflect and philosophize about how people operate and about whether God really exists. And if he does, does he know or care about my tennis career or is he busy working on the world's major problems?

Michael Chang had this tremendous desire to spread the word of God and Jesus. On every autograph he gave, he wrote, "Jesus loves you." In interviews, he would talk about his undying love and belief in God, how he believed that God picked him to win and cared about his forehand and backhand. A lot of people criticized Chang for his proselytizing, wondering why God would care more about Michael Chang's forehand than about all the wars and poverty and diseases in the world.

I believe in God, but I would never be as outspoken as Michael was in his beliefs. I never judged him, though, for the way he went around telling people about the positive effect his belief in God had had on his life. Tennis pros know a lot about faith. Without faith in ourselves and in our games, we never would have made it to the top. We always think and hope we can win, because when we refuse to give up, we have the greatest chance of realizing our goals. This is the way most of us bring a pious belief and attitude into our lives.

It's late, and these are the times I find myself drifting into pondering these deep thoughts — especially when the television in my room has no English channels on it except CNN. How many times can I hear the news and that song they play filled with trumpets and drama? I've got to hit the lights and get ready for Spain tomorrow. I'll need God, my forehand, backhand, and maybe Chang to lend me a little of his speed to beat Robredo.

MAY 20

I won, I won, I won, I won. I won. It's the only thing people care about, right? I lost to Robredo in three sets yesterday, but defeated 12th-ranked Joachim Johansson today, 6–3, 6–4. I'm feeling numb with confidence. I've got that untouchable feeling. Life doesn't suck, after all.

Everybody notices when you win. Even the lady serving lunch gave me a bigger portion of chicken, saying, "You deserve it." Front-running is so prevalent in sports, and hence, life. It's winner takes it all, and the loser might be a good sport, but he's also just a loser. Oh well, it's the game of life. You can ante up or fold. Here's my ante, come on, bring it to me, life. I'm ready for the French Open.

Here's my little French rap:

Ladies and gents will be jumping the fence to catch a glimpse of Vince at the French, he's so intense, doesn't give you an inch, I went from sitting on the bench with a dollar and fifty cents, to a corporate account at Merrill Lynch, but let me know what youse think, when you see them dragging me off the links, at Roland Garros, cause Spadea will break you down like a broken arrow, a golden pharoah, fighting to be the hero at Roland Garros, I'm tennis's Robert De Niro, and I'm representing South Florida, champagne pouring out, that don't rhyme? Shore it does, trying to keep up with the Joneses like Norah does, peace out, I gotta start jump roping, before I leave Paris without the crown at the French Open.

MAY 23
Paris

It's game time. I blazed out of bed today — hardly slept a minute — excited. When I was younger, I would have woken up nervous and filled with self-doubt, apprehensive to go out for my first match of a Grand Slam. But as I get older, I feel how precious these opportunities are, and I'm thrilled to have a chance to change my fate in the game with the possibility of getting red hot for the next two weeks.

I feel good about playing Albert Costa of Spain, a former French Open champion in 2002. Maybe it's not the best of draws, but he's been in a downward spiral for the last year or so. The schedule had me playing the fourth match after an 11 a.m. start, so there was no need to rush to get out of bed or get to the courts. I'm just in an anxious mood and wide awake already.

When we finally go on — it's been a slow day — they've put us on the last court in the complex. (They must have talked to the Australian Open tournament directors.) But here there's a packed crowd in the limited bleacher area, and as the match starts, we're like two thoroughbreds breaking out to the sound of the gun. We're both hitting heavy, smothering, big-spin winners. Albert throws in his deadly drop shot to make life even tougher on me, but I hold on like a cowboy at the rodeo, herky-jerky, but managing to do whatever it takes to stay in the ring and draw first blood.

I'm hitting more aggressively than ever before, and I'm moving him all over the court, almost the way Agassi makes his opponents scurry. I take the first set 6–4. Costa has an incredibly heavy forehand, it spins and moves high like a tidal wave, and threatens with depth and pace. He may be turning 30 in a little over a month — not that that's old — but he still moves like a gazelle. His backhand is one-handed, and can be devastating when he takes it up the line, or when he disguises it with a feather-touch drop shot.

The second set is a grind, with me trying to sustain my level. I'm beginning to feel fatigued a few times after long points, but I tell myself I have to stay aggressive or else he's going to wallop me with his forehand and his comeback attitude. Costa goes up 6–5 and is serving for the set, and I have no choice but to hit harder. I can't wait for a champion like Costa to give it to me. I ambush him with swinging wide shots, and follow it up with daring net play. I break him and send the set into a tiebreaker and win that with convincing power, defense, and finesse.

Now I see him shaking his head as if he didn't imagine me capable of this. An American not named Agassi taking down a Spaniard who's an expert on this surface. Not possible, he thinks. Sorry, Albert, today it is. I keep the smackdown going, and he dissolves completely in the third set, 6–2.

"Game, set, and match, Spadea," I hear the umpire call out. What a feeling! Everything felt flawless until match point. Serving at 40–0, we entered a long rally, and as he came to the net, I ran full speed for a running backhand passing shot — my favorite. But as I completed my stroke, I felt something tighten up on the left side of my stomach. My shot landed in, and I raised my hand in joy and victory, only to have this side stomach muscle rebel and cramp up.

It was strange. I wasn't dehydrated, but something was hurting. I quickly shook hands with Costa, wanting to get to the trainer's room, but Pam Shriver of ESPN waved me over for a post-match interview. I hurried over and we talked for a few minutes, reflecting on a good day for me, but a bad day for Americans. Andre had gone down with a bad back, and besides Roddick, Blake, and myself, there were no more Americans left in the tournament. In the back of my head, I knew something wasn't right with me, too. I didn't feel comfortable even standing still, and my second-round match against Tommy Haas was scheduled for tomorrow. There was a spasm in my left side, and I struggled to carry my bag back to the locker room.

A few hundred feet from the center court stadium and all its amenities at Roland Garros — a walk down a boardwalk — is the smaller stadium, the Suzanne Lenglen court. The third feature court here resembles a bullfighting ring, being circular and intimate. This is where I played — or attempted to play — Haas.

I felt like I had been stabbed in the left side of my stomach. I couldn't sleep or turn over during the night. I shouldn't have even walked on the court, but I tried wearing my red badge of courage. But right from the warm-up, I felt a constant throbbing that caused an ache close to agony. It was making me feel lightheaded. On my serve, I couldn't lift my left arm to toss the ball normally. I knew this would be ugly, but I had been told by a doctor I couldn't make the injury worse by playing.

We started the match, and I figured my only chance was to go for broke. I hit with abandon — and a lot of discomfort — and I broke Tommy's serve in the first game, then I held to take a 2–0 lead. I was serving at no more than 90 mph, but I was grinding through it. I was hoping to gain momentum from my positive start, but I knew that even if I somehow won a set, trying to win two more would be debilitating. Haas caught on to my weakness, and played solidly enough to win the first set 6–4.

He was a little tight in the second, and I broke serve again, but I just couldn't hold my own serve. Haas took the second set 6–3, so I went ahead and put myself out of this misery and embarrassment by retiring. I shook Tommy's hand and told him I was injured. My French Open dream that had seemed so heady just 30 hours before was over for another year. After the comeback from my shoulder tendonitis, to have suffered a new injury I didn't know how long would take to heal felt like a huge setback. I had regained my form after taking a month off, and here another freak injury puts my ranking, job, and career back against the wall. At my age — at any age — it doesn't feel very fair.

PART IV

THE CROWN JEWELS:
WIMBLEDON and THE U.S. OPEN

JUNE 4
Boca Raton

I know I said earlier that I only spend a few weeks of the year in Boca these days, but this has not been a typical year. I'm out of the two Wimbledon warm-up tournaments rehabbing this abdominal pull I have. A doctor told me there is usually a four-to-six week rest period for this type of injury, but I'm going to try to make it back for Wimbledon in less than three. I've got the same injury Dwyane Wade of the Miami Heat just suffered in the NBA playoffs. It's a rib muscle strain, technically called an "oblique muscle pull," and it feels like that pain you get in your side when you're running, except a little more intense. It makes it hard to breathe without feeling a stab of pain.

Injuries are the toughest obstacle a pro athlete has to overcome. We make our living with our bodies, and tennis is especially difficult because it's an individual sport in which our ranking goes down if we don't play and win. In a team sport, if you're one of the top players and you get injured, and it's not the playoffs, the team can put you on the disabled list until you recover. In most cases, when you're healthy again you get your position back. In tennis, depending on how long you're injured, your ranking can drop as far as a thousand places. My ranking dropped from No. 19 to No. 43 when I took the month off to rehab my shoulder injury. Now when I return, my ranking will probably be somewhere in the 50s.

It's bad, but I have no other option than to deal with it. Injuries can make you feel like you're one step slower, not as strong or fast. Injuries often disable your mind more than they do your body. I don't believe in career-ending injuries. I think tennis players get too intimidated by the setbacks of injuries and surgeries. There are players who say they retired because their knee was torn up or their back was never going to be the same. But look how Thomas Muster came back after a car hit him and crushed his leg. Obviously, there are clinical issues you have to address, but right now, if I had a serious injury that knocked me out for the rest of the year, I'd still be back next year at age 31 trying to make a comeback. Worst case scenario, I can go back to the Challengers and do it all over again.

It's just a couple of weeks shy of five years now since I set the record for the longest losing streak in the history of pro tennis. I wasn't even aware of it when I set it. I lost to Sebastien Grosjean in Nottingham the week before Wimbledon 2000, and this reporter came up to me after the match and said, "Hey, do you want to hold a press conference. Your loss just broke the world record for consecutive losses on the pro tour."

I did the press conference, but I thought it was ridiculous

how the British press embellished the whole thing. The previous record-holder had been an American player, Gary Donnelly, who'd set the previous record of 20 straight losses in 1987. I knew of him because I had actually once been a ball boy for one of his matches at the Lipton tournament in Miami. I think he also once held the record for having the fastest serve in tennis. I knew I was losing a lot of matches, but I didn't know they even kept track of such a record, or that I was close to breaking it. They counted my three losses at the World Team Cup as part of the losing streak, and I thought that was ridiculous. They don't even award ATP ranking points for those matches, and you can easily lose three in a week like I did.

When I beat Greg Rusedski in the first round of Wimbledon, the headlines in the papers were: "Rusedski Loses to Tennis's Worst," "Rusedski Slain by Man Who Could Not Win," and "The Biggest Loser Ever Overcomes Rusedski's Nerves." That's the British press for you, but I thought it was a bit pathetic of the journalists to write such condescending words. Last year, when I made it to the round of 16 at Wimbledon, I took a lot of pride in that result. I felt like saying to the British press, "See fellas, I'm not so bad."

The British press covers tennis with much more fervor than the American press. But over my career, I've had to learn how to deal with both. As a tennis player, you develop little idiosyncrasies that lead you to believe you're going to be a champion. These habits become an attitude and sometimes, we can get a little carried away with these attitudes. Serena Williams will win a match, and afterwards when the press asks her when she wants to do her press conference, she'll say, "In an hour." Does she really need an hour after a match before she talks to the press? Maybe she does, but me, I'll do press 15 minutes after I finish a match. All I need to do is take a shower, throw some ice on any sore body parts, and I'm ready. I know I can stretch and get a massage later.

At the same time, I don't want to walk in with a wet T-shirt and drop my bag, just to appease the reporters. Each player has his own system. I try to show some humanity to reporters, but when one approaches me and says, "Hey Vince, I know you have a match at four today, but do you want to do a radio interview with me at two?" I have to show some discretion and say to myself, "What's the right thing to do? What's going to make me play my best?" I need to keep my edge.

JUNE 8

Besides the fact that our season, at 10 months long, is ridiculous, here we have the Oscars of tennis, Wimbledon, and it is held only two weeks after the French Open closes the clay-court season. The European clay-court spring season is nine weeks long, the American hard-court summer is seven weeks long, but there's only four weeks to the summer grass-court season and two weeks of tournaments leading up to Wimbledon.

The transition from playing clay-court tennis to grass-court is hard enough, but why not make it easier by adding another week between the French Open and Wimbledon — by taking a week off the relatively unimportant fall indoor season — and making the Queens Club Tournament in London a Masters Series event? The Australian Open has the same problem, coming at the beginning of the year with just two small warm-up tournaments preceding it, but this shouldn't happen at Wimbledon, the crown jewel of tennis.

JUNE 12

This disturbing news item appeared in the *Mail & Guardian Online* (www.mg.co.za) today:

> "Irakli Labadze, a Georgian last year ranked 42nd in the world, will be accused at a court hearing in Austria this week of conspiring with a professional gambler to make money by 'throwing' a match.
>
> Tennis authorities are watching the case nervously amid growing fears that some players and their associates may be profiting by using gambling websites to place bets on matches in which they know the result in advance.
>
> Labadze fell under suspicion after he unexpectedly lost a first round match in last year's Raiffeisen Grand Prix in the Austrian town of St. Poelten to an unseeded local player, Julian Knowle. Martin Fuehrer, a gambler with whom Labadze is friendly, celebrated after he won 17,000 Euros after betting 10,000.
>
> But when he went to collect his winnings, the bookmaker, Cashpoint, refused to pay out. . . .
>
> Justin Gimelstob, an American player, has warned that corruption may be going undetected and that tennis is an 'easy' sport to fix. 'It's 100 percent possible and I have my suspicions,' he said."

On top of these allegations, the ATP has exacerbated charges of gambling in pro tennis by giving the main sponsor spot for the tournament in Kitzbühel, Austria, next month to a gambling operation called Betandwin.com. Spectators can bet live on their cell phones after each point.

The ATP has to take a serious look at gambling. Instead of trying to win matches on the court, apparently players must be looking for easier ways to make money.

JUNE 18
London

I've arrived in London. After a second day of practice, my body is sore. Gosh, I'm falling apart. I've never felt this brittle before. I practiced with Lleyton Hewitt today on the Wimbledon courts. We're allowed 30 minutes to practice on the actual match courts to test the surface and get a taste for the days to come. So I used my 30 minutes with Hewitt. He's an amiable guy, generally speaking.

"Hey mate, how you going?" he asked me. I was "going" fine, but in American English, I told him we say "How you doing?" He laughed. Lleyton's not the type of guy to break the ice and try to be your best friend, but if you're nice enough to him, he's cordial and cool back.

We hit some balls on the bushy grass of Wimbledon (the courts seem to be playing somewhat slower than usual, especially when the ball lands short — it just dies out). We worked hard for an hour — exceeding our time limit — and played some games. Actually, he kicked my butt. I felt slow, slightly erratic, and sore. Lleyton was hitting the ball well.

On the grass, he hits more of a flat sidewinding spin off both sides. His backhand is second to none, on a par with his foot speed and determination. His forehand is good, but can occasionally break down. His serve is crisp, well-placed, and speedy for his height and weight. His Achilles' heel is his volley. He doesn't hit weak volleys exactly, but they are only serviceable, and I think he needs to improve them if he wants to win another Slam.

"Who do you play, Vince?" Lleyton asks on a changeover. It's the most overasked question in the days just prior to the tournament, because it kind of eases the tension.

"Rafael Nadal," I repeat for the sixth time in two days.

"Oh, that's not so bad, that's a winnable one," Lleyton's coach, Roger Rasheed, states.

"Yeah, well," I chuckle, "he won't be hitting as flat and effective as Lleyton." They chuckled also and then we shook hands and parted ways.

My first reaction when I heard that I was going to play Nadal was, "Oh, my God. If I can recover and get well fast, I have a good chance to win and make good headlines." Another one of my Vince Spadea Can Beat Any Player, But Who's Vince Spadea? style headlines. It's my chance to be famous for 15 minutes again, I thought.

I ran up to the lunchroom and people were standing in line to get food, while others were sitting, eating, talking, and watching. What a scene! An African-American girl named Angela Haynes stepped up behind me and asked, "What's up Spadea?"

"Just chillin', you?" I holler back. She was listening to her iPod, so I asked, "Whatcha listening to?"

She goes, "Jay-Z."

"Ahh, one of my faves," I tell her. I let her know what was up and she said, "ok, now you're talkin' my language." I recited a few lines of Jay-Z's and she laughed, saying, "You funny." She told me she was from Compton. How interesting, another girl like the Williams sisters making it out of the hood. Good for her, and good for tennis.

In one of the London papers, the sports headline read, "Nadal Plays Eccentric American." I actually liked that. It means I'm starting to be regarded as someone who's different. Maybe not Dennis Rodman different, but it's a start.

JUNE 21

I got a few patch deals for today's match, signing with Geico and Nivea Sportscreme. When you play a player with as high a profile as Nadal on Centre Court at Wimbledon, he makes so much money, he makes you money. I would never have gotten those deals if I were playing Joe Blow in the first round.

I walk onto Centre Court with Nadal at about 5:30. Opening day matches on Centre Court don't start until 2 p.m. and Henman had just had a long five-setter in the first match of the day with Jarkko Nieminen. We went out and the war was on. At first I was nervous. I was playing on a court that everyone talks about as being immortal tennis grounds. It has this superhuman atmosphere with all the great championship battles that have been played on this lawn, and I was finally there where it had all happened.

I had never stepped out onto it before. They don't allow you to practice on it, they don't even allow anyone to look at it. To a certain extent, they get a little carried away. The English act like they're too good for this, and too traditional for that. But it gets to the point where — just like you can't play the game with wooden rackets anymore and women can't play in wedding dresses or men in blazers — enough with the pomp and circumstance, let's roll the balls out and play. When you walk out onto Centre Court to play a match, you're a part of Wimbledon history and everything that's happened there. But at the end of the day, it's still just a tennis match.

It's compact and crowded. I didn't have to bow or anything. There's a buzz in the crowd. They're acting like someone significant has just walked onto the court, and I know it isn't me. Nadal and I didn't say anything to each other before the match. I had been demoted to the unseeded locker room after I'd been in the seeded one over the last two years. The seeded locker room has much bigger lockers, and they have your name on the top of your locker. There are people like Fred Stolle and Stan Smith hanging around. There's a small, private trainer's room. There's much more service. The bathrooms are equipped with the top shower gel of the month, and shampoo and conditioner, and plush shaving cream with razors. It's a great feeling.

Andy Roddick chooses not to partake of the amenities of the seeded locker room. He eccentrically goes into the unseeded locker room instead. I've heard that he doesn't like the aristocratic, seeded locker room atmosphere. He's an everyman type of guy who doesn't like the first-class treatment. Besides, he started off in the unseeded locker room, so it's a superstition with him now. Roddick comes from money, but he likes hanging out in simple bars in Austin, Texas, where he lives. It's a little small-town America attitude, and he's originally from Nebraska. I think it's cool that he does that, but I felt kind of shafted when I walked into the unseeded players' locker room. I stopped believing in myself for a moment.

As the match starts, I think, "Okay, when am I going to break him and win 6–2, 6–2, 6–2?" I know Nadal fancies himself winning Wimbledon one day, but he isn't a grass-court player, and I had a good result here the year before. I feel like my game is a little more suited to grass because I have the ability to hit the ball flatter than he does. My strategy is: "Don't throw up on Centre Court." No, I want to stay on the baseline, take the ball early, try to come in when the opportunity presents itself, and throw a slice down to his forehand every once in a while. I don't want to let him get into a grinding clay-court rally. I wanted to flatten the ball out, so it skips into him and he might start hitting the ball late.

I also want to take advantage of his second serve which is weak, only 85–88 mph. On clay, he can get away with it, because no matter how much you attack his serve, the ball bounces higher so it's harder to hit a winner. And then he is so fast in retrieving balls — exceptionally fast, and equally good at swinging on the run. He doesn't slice on the run; he takes full swings in full stride.

I start doing some of those things, but my whole body feels locked up. My back is really tight, and I'm having a lot of trouble swinging through the ball and getting a lot of power on my shots. I feel how Agassi probably felt at the French, where he lost in the first round to Jarkko Nieminen when his hip went out on him. I had been hitting hard for the last four days before the tournament, trying to get back my normal pace, but all that hard practicing after three weeks of bed rest is coming back to haunt me.

Grass is not a forgiving surface, even though it feels like it is because it's so soft. But really you're slipping and bending lower reaching for balls. It's softer, so you use your muscles more to balance yourself. The harder the surface, the more rebound you get, so you don't have to use as much muscle to stay balanced. It's not a pounding feeling playing on grass, but you're sinking so it makes you go deeper into your muscular fibers. The more days you play on grass, the more sore you get, and that's not true when playing on hard courts.

I hold serve and go up 2–1, but the pain is getting to me and I think, "I don't know if I can keep this up." I can't break him, I'm just trying to hold my own serve and get it to a tiebreaker. But he breaks me at three-all and he runs to his chair pumping his fist. It's good. He's into the match, and if he was killing me, he wouldn't need to do that. He looks into the stands a lot at his uncle, because a young player is not normally programmed to be this good. He doesn't really have a mind of his own yet. Most prodigies are guided and controlled by some surrogate father or mentor who is really pushing the buttons. The prodigy tennis player is the great athlete, and he has the good sense to listen to his coach. But the underlying desire to achieve starts with the older coach, who instills it in the prodigy.

I remember when Roddick was first coming up, he would look up at his coach, Tarik Benhabiles, after every point. If he hit an ace, he looked up at Tarik with an expression that said, "Can you approve that? Tell me you approve of that ace. I can't go on to the next point without your approval." If he lost a point, he'd look up at Tarik with an expression that said, "Tell me what to do now."

When you're young, you're innocent and scared, and you're constantly entering uncharted waters. You need somebody with a strong personality and confidence who's going to take charge and guide you through the initial impasses. McEnroe was the exception, but that's the New York in him. You talk to a 17 year old on the streets of New York, and he'll not only tell you where to go, he'll tell you what's up. At least, he'll think he knows what's up.

I am feeling stiff, so I take an injury timeout and have the trainer come out and look at my back, but there's not a lot he can do. I ask the trainer, "What the heck is happening to my body?" He looks me over and says, "I don't think your back is that seriously injured. You're just going to have to ice it after the match and get some treatment, and see how you feel in the morning." At 5–4, Nadal preceeds to steamroll me, winning 6–4, 6–3, 6–0.

Players are taking more injury timeouts these days. Look at Mariano Puerta in the French Open finals. He was down 3–1 to Nadal in the first set and serving at 15–40. He's missing balls, he can't move. Everybody's thinking, "This is going to get ugly. He's going to get killed by Nadal. This is going to end fast."

Puerta walks off the court in mid-game. The trainer comes out and starts working on Puerta's groin or something. Three minutes later, he's out on the court a different player, and he grinds back. He holds serve, breaks Nadal, and wins the first set 7–6.

I could not believe how fast the match turned around after he took that medical timeout at 1–3, 15–40. If he hadn't been allowed to just walk off the court, he would've tanked away the game. It would've been a 6–1 or 6–2 set, and the match probably would have snowballed from there.

I don't see these injury timeouts as a big problem yet — most of the players aren't abusing the rule. When a player does call a timeout even though I know he's not injured, I just look at it as more adversity I have to deal with. You want to bring more adversity, just keep bringing it, I say. How bad is it going to get? It's just gamesmanship. If a guy wants to pull all these games and tricks, I look at it like it's a rain delay. I don't look at it as a purposeful ploy. It's just something that happens that is unfortunate and annoying. I'm not going to make a big deal about it and get stressed out when some guy is doing something within the rules. Maybe the rules should be changed, but the tour has allowed players to act this way by allotting all these injury timeouts.

I went and got my prize money of about 9,000 pounds — which is like $18,000. I say to myself, "I'll take a five-hour flight for this kind of payday any time."

JUNE 22

I'm hanging out with my buddy in London at an Italian café, and this gorgeous, tall, leggy blond walks by.

"Hey, are you from somewhere?" I call out. She looks at me, makes some funny gesture, and just keeps walking. She starts walking down this big, busy street and sits down on a bench, so I run after her. These two guys sitting next to us at the café are laughing at me, but they say, "That girl is hot." I look like a desperado running after this girl.

"Hey, I had to come here and say hello." I say, as I run up to her. "You know where Harrods is?" Harrods was right next to us. She laughs.

"You like tennis at all? Do you want to go for a drink? Because you seem like a great human being."

"Actually, you know," she says, "I'm from Poland, and I think it's very romantic that you just ran after me in the street." I thought she was going to tell me to drop dead, and start talking on her mobile. But she's totally warm and we have a nice five-minute conversation before she says she has to run off to a modeling job. But she gives me her number and tells me to call her.

The guys are still laughing when I make it back to the café, but not so hard anymore, because I'm holding up the piece of paper with her number on it. I call her later and we hang out. I pick her up at her apartment, and we go to a pub and have a beer and get to know each other.

"I'm trying to do whatever it takes to make this happen," I

say. "What's it going to take? I just want to meet someone, fall in love, and get a life. I'm 30 years old and I'm done with the whole email and nice-to-meet-you rap. I like what I see in you, I just want to see if I like what I hear."

She's like, "Oh, you're very cool. You're very much my type." She lights up the pub with her smile. She has bright features and is 22. Her name is Gosh, which is apparently a classic Polish nickname for Margaret.

"That's one of my favorite words," I say, "because I never take that name in vain. We're going to get along really well, even if I get mad."

But I was out of the tournament and leaving the next day. It was okay, she was a little bit of a free spirit anyway, and they're tougher to tie down. She sort of had that model disposition of: "Just because I look good, I can say the most idiotic things and still be really likeable." And it got to be not so likeable after a while. I can get tired of girls — even gorgeous ones — very quickly.

JUNE 26
New York City

I jumped out of bed at 9 a.m. Oh, the aches and pains of being 30, staying out until 2 a.m. last night at the hotspot Butter. Bruce Willis made an appearance, checking out the young ladies. What is he, like, 48? "Bruce, you're gonna die hard, goin' out lookin' for girls your daughter's age."

It helps that I don't drink, but I still feel like I'm coming down with a cold, burning the candle at both ends. I'm sore and I have to rush out to Queens to start my new coaching partnership with Argentinean Gabriel Markus. I have to be at my best — alert, moving my feet, and full of energy. Right now I'm barely awake.

Cabbing it from downtown Manhattan out to Forest Hills, Queens, is a $30 dollar affair. Of course, I'm running late so I stop in the gift shop for a breakfast of a granola bar, Rice Krispie treat, and a good ol' bottle of H_2O.

Markus and I train hard for an hour and a half. We work on hitting approach shots and coming up to net, on my volleys and forehand drives. It's still grass tennis training as I'm getting ready for the Newport Hall of Fame Championships.

Seeing these guys playing in this Challenger is making me sick. It reminds me of when I was lost, trying to find myself, my game, and my head. It's humbling and therapeutic to come back here. I feel it sparking a fire under me to stay away, for as long as I can, from the Challenger life.

I had to blaze out of Forest Hills right after practice, wearing my wet T-shirt on the subway. I've only ridden it three times in my life and I'm not a fan. I feel claustrophobic, unsettled, and grossed out. But, what the heck, why not live a little, and make some changes?

I have a backpack with two rackets in it, and I look like a weekend hacker, soaked in sweat, heading for Manhattan as 8 million strangers all bump into me. Saying, "Excuse me," doesn't exist in New York City. Instead, New Yorkers just say "Get the hell outta my way," with either their mouths or eyes. I don't feel like an elite athlete today — eating a granola bar for breakfast, riding the subway in a sweaty T-shirt. I'm bushed from last night's partying and today's grind of a practice.

I eat dinner at a hot sushi place in Tribeca called Nobu. I sit alone at the bar because a friend canceled on me at the last minute, which sucks. Sarah Michelle Gellar and her husband, Freddie Prinze, were having their dinner a table away from me and they looked bored. I thought, "What have they done lately?" They were a hot couple a little while back, but I haven't seen them in the news lately. That's all anyone cares about, it seems. Who's the latest and greatest? What have you done lately? If you don't stay on top, the press tunes you out and turns its attention on someone who *is* making things happen. I want that someone to be me.

I need to make a mini-comeback from this latest injury, and get back on top. It's my only option, my only passion — unless I want to sit at a sushi place picking at seaweed, frustrated with my future, like Sarah Michelle and Freddie appeared to be. My ranking has dropped from 18 to 55 in two months. Talk about brutal. At the beginning of the year, I saw myself breaking into the Top 10. Is that a realistic goal or am I chasing a pipe dream?

JUNE 27
Forest Hills, New York

Gabriel Markus, an Argentinean, has had great success in the past few years coaching Nicolas Massu and David Nalbandian, among other South American players. He has seen me around the tour, he just wants to start our practice sessions here, at the Challenger being played out at Forest Hills, the former site of the U.S. Open. Markus is also coaching Giovanni Lapentti of Ecuador, the younger brother of Nicolas, who is playing out here.

I'm hoping Markus is the coach I've been looking for. He's a former player who got to No. 36 in 1992, and he's got a good feel for the game. He's mentioned some technical things already, like getting my toss more out into the court — it's too far behind me now — and staying down more on the follow-through of my forehand. He hits the ball well, and can handle himself against me in points and in drills. He's all about working hard; he's already asking for extra practice time, trying to work ways to get us more hours on the court and more competition in practice situations. So I'm ready to put in the effort and get that edge. I think over time, he can help me a lot. We're going to have a good week of working out here, hitting a lot of balls, and then I play the Hall of Fame Championships in Newport next week.

In the larger tennis world, Guillermo Canas, the No. 8 player and an Argentinean, is under investigation for failing a drug test at a tournament in Acapulco in February. He's pulled out of Wimbledon, and has said he didn't knowingly take any banned substance and that he believes he will be vindicated.

Steroid use has gotten out of control recently, but tennis should be praised for the strictness of their approach. I've been tested in the past, but this year I haven't been, and I hope that doesn't mean the ATP has become more lenient. I got blood-doping tests at Monte Carlo, and once they did a random check in 1999 in both London and at my house in Boca Raton. They also checked me at the Olympics in 2000.

Still, players continue to take steriods. I can see who's used them by the way certain players perform, and the way their bodies have changed. Canas's suspension is not surprising to me. It's gotten to the point where the drugs are everywhere and the penalties are going to have to become harsher to stop it. If you blatantly cheat and become an imposter in the game — which is what these guys are doing by taking steroids — you have to be dealt with harshly.

But there have also been incidents where players have been falsely accused. Horst Skoff of Austria had an incident where he launched a big lawsuit against the ATP contesting the way they tested him. And I think he won. Greg Rusedski won his appeal. Guillermo Coria had an appeal that showed the companies making approved vitamin and mineral substances were sort of corrupt in the way they operated their labs.

But if you're a fan and you read that six guys from Argentina are accused of steroid offences, you'd have to think that something is going on. Argentina has abused the system with Coria, Canas, Juan Ignacio Chela, and Puerta all testing positive. They're claiming it's a dysfunction in the standards and approvals their country uses to legitimize medications, but I'm not buying it, and neither is the ATP. The Argentineans practice on the court for two hours a day, then they must practice in front of a mirror for two more hours saying, "I'm not guilty."

These guys are ruthless out here. We're all guys who go out and bang balls at each other for hours upon hours, year after year, to get ahead. We're going to do everything we can to improve our chances to succeed. I've never attempted to cheat, but I've learned that to be a success, I have to focus on whatever it takes to win. Some players are taking ATP-banned substances to get something that they want. Unfortunately, these players have crossed the line.

With Puerta, a player suspended for steroid use in the past, then making it to the finals of the French Open, it's a very bizarre situation. What's his story? Is he clean now? Is he this fearless guy who's great for the game because he goes out and fights like a dog? Was he really guilty in the first place? It's all very weird and murky. [Editor's Note: Puerta was banned from competition on the ATP tour for eight years in December after the International Tennis Federation confirmed that he tested positive for the banned stimulant etilefrine, following his French Open final defeat.]

Steroid use is a serious issue in tennis right now. Players are talking in the locker room about what these drugs do for a player who takes them — body, legs, and mind. I remember back in the day when we used to have player meetings, Michael Chang would get really worked up talking about steroids. He suspected players who had extraordinary results on clay, like a very well-known Austrian and several of his Spanish contemporaries. Chang was starting to slow down in his game — the way I have felt this year physically and mentally — and he saw these guys getting stronger, more muscular, and beating him. He was having a tough time coping with it. It's a disturbing feeling to be working hard and not achieving the same results you have in the past. I know. Chang was angry because he was clean and playing fair, and it was possible that others weren't. Chang's game was a war of attrition, where fitness was the key element — which player was more willing to stay on the court and battle. He didn't like that another factor was being thrown into the mix.

Each individual player has to draw their own moral line concerning steroids. What's the difference between a masked gunman robbing a bank and a tennis player taking performance-enhancing drugs to win more matches, gain an unfair advantage, and steal opportunities away from his peers? In my mind, the only difference is that people see the gun. I don't think a large number of players are using steroids, but if it's even a few, it's a disgrace, not only to the sport of tennis, but to the human race. It's a malicious sign of desperation, disrespectful of the supposedly even playing field and fairness of sports. Worst of all, it's a crime what these offenders are doing to their bodies, minds, families, and futures — all for the sake of gaining money and status.

Certainly, they are victim to the pressure applied by the avaricious, bizarre, and superficial world we live in. Nonetheless, these pressures do not justify their actions. In the end, they will have to face the penalties, feelings of guilt, nights of sleeplessness, and the bad karma. So far, the caught offenders are mostly from South American countries where the conditions are dire; but it comes down to the individual making a decision to play fair or to defraud. With the stakes getting larger as the game becomes more international, even with a stiffer testing policy, it will be an uphill battle to maintain a fair playing field. This is the beginning of the weeding out of these steroid abusers, but we're not close to reaching the end. Because I am clean, my results can only get better now that the cheaters are getting caught.

As for Nadal, he's the real deal, no doubt. Jim Courier was the real deal, too, and he won four majors. If Nadal can match Courier, that would be an amazing feat. I don't think he can keep it up for the next three years. He's not Courier, and he's certainly not Borg. Spanish players have a reputation for having great years, then just losing their dominance. Nadal works too hard to win. He is a warrior and has a great fighting spirit, but he doesn't have Borg's serve, and defensive players, for the most part, don't win majors. I know Wilander won seven, and Hewitt has won two, but if I had told you back in 1989 that Chang wasn't going to win another major, you would have laughed, too.

JUNE 28
New York City

I feel like I'm in a post-Wimbledon downward spiral. It's a deadened, dull feeling, but it hasn't really hit me yet just how destructive it is. I'm losing in first rounds of tournaments, out early in the week, just sitting around not able to get into the doubles draw or make much in prize winnings. I normally wake up in the morning with a passion for tennis and a purpose — to work hard to be the best; lately that has been waning. I look at the other players and say to myself, "Why are these guys doing this? This lifestyle's so dull." That's how I'm feeling these days.

I've got to break out of this negative vibe. I've been staying out late, carousing, feeling depressed. My mind and body feel sluggish; I feel slow in practice. It's knowing I'm losing ranking points every week. I'm losing to players I used to beat and seeing younger players doing sprints on the sidelines, hungrier than ever. I'm like, "Gosh, I've been at this tournament seven times already. I ran those sprints ten times over. I don't feel like doing any of them now."

My sister Luanne has a great spirit. She helps me out a lot. She's married with children now and it's great to see her living a stable, down-home life when my own life is so unstable, high-strung, and jet-setting. Sometimes I envy the life Luanne leads; I think it's more peaceful to live the way she does. Luanne's a great inspiration to me in a lot of ways: she's a fighter, she's smart, and she's accomplished a lot. Every morning she calls me at 10:30 to make sure I have my schedule for the day. I don't get to the city much to visit her; it's more hectic here.

I'm staying at the Hilton Millennium downtown. When I open the window, I look out at Ground Zero. I'm 12 steps from the gaping hole where the Twin Towers used to be. It's kind of weird and depressing staying so close to such a strong reminder of the terrible tragedy and hardship that goes on in this world. But it's also a symbol of the American will to triumph over terrorism.

There is crazy security at this hotel. When I checked in the other day, my room wasn't ready so I stored my bag behind the front desk and went out for a while. When I came back to the hotel, a clerk asked, "Can I help you?"

Apparently, I looked a little bit suspicious with my long hair and facial growth, carrying a knapsack with two tennis rackets sticking out. I said, "Yeah, do you guys have a bathroom here?"

He said, "Are you a guest of the hotel?

And I said, "Yes I am."

He was like, "Are you sure? Where's your key?"

I said, "Actually, I have to go get it now. I was supposed to check in earlier but my room wasn't ready." He was making me feel like I really was a suspicious character.

He walked to the front desk with me to check if I really was staying at the hotel, probably thinking he was going to catch me in a lie. I showed the front desk person my ID and they gave me my key. I gave the clerk a look that said, "Nice try, buddy."

Being back playing at a Challenger feels like, "Oh God, I can't believe that I had to go through this and I never want to have to go through it again." When I went back to playing Challengers in 2000, after six years in the big leagues, I felt like a complete nobody. Waiting out rain delays just so I could play in a practice match to prepare for my real match, which if I won, I'd make $200 at best. I needed those points to get to the next round — which I had to win to get more points. Once I got to the quarters, the tournament really began. But if I didn't make the quarters — where I could win 12 ranking points — I wasn't going anywhere. I'd only go from, say, 250 to 248 in the world.

I felt I was far from reaching my destiny or even my capability to make a living. I'm not even talking about being a star. Making a decent profit after paying for all my expenses was my main concern. It's hard to see some of the same guys sitting in the players' lounge five years later. I still see Mashiska Washington, who has been playing these tournaments since

1996, and his father, William, who groomed Mashiska and his older brother, MaliVai. Thomas Blake has been out here since 1997. Dusan Vemic — part-time player, part-time I don't know what. Keith Crossland, who's the tournament director, used to be an umpire in the Satellites in Hawaii where I played when I was 17. I've got to get out of this place.

JULY 3

Recently, I bought John Steinbeck's *Travels With Charley*, and F. Scott Fitzgerald's *The Great Gatsby*. I figure if I'm writing a book, I should read some of the classics. The only book I've read cover to cover is the *Kama Sutra*. I read every line of that book. Truth is I'm not much of a reader. I think the only reason people read books is just to say they have. But for me, reading a book is like watching a movie — I can hardly get through the two-hour period. With the exception of guys like Paul Goldstein, I don't see too many tennis players reading books.

I didn't want to watch much of Wimbledon on television after I lost. But I was walking past a department store the other day and in their window, a TV was tuned to Wimbledon coverage. Justin Gimelstob was playing Lleyton Hewitt on center court. Gimelstob was diving on the grass like he was Boris Becker in his prime. He probably felt, "Hey, here's my national television time. I haven't gotten this kind of exposure in years. I'm going to milk this for all I can. I'm going to run, jump, get to the net, dive, and yell out like a dirty Jersey boy."

When Gimelstob came onto the tour in 1996, he had a game that money can't buy. I'm not saying he was a great player, but Nike and other sponsors gave him endorsement deals worth a lot of money. He's had all the best coaches.

While he's been a good doubles player and has suffered from some injuries, he's not the most naturally talented player in the world. He works hard, looks like he loves the sport, and has a pretty good attitude, but he hasn't come close to living up to what people expected of him.

In this regard, he's not alone. Tennis is filled with players who were top juniors or collegiate players but never really panned out in the pros. Jeff Morrison is one of those guys. He won the NCAA championships, beating Blake in the finals, and one year he made it to the third round of Wimbledon. He has a good game, but he doesn't have the mindset for the pro game.

There is no prototype for a champion player. We've seen a lot of different kinds of players get to the top: Wilander, Chang, Becker, Agassi, and Sampras. These guys are the ultimate in tennis, but their games were so dissimilar. What they did have in common was their drive to win, and single-minded pursuit of championship titles.

It's hard to pinpoint why certain players with talent don't make it. Morrison is a laid-back guy (he comes from West Virginia) and is sort of a Howdy Doody, happy-go-lucky guy. He talks your ear off in the locker room and doesn't really put the time in on the court. I think if he had had the right coaching and more hunger, he would've gone further.
I can tell when a guy doesn't want it bad enough. Did you see Venus walking to the sidelines in the finals of Wimbledon when she was down a break? Her ears were steaming and she was so focused on her mission. She was saying to herself, "Nothing is going to stop me from winning this title. Not wild horses or Lindsay Davenport."

She had that Hewitt look. But I can see the difference between Hewitt's look now and when he won Wimbledon in 2002. He's lost that extra edge. He lets things slide a bit more now than he did in the past. He's not as vicious or as adamant in his approach anymore; he used to refuse to lose or take errors in stride. Sampras lost that look, too, for a couple of years, but he got it back and won the U.S. Open in 2003. There's that little complacency that hadn't been there before, a lackluster approach.

I can feel it creeping into my game now. Everything I do, say, and breathe doesn't revolve around what my goals are in tennis. To be a champion, there's no middle ground. You have to be very intense. Federer has that look now. I can see it in his eyes.

Today in the Wimbledon finals tiebreaker against Roddick, Federer was already up a set and two mini-breaks, but then he lost both points. He might have been thinking, "I should be up 5–0 now in the breaker and ready to take a two-set lead." He could have hit the panic button, but champions press that button a lot less than most players. They have a lot more confidence to do the right things throughout a match and they come out on top.

JULY 4
Newport, Rhode Island

Happy birthday, America.

I received a penalty point in my first-round match here at the Hall of Fame Championship and got fined $1,000 today by the umpire. I immediately called out the tournament director, Mark Darby. I normally don't act up on the court, but the umpire was calling balls out against me and I got irritated with it. I don't like seeing an umpire showing preference to an opponent because of his reputation. I know he thought that my opponent, Alexander Popp, was a good grass-court player, because he's reached the quarterfinals of Wimbledon twice. I felt like I was playing the No. 1 seed, with the umpire calling balls in when they were out because he's thinking, "This guy's been in the quarters of Wimbledon, so his shots must be landing in."

I just said to the umpire, "Listen, buddy, you're acting like a loser now." It was an act of rage. When Darby came out, I asked him, "Does using the word 'loser' constitute a penalty ten-out-of-ten times? Just out of curiosity. I'm not trying to argue I'm right or wrong, I just want to know what you say."

Darby told me, "If you call the umpire a loser, you're going to be penalized," so I said, "That's all I want to know. Thanks." Really, I just wanted Darby to know why I got a point penalty. I didn't act up all that much. I thought, "Let's get down to business before this match slips away." I lost the first set 6–4, but came back to win the next two pretty easily. After the match, Greg Rusedski, who I guess saw me get the penalty point, told me, "Vinny, you're not going to be fined a lot of money for calling a guy a loser when you didn't even swear."

JULY 5

Here's a story that illustrates the complexity of meeting women on the tour. As I was hitting a serve against Popp yesterday, I noticed this girl in the stands who looked amazing. She was voluptuous, probably like 21, and just out-of-this-world perfect, like a gift from Paradise. I felt myself getting distracted, so I made up my mind not to let her upset my game. I'm not going to let an attractive girl — I don't even know what she looks like up close — ruin my focus. I can't achieve greatness in tennis if I'm constantly looking over at some hootchie-momma-looking girl.

Later that night, as I was walking from my hotel to a restaurant for dinner, this weird guy I know from Los Angeles saw me and said, "Hey, Vince. Where are the ladies at?"

I said, "Oh yeah, they're around." Right then, this young, attractive girl walked by and I said, "There's one right now. How you doing? What's up? What's your name?"

She stopped. She was on her cell phone, but she said to whomever she was talking to, "Hey, I got to call you back."

It was then that I got a real good look at her and I said to myself, "Uh oh, this one's young. She's like teenager young."

So I said to her, "You're like 17, right?"

She said, "No, no, no, I'm 22."

I said, "You're like 20? I'm sticking to 20. But, you know what? We're going to stop talking right now. I'm hungry and I've got a life to lead."

She said, "Where are you eating? I'll walk you to your restaurant."

I said, "No, I don't even want to walk with you because you're under age. Even talking to you is a crime."

So I walked alone to the sushi bar I like in the harbor area. As I'm eating, I see the young girl I was talking to on the street walk by with her family. I recognize her sister — she's a 24-year-old girl I hooked up with last year at this same tournament. I tried to keep in touch with her, but it didn't work out. She came into the restaurant and said, "Vince, what are you doing? My 16-year-old sister says that you were hitting on her."

"I wasn't hitting on her," I said. "I was trying to protect her."

Then she introduced me to her other sister — it's the girl from the match. What a family. I had hit on the oldest and the youngest sister, but the one I was really infatuated with was the middle sister. Just my luck.

I'm back sitting at the same sushi bar, eating alone again tonight after beating Karol Kucera, when this girl comes up to me and says, "Hey, how's the sushi treating you?"

I said, "Pretty good." She was very pretty, and at least 30. She said she went to Brooklyn Law School — and then she said something that kind of turned me off — she told me that she'd stripped for her thesis. She did her thesis on stripping, working as a stripper at Scores in Manhattan. She was wearing a miniskirt, and she had a big fake rack — cleavage reminiscent of the Black Hole, it never ended. She was an Italian-looking girl who did not have a stunning, outstanding face, still she was attractive all the way through.

On a scale from one to 10, she was about a 38 DD — her hug goodbye nearly punctured my chest — and she was really interested in me. Within five minutes, she said she wanted to move down to Florida and organize my life. It was kind of like a line I'd give to some girl, but this time the girl was giving it to me. She felt like I had a lot of "po-tential." I said, "In what!?" All she knew was that I was a 30-year-old wannabe pro-tennis player. She had no idea I was a professional player. She thought that I was starting from scratch, still trying to make it as a Challenger-level player. She knew I was a writer who wrote rap songs, and I told her about this book I'm writing, and that I was an actor who was moving to Beverly Hills.

"There is a lot of potential in you," she said again. Then she said, "Your hair is the only thing you have going for you." I had it long and pulled down. So I said, "Maybe I should get a haircut so you will leave me alone." She had a sister who was looking to give out a blister — she was pretty hot herself — and they had a pretty good one-two punch going at the bar. A lot of guys were coming up to them. But we parted ways.

A doubles player here — who shall remain nameless — told me of an encounter he'd had in the hotel elevator this afternoon. He was riding it up when he happened to bump into the ample breasts of the girl standing next to him. He said, "Hey, I'm sorry. But if your heart is as soft as your breasts then I'm in love." Then she said, "If your member is as hard as your elbow, meet me in Room 106."

JULY 8

My backhand is my most natural shot, and I used it today to dismantle Dusan Vemic, a Challenger player who hits a lot of quirky slices and drop shots that, on grass, can make for pretty effective and annoying balls to run down. Even though I have a lot of confidence in my backhand, I still have to be on top of it to hit it well. I have my checklist of what I need to do, and I go over it from time to time in my mind. I don't just slam it and expect it to go in.

First, I have to make sure I'm down, bending my knees, and that I hit the ball out in front and finish with a good follow-through. Whenever I miss, I think about why. Did I not move my feet and get under the ball? Did I not have good racket speed? Sometimes, I'll need more rotation or I can hit it perfectly, but I targeted the ball too close to the line and I miss. Did I aim too tight, or did I get lazy? Even though my backhand is natural, I use this checklist, because I'm working on other aspects of my game so much I don't want to forget about my baby.

Even if I hit it right, and I have two hands on my racket giving me more strength, it's hard to hit outright winners off my backhand. With the exception of Agassi, who hits back-hand winners down the line, there aren't many players who have potent backhands. Even Federer hits more winners with his forehand. His backhand is just a complement stroke. There's more room to see on the forehand and you can release further out, for an elongated meeting point. The backhand is more tangled because you come across your body when you follow through.

Federer has glorified the wraparound finish stroke on the forehand and made it famous. But I think the old school, classic swings are the best. They're the most effective and most correct way physiologically to hit the ball. The wrap-around is most effective when you're hitting on the run and you're not quite in position to set up a more conventional shot.

I've played all of my matches in the stadium here on one of the two center courts. The stadium in Newport is the closest thing tennis has to Boston's Fenway Park. The bleachers are filled with wooden chairs and there are red wooden scoreboards with removable numbers in all four corners. The grass is a nearly perfect green, with only two golden patches of dead grass showing where the server stands on the deuce and ad sides. When you walk into the International Hall of Fame grounds off Bellevue Street, four people dressed in old tennis clothes, wearing long pants with suspenders over button-down long-sleeve shirts, are playing doubles with old wood rackets.

I think it's tougher to play on the outside courts, which are situated side-by-side with only one idle court between courts with matches on them. I had to play on them once when I played the qualifying tournament here, and it was like standing-room-only. The fans were right on top of us, and if I hit a serve that penetrated the netting at the back of the court, it could hit someone right in the chest. I had to play with even more tunnel vision and stay strong.

I look at my strings a lot when I'm playing, but what I'm actually doing is looking for the meaning of life. Seriously, I've been having a long-term relationship with my strings, and sometimes it's good to have conversations. No, actually it's just a simple concentration technique that most players use. It's like if you want to give a good speech, you want to look in one direction, and then shift your head and eyes to another direction. But you never want to focus on anyone in the audience because that might distract you. Looking at the strings gives me a non-distracting point of reference, so I can stay focused on what my goal is. You won't see many tennis players looking up into the crowd between points the way baseball players in the field do between pitches.

Grunting when hitting shots is another way top tennis players stay focused. There aren't many players who don't grunt today when they hit their shots. Federer is like Sampras in that he doesn't grunt. Muster was famous for it, and now Nadal is a big grunter. Of course, a lot of the women today, like Sharapova and Serena, let out big yelps as they hit. I once had a coach, Nels Van Patton, tell me, "Y'know what, you should grunt no matter what on every shot, because then, even if you lose, everyone thinks you were trying." I didn't take his advice totally to heart. I tried it, but as soon as I lost, I stopped.

The word is that Agassi is going to play Indianapolis in two weeks. I think at this point he's playing for enjoyment, and to try to eke out a few more titles. I think he's also playing out of fear of losing his life. It's almost a fear of death he has right now, like a surrogate fear of death specific to tennis. I think that's very normal, and close to what I'm thinking these days. I think a lot of players at our age think this way.

He even said in an interview right after he'd lost to Nieminen in the first round of the French Open with the bad back: "It's all that I know how to do until I can't do it anymore." But I don't think he'll hang around the way Chang did at the end. Watching Michael lose that way made me realize even the greats can start losing for good at any time.

At the end, Chang was getting beaten up in the Challengers. Some of the players wondered, "What is he doing? Why doesn't he stop the bleeding?" But if I lose my ranking, I could see myself going out that way, playing the 35-and-over Florida championships. Chang can look back and definitely say, "I didn't have any majors left in me. I didn't even have any Challengers left in me." Sampras doesn't know that, and I think Andre wants to be sure he doesn't have any majors left in him before he leaves the scene.

JULY 10

I played Greg Rusedski today in the fifth ATP tournament finals of my career, and blew a huge chance to win my second ATP title. I broke his serve at three-all in the third set, and I thought it would be pivotal since I hadn't lost my serve once to that point, a stat that is rare for me. Unfortunately, then all hell broke loose.

Serving at 4–3, I didn't get one first serve in the entire game, and Rusedski started pounding his ground strokes and putting pressure on me. I should've been the player pounding confident, aggressive groundies, set up by a strong serve. But I failed to execute; my serve broke down, my forehand and backhand landed short, or worse yet, out, and I just felt helpless out there.

Fatigue, anxiety, and choking all played a role in my breakdown. There's a fine line between choking and getting tired, and I'm usually able to negotiate between the two and stave off a collapse like I had today. Blatant choking involves not being able to hit simple shots and easy sitters in the court. Nerves dominate your body and you can hardly swing the racket, leads are blown like bubble gum, and you double-fault more than usual. I didn't do all that. I got slightly tight, and because I haven't been able to train properly with my injuries, my legs and arms felt heavy and weak. I feel like I almost stole this title without preparing correctly — which is kind of a boost for my confidence — even though the second title of my life was sitting eight points away against Rusedski, the defending champion and a grass-court specialist.

I have to hand it to Greg; he just didn't miss any balls, especially from the baseline. I was on my heels from the start of every point, and then he kept coming in with slice back-hands just inside the baseline that hardly bounced off the turf. Rusedski has a lethal weapon in his serve, but he also has one of the most lopsided games on tour, with the rest of his artillery often left sitting dormant in his tennis bag.

His serve usually determines his destiny. He's a lefty and that's to his advantage. Lefties have an innate advantage in the way the game is designed, as the ad court decides so many big game points and a lefty serve has a natural slice that is especially effective when playing a right-handed player. Rusedski has a brilliant slice-serve out wide, taking righties off the court on the ad side. He had the fastest serve on tour until Roddick showed up, and at almost 32, he remains among the top in hitting rocket-speed serves.

But the rest of his game is dubious. His volleys, many times improved and now solid, still won't be mentioned in the same breath as Edberg's, Cash's, McEnroe's, or Laver's and his ground strokes are sloppy. But when he's zoned in —

like today in the third set — his slice stays low and sharp and he can blast an unexpected winner off his forehand.

I like Greg. His arrogant attitude has been criticized by players on tour, but I find him funny. He's an amiable guy, who talks confidently, but I sense a slight feeling of insecurity mixed in. He's always been cordial and professional with me. I remember playing him in the boys' 12's Orange Bowl Championships and seeing a kid who traveled with three coaches and was always jumping rope and working out like he was already a pro. His parents told my parents, "Greg is training to win the U.S. Open one day, and he will." It was kind of humorous, a stern statement to make for someone so young, but Greg actually did make it to the Open final in 1997, losing to Rafter in four sets. So I give him credit for sticking to his passion and dream, even though he didn't quite achieve it. He's made more than $8 million in his career — $2 million coming in one paycheck when he won the Grand Slam Cup one year in Germany — and he's still winning titles.

There are times in a match when I feel that I'm up against a superpower. No matter what I do, the outcome seems predestined, and that thought becomes a belief that takes over my mind and body. It's negative thinking, of course, but it sure seems stronger than that when it clouds my mind and paralyzes my body. I try to fight through it until the final point, but today I couldn't, and this day belonged to Greg, who's now won his second tournament after the age of 30, while I'm still searching for my first.

So I sit here alone in my hotel room with Godiva chocolate and an unopened bottle of champagne I bought for myself earlier in the week in hopes of a celebration with who knows who. I feel physically plastered and mentally wasted. Feeling unfulfilled, I take a bite out of my chocolate and a nasty raspberry filling spills over my lips. I was hoping for a caramel inside. Tennis is a lot like life and life, in the famous words of Forrest Gump, "is like a box of chocolates. You never know what'cha gonna get."

JULY 11
Boston

I got to bed at 3 a.m. after I caroused around Newport for one last night, doing some serious thinking this time. I typically overanalyze the details of matches after a loss, especially an important one like yesterday's final. I had to wake up a few hours later as a car picked me up at seven to take me to Boston, a two-hour drive. I had booked an exhibition match a couple of weeks ago that consisted of a one-day kid's clinic, a televised match on the Tennis Channel, and a party afterwards at a mansion. All in all it's more money in my bank account by midnight, a "thanks for coming, thanks for having me" tennis extravaganza. It sounded easy enough on paper, but boy did I struggle through it today.

The concept for the exhibition match was interesting. It's a show called *The Grinders*, a televised series about struggling and unheralded pro tennis players trying to make it to the top by playing lower-level pro tournaments around the world. The series follows three young players giving an inside look at their lives and tennis careers. I was asked to do this guest spot in an episode by playing one set against the three grinders, Todd, Jonathan, and Carlos (Jonathan is Jonathan Chu, a New Yorker and the former No. 1 player at Harvard, who is now ranked around No. 900). They alternated playing two games each against me, and I had to hold them off.

I did by the score of 6–2, but the main problem was that I had finished a week of playing grass-court tennis, and this match was held on a red clay court in the backyard of an estate. There were 150 special guests watching, and after dusting off the three grinders, I then had to play a final set against the player who'd won a round-robin tournament amongst the three of them earlier in the day. I played Todd, and won again, 6–2.

The last thing I wanted to do was lose a televised match to a low-ranked player after just losing to Rusedski in a final shown nationally on Fox Television. But they were tough competitors ready to battle, and if I'd lacked focus or will, they could have beaten me. The difference at the pro level between No. 50 and No. 500 is not so much physical, but a matter of craftiness, experience, and competitive fire. I'm glad I got the job done without embarrassing myself.

There was a nice party afterwards at this beautiful estate, and my parents surprised me by flying in from Florida to escape a hurricane. My mother's Colombian relatives all live in the Boston area, and my parents had come up to see them as well as me. It was nice to see my parents again. It's funny with parents, you miss them when they're not around, but when they're around, you end up disagreeing over minor things and it can get frustrating. Even though I'm turning 31 in a week, they are as concerned about me as if I were still their little boy. Sometimes their concern becomes annoying and aggravating, but we're still all happy to see each other. Welcome back to the family, Vince.

JULY 12

I shopped around Boston today — I'm a guy, but I like to shop for clothes — and speak of the devil, I ended the day watching Patrick Rafter play in a World Team Tennis match

239

on a converted tennis court in the Harvard Hockey Rink. Team tennis in America is a pretty big deal. It kicks off the summer season leading into the Open. On each team are three girls, three guys, and one coach. The teams travel and play one another in consecutive nights for about three weeks. The big-name players don't usually play, but James Blake, Roddick, and Agassi have played in recent years. I've never played because I'd rather be playing tournaments and winning ranking points, and because the most I've been offered by a team for the three weeks is $30,000. A guy like Blake probably gets $20,000 to play one WTT match. I have to face it — Blake is the guy everyone loves and I'm the guy everyone cringes to love. Usually teams consist of up-and-coming tour players, a step above the grinders I played yesterday, and the drawing card — a legend like Rafter or Becker or McEnroe.

I have to admit, I'm here to see the Australian recent retiree with two U.S. Open crowns and looks that rival Hollywood's best. I knew him as a gentle, easygoing guy. Rafter walks out onto the court, and he looks alive and well, his hair cut short and clean, his demeanor humble and reserved as always. His two titles at Flushing Meadows transformed him from a struggling pro into an icon of the game. He stopped playing at 29 when his game was ripening, due to travel, family issues, and shoulder surgery. But really I think it was complacent thinking that became his real detour back to a modest and obscure life in Australia and the Bahamas. Rafter was a late-blooming classic serve-and-volleyer who caught his country and the tennis world by surprise with his work ethic, an NBA vertical jump, a competitive drive masked by his stoic character, and a face loved by every female on the planet.

The cheers welcoming him back prove that the fans

haven't forgotten him. There are lots of youngsters in the stands who could barely remember Rafter, but I'm sitting in the crowd reflecting on our past battles in Philadelphia, London, Miami, Los Angeles. I only beat him once in all those tries, but I enjoyed the matches because Pat played with such sportsmanship and fire.

It's strange to see him now in this fringe setting. I can't imagine what they must be paying him to hop on a plane to Boston from Down Under to play again. What price could lure a guy of his stature? He's had it all: $11 million in prize winnings, being named *People Magazine*'s sexist man alive, married to a beautiful model, a father, and still an international hero. Here he is standing on a tennis court in Boston in front of 2,000 people, waiting to return the serve of Thomas Blake, James's older brother and a Harvard graduate, but ranked No. 400 — a struggling pro. The price tag has got to be just plain love.

Tennis players love this sport, and we miss it to death when we retire. It's as much a part of us as the arm that locks into our shoulder socket. When we lose it, we will cross the world to find it again. For one last match we want to be the person we once were, playing in the sun or in a converted hockey rink, it doesn't matter as long as we can chase the ball down and tattoo it back over the net. Just for this one transformative moment, Patrick Rafter, the ubiquitous volleyer, is gracing a tennis court again with his sturdy frame and famous transition game.

Tonight he looks rusty, and as I sit here and relish the joy of being a tennis fan, with my popcorn in my hand and my cheap seat at the top of the arena, I want to jump down onto the court and take over for Blake, to be a part of Rafter's night, engage him in a crosscourt rally just one more time, for one more moment.

Indianapolis

Tomorrow is my birthday, boys and girls, and I'll be 31 years old. Can you say 31? It's strange how when you're a kid, you can't wait for your birthday to come, and when you become an adult, you can't wait for it to pass. I feel a little achier after matches now than I did when I was younger. There are athletes who are invincible at 35. Karl Malone was 40 and fit as a fiddle. Ken Rosewall, Laver, Connors, and Pancho Gonzales all had tremendous longevity in their careers. Rosewall was in both the Wimbledon and U.S. Open Finals at age 39. I think I want it as much now as I did when I started. That's probably the most important question I ask myself now. It's got to come from how badly I want it, and I still feel positively obsessed.

I saw the Golden Boy of American tennis on the practice courts here at the RCA Championships, Andy Roddick. He was talking to me about the ESPYs. I don't have much of a rapport with him. I think maybe he has a problem with me. I'm like a guy who wants a piece of his pie, and even though I'm a distant threat, it's annoying to him. I might steal some of his greatness; I might start taking food off his table. In sports, you never know what's going to happen.

It's brutally hot out here, and Markus just had me running side to side. This is the first week of real humidity and I'm going to have to fight through it. I'm working hard so I can get ready for the summer heat. If I'm with Markus for a full year, I think I could see some good results.

I felt pretty bushed and out of it after the practice. I checked Dr.Com out for "encephalitis" and "depression." I got a mosquito bite on my head in Newport and I figure if I have something major wrong with me at my age, "what will be, will be."

I have this beautiful two-bedroom suite in the Westin with a wraparound view of the city. There are two televisions and a living room, and the tournament gave me an appearance fee plus RCA equipment. This girl I met in Indian Wells last year came up to my suite tonight at 10, but she was good and left at 11:30. She wanted to explode, but I told her no, and she was good, she knew that I had to get my rest. Before she left, she told me that she'd had sex with one of the other players the night before.

"It was the worst sex," she said. "Kissing him was like kissing a 17-year-old boy. He felt guilty about everything we were doing. He was not a man of control."

Being able to invite women up to my suite reminds me of when I dropped back down to playing Challengers in places like Tulsa, where I stayed in Motel 6's with my coach and ate at Denny's. There was no suite to invite a woman up to. When my coach picked up this girl at Wal-Mart, they went to her car to make out. You never know when the ride is going to end.

I've got Robby Ginepri tomorrow and it should be a real challenge. I beat him at NASDAQ in the first round 6–3 and 6–4, and he beat me at the beginning of the year in Auckland.

JULY 19

If you look up "winning" in the tennis dictionary, you see a picture of a champagne bottle. Under the word "losing" is a picture of a coffin and people around it dressed in black. I climbed in that coffin tonight and got buried.

I lost to Ginepri, and now it's midnight and I feel like crap. This is no way to celebrate a birthday. My body feels drained and heavy, like I'm trying to walk underwater and every step is a major effort. I can't get out of bed. I sleep 10 hours and wake up feeling like I haven't slept a minute. I don't have a sore throat or a fever, stomach problems or nausea, but I'm feeling delirious, disoriented, and exhausted. I couldn't see the ball tonight. Robby played well, but I wasn't even into it. It was an out-of-body experience, and I didn't know where I was out there.

I'm a little worried. Do I have mono? Am I depressed? Do I have some sort of flu, or worse? Is this just life at 31? I got on the Internet like a hypochondriac and Googled my symptoms so I could get a head start on my diagnosis. According to the Internet, I could have any number of illnesses and diseases, which didn't exactly put my mind at ease.

What a day. It's my birthday, and I'm alone in a hotel room suffering through online descriptions of sickness. I lost again, and I feel lost again. I've got to find out what's wrong with me before I worry myself sick. Why did my serve suck tonight? I'm sleepy and I haven't showered yet. I'm going to eat a Balance bar and sleep this pain and exhaustion away. The more I think I know, the less I understand. Everything I've learned about life I can sum up in three words. "It goes on . . ."

JULY 22

I feel like describing my day by using the word "then" a lot.

I woke up today with a headache. Then I had breakfast at Starbucks, and then lunch with a pretty Indianan girl named Autumn at PF Changs. Afterwards, I took a Tylenol. Then I said goodbye to her, took a car to the airport to catch a flight to L.A. Then the flight was delayed two hours from 6:30 to 8:30 p.m. Then I flew four hours and had a guy from Africa talking to me the whole time in a broken accent about tennis. Then I got picked up and arrived at the hotel past midnight. Then I walked to an all-night diner to eat a quick sandwich. Then I passed out on a king-size mattress with all the lights in the room still on.

JULY 23
Los Angeles

Lovitz called me today and said, "Hey, you want to come to a party with me tonight?"

I said, "Sure." I was alone. Markus was staying in a hotel 20 minutes away with Lapentti. I'm beginning to feel that sharing a coach with another player is not the way to go.

It turned out to be David Spade's birthday party. The party is in a small room at the Buffalo Club in Santa Monica, a classy upscale bar usually filled with making-it, entertainment industry types. It has the ambience of a gentlemen's club with a dimly lit interior, soft leather booths, and bar stools.

I hit the buffet and Arnold Schwarzeneggar walked up to Jon and me. I had met him once before at the L.A. Open three years ago. He had eagerly asked me about a match going on between Gambill and Michael Joyce. I didn't address him as "Governor," but when Lovitz imitated the way Arnold always says "Galifornia" instead of California, I joked, "I didn't know you could be the governor of a place you couldn't pronounce. What's Galifornia?"

Lovitz was talking with Jim Carrey. He's a big, tall, very

normal-looking guy, and he was dressed conservatively. When Jon introduced us, Jim said he loved tennis, and just once would love to burn Agassi on the court. He asked me questions about Agassi and I told him, "Don't worry, Jim. I'm still up-and-coming. I'm still blossoming. I'm not just chopped liver. I made the Olympic team. I'm not just here to serve the hors d'oeuvres, y'know."

I was trying my comedy out on him and he was cordial, but he looked at me like, "Why are you trying to hang with me? I make $20 million a movie. So cut it out."

I turned around again and Jon was talking to Pamela Anderson. I didn't get too much into it with her, not wanting her to think that I'm just like every other guy, only interested in gaping at her. I wasn't going to hit on her. When someone's single and attractive, I can make a play for her if I like — it's a free country. Women usually enjoy the attention I give them; it's the men I hear grumbling about how I approach so many women.

I've heard them say, "Spadea's probably homosexual. He tries to pick up all these women and then he says, 'No one's good enough for me.' That's because there isn't a woman or species that fulfills his requirements."

I'm not gay. My problem is that I'm overly interested in women and the relentless pursuit of perfection. There are a lot of women available in the tennis world and it makes it tough to choose. I've learned if I like a girl, I should keep calling her and try to see where the relationship will go. It's exhausting to always think there is another woman who is better, smarter, richer, prettier, and more outgoing than the one I'm dating, and frankly, it's also immature and shallow of me. Every woman has her strengths and flaws and I'm just looking for the one that I can embrace, cherish, and have the best time with, regardless of her attributes and shortcomings. Bottom line — the girl who sparks my interest and who wants to be with me is the best one for me.

A certain amount of indecision for a single male in his early 30s is normal when it comes to choosing a woman. Every guy goes through it before settling down with someone he enjoys as a person, regardless of whatever physical imperfections she may have. We end up connecting with someone in our souls and not just our loins.

Another problem of mine is I philosophize too much. Growing old with one person is a great dream, but at the same time, humans have this incredible urge to lust after beautiful, young flesh. It's not reality we're seeking; it's a temptation that really shouldn't be pursued. I hope that one day I'll understand this and get married, try to attain the white picket fence, American Dream life.

But what is the definition of normal? Is it getting married and having kids? If normal is doing what most people in society do, it's also conformity, a sign you're somewhat insecure about forging your own path. I don't like being normal and following along with the majority just to fit in.

Just then the champion of non-conformity, John McEnroe, called out to me, "Hey, what's up, buddy? What are you doing here?" He was sitting on a stool at the bar with a cigar in his mouth. He walked over to me and started talking about my match with Nadal.

"You go to Wimbledon and you tank?" McEnroe said. "Who tanks on Centre Court of Wimbledon, losing 6–0 to Rafael Nadal, who then loses in the very next round?"

"What are you talking about?" I said. "I hurt my back. I was injured. I was just trying to make a good impression and the guy wiped me out." I was going to add, "Not everyone's as good as you, John," but I didn't.

JULY 25
Los Angeles

Playing Zach Fleishman here in the Mercedes-Benz Cup at the UCLA courts was one of my best possible draws. He's an inexperienced qualifier, who's been on the Satellite tour for several years. It's a good match to break into a tournament with, because I can play mediocre and still win. The problem is that I didn't play mediocre — I didn't even play poorly — and I lost to a guy ranked No. 375, the lowest-ranked player I've ever lost to in my career.

I played an insanely disturbing, numb match. I was lethargic, and this malaise I continue to suffer from zapped the spark out of my body and mind. My painful performance gave a helpless Satellite player, in his words, "the biggest win" of his career. I'm glad somebody thinks I can still play this game. Zach fought and played well; I've got to give him credit.

I'm going to my doctor's office tomorrow to get blood tests done. I need to find out what's wrong with me. I can't work on my game until I know what I'm dealing with here.

JULY 30

All the tests came back negative. I still feel groggy, but I'm going to fight through this. I pulled out of the tournament in Washington, D.C., to rest up. With no one to practice with, I decided to go down to a park in West Hollywood and hit some serves on the courts there. As I walked up to the courts, I saw an older man in his mid-50s, I'm guessing, sitting on the bench with his racket bag and tennis outfit looking excited to play.

"Are you waiting for someone?" I asked curiously, trying to see if I could use the one remaining court to practice my serve on before his partner showed up.

"Yes," he said, "my friend should be coming in 15 minutes. Are you looking for a hit?"

I gladly agreed, though I was sure this guy couldn't keep up. I started slow, warming into my full swings. The guy wasn't a beginner. He had some feel for the ball, and was countering marginally back and forth, giving me some rhythm. We chatted as we hit a few balls, and he told me that he was a film producer. I told him I taught tennis. He didn't recognize me — which in a way, was good, but in another way was frustrating — nobody, not even a tennis player, knows who I am.

He paid me some compliments on my strokes and asked me if I'd ever played on television. I said "sometimes," but smiled and I think he took it as a no. We had some fun and played some points. He looked like a kid in a candy store, tripping and stumbling to handle my regular shots. I wasn't trying to torture or demean him, but I hadn't hit in days and I needed to get in some practice. Then he asked me to bring it harder and with more spin. He was a competitive guy looking for a thrill on the weekend.

We played some points and I aced him. I hit him body serves that had him diving for safety, and one time, when he returned it, he followed his shot and ran up to the net vigorously. When I legitimately missed a passing shot wide, he smiled triumphantly. The door behind me creaked open and another middle-aged man emerged with his tennis bag. I thought our practice session was over, but my partner called out to his friend, "Hey Harry, try to return this guy's serve. He's just a teaching pro, but he's got a good one." His friend hurriedly fished his racket out of his bag, and I gave him what he wanted, a Sampras-like torpedo that painted the middle line for an ace.

He looked at me and wiped his brow. "God, you sure are pretty good for a teaching pro," he said. "That shows you how tough the real pros must be. I won a contest once and got to play against a real pro, but he wasn't very highly ranked. His name was Zach Fleishman and he just made it to the second round of the pro tournament this week in L.A. You should think about giving the pro tour a chance yourself. You hit your serve much harder than he did."

I thanked them both, gathered my stuff, and left.

AUGUST 7
Montreal

Montreal is a good transition back into the tennis scene. The people are friendly, the city is distinct with plenty to do, and the tournament is great. There are big crowds, a hot summer sun, good hospitality for players, a nice hotel, and huge stakes at a Tennis Masters Series.

I walk into the player's lounge and see Nadal sitting on a sofa listening to his CD player. I'd have thought he would have graduated to an iPod by now, but whatever he's doing is working for him. He always listens to his music before matches to inspire him. I still use a CD player, too. I have two iPods, gifts from the Olympic team and the NASDAQ tournament, but I'm too lazy to figure out the downloading system. Funny, but somehow I'm not having the same results on the court that Nadal is after listening to *my* CD player. Maybe I should get it checked.

Roddick's in the locker room getting congratulated by players for winning at Washington last week. I'm running for

the trainer's room to get my knee tendonitis — a new injury
— worked on after a terrible practice where I lost a set to a
Canadian junior, and moved like a man who just drank a
12-pack of beer. The trainer's room is packed — it's always
packed. Players are in there like there's a sale on, getting
free treatment, taking the best care of their bodies. The massage list is jammed on the half-hour until 9 p.m. There are
plenty of tables and therapists as Canada goes all out provid-
ing medical assistants. But the doubles players monopolize
the massages.

AUGUST 8

Monday and my match against qualifier and veteran, Jonas
Bjorkman of Sweden, begins. It's another good draw for me
considering Jonas's singles game has dropped in recent years
and everyone else in the draw is a Top 40 or better player.
The other first-round matchups at my time slot are Roddick
vs. Mathieu and Nadal vs. Moya, so mine looks good. I see
Darren Cahill, Andre's coach, in the bleachers scouting our
match on a back court, as the winner faces Andre in the second round.

   Jonas wins the toss and serves out a love game. My
mindset is to beat him bad, but I start the match not putting a return of serve in the court. I serve and lose a close
rally, double-fault, and then miss an easy forehand and
blame the 20 mph wind for his return winner that blows
back into the court and breaks me. I cannot function. I'm
not seeing clearly, as if I'm looking into a blurry haze or a
windshield during a thunderstorm. My confidence is shot. I
play on.

   I can't break Jonas. He is playing aggressive, sound tennis

and pumping his fist like a rookie looking for his first big win. Jonas is a great competitor, a classy, friendly guy who everyone on tour likes. He even travels with his family a lot. But that's no reason why I should lose to him.

But I'm like a lemon car huffing and inching its way up a long hill with no end in sight. Lifeless and fizzled, to my dismay I hit one last wild ground stroke out of the court. It hits the fence on the fly, and I'm on the losing end of a 6–3, 6–2, pasting. In the locker room after the match, Cahill walks up to me and says, "Vince, bad luck today. I hear you're writing a book, what's it about?"

"Oh, not much," I say. I didn't want to tell him his client plays a prominent role in it.

I'm starting to hear a few comments from the other players concerning what I'm writing. I'm not worried about what they think. I'm just a squirrel trying to get a nut and I've got a book deal. Hey, more power to my publisher for buying a book that is going to provide a true representation of who I am and what the pro tennis tour is all about. I believe in being moral and telling the truth, so the idea that I shouldn't write honestly about what I hear, see, and think about the other players and the game is nonsense. We all have an opinion, and this is the land of the free and the home of the brave. But unless I start winning again, no one's going to care what I write about anyway.

AUGUST 10
Boca Raton

I wake up this morning to hear a message on my cell phone from Pete Fischer. "Are you done, Vince?" he asks. "Are you calling it quits?"

I'm back in Boca yet again, taking more medical tests as the malaise continues, and getting physical therapy for my knee. My doctor tells me I have the cholesterol level of a baby. I've been on the road for eight straight weeks since Wimbledon, and I need to regroup if I'm going to try to play the Masters Series event in Cincinnati next week.

My six-week trial with Markus is over. I canned him. I already have a reputation for dropping coaches, so I guess I'm just adding to it now. I had contracted for him to coach me through the U.S. Open, but it's not working out, so why prolong it? Sharing a coach with another player just doesn't work. I have no one to eat dinner with, and he didn't even get my rackets ready for me before matches. He would poke his head into the locker room and say, "Vince, everything good? I'll be in the players' lounge."

I know I've had a lot of coaches, but I've tried to respect each one and work with them as a team. I have to be intrigued by the way a coach explains a strategy or stroke technique. If the rapport isn't quite right, I try to make an adjustment to keep the relationship going so we both make progress.

Markus and I lacked the right camaraderie. I like it when I can interact socially with my coach because I don't have established relationships with the other players on tour. Markus and Lapentti would eat dinner out much later than I liked. They eat dinner at 9:30 p.m., while I like to eat at 7:30 and go to bed by 10:30 or 11. It grew lonely sitting at a bar and eating dinner alone, or trying to find some entertaining excursion to go on. I'd just go back to my room, turn on the TV, and be bored.

The bottom line is that Markus didn't give me the impression that he was 100 percent with me. He was courteous, but I didn't feel he made a deep commitment to do what was necessary as my coach to make me a top player.

AUGUST 14
Cincinnati, Ohio

The Cincinnati Masters tournament is one of the best places to play in the world. It's technically in Mason, Ohio, but I guess Cincinnati sounds more prestigious. The people are really nice and enthusiastic about tennis, and the tournament feels like it's the biggest thing to hit Cinci since Pete Rose's headfirst slide. Every time I meet someone from here, no matter where I am or what age they are, they talk about this tournament like it's their job to promote it. Pro tennis players in Cinci are treated like the Beatles on a live stage. Okay, I've gone too far, but then why does my hand cramp from signing so many autographs when I'm only like the 50th-ranked player in the world? Seriously, if every city and every tournament had this type of fanfare going on, tennis would replace hit television shows and U2 concerts as the most happening entertainment in the world.

My father accompanied me on this trip. It's been a while since we traveled together, and I'm enjoying his company. I miss those early days when he and I would plot our run up the rankings. My first-round match is against a qualifier from France named Gilles Simon. I think even the French don't know who he is. The only time I ever saw him was when he played in an exhibition mixed-doubles match at the French Open before the event started. He was playing with a host of greats: Marat Safin, Justin Henin-Hardenne, and Steffi Graf. It was quite amazing to see Steffi back on court, laughing and playing doubles.

Now this unknown is my opponent in the first round. It's a good chance to break my four-match losing streak. I play my best first set of the year, hitting aces, going for broke, backhand winners down the line, knifing forehand volley angle winners. In 25 minutes, I win the first set, 6–2.

I'm playing through my funk with subconscious winners and timing. But then I start to analyze, realize, and criticize — the three big no-no's for a tennis player. I miss one ball in the second set and completely lose confidence, resorting to playing a pushing, grinding game. I back off from the baseline and play not to lose; waiting for this carefree first-timer Frenchman to take his cuts. He may be inexperienced, but he's also talented, and he hurts me early to go up a break. The crowd starts cheering me on and giving me the will to make a comeback in the third set after losing the second set, 6–2.

But I don't believe in my game and I'm still not seeing the ball well. Simon steps it up and breaks my floundering serve, and although I get a break point back, I can't convert it. "Game, set and match, Simon," the umpire's voice shouts out like a judge's sentence.

I wanted to win, I tried to win, but mentally and physically, I'm just not right. It's like I'm up a creek without a paddle. I'm not going to write in this diary again until I win a match.

AUGUST 22
New Haven, Connecticut

Stop the presses, Spadea wins. I played a great match today and beat an up-and-coming Italian player named Andreas Seppi. I'm not going to jinx it by writing anything more.

AUGUST 27

It's Arthur Ashe Day at the Open, a day of entertainment and exhibitions to kick off the tournament and honor the memory of the great Wimbledon and U.S. Open champion, humanitarian, and author. I'm going to be the MC for a couple of corporate gigs taking place on tournament grounds.

I walk into the nearly empty stadium, just to relax and listen to a teen band warming up for their performance later in the afternoon. Kim Clijsters is practicing with Anastasia Myskina. I sit down two seats away from Clijsters' younger sister. I ask her, "Do you like this band? Who is it?"

She says she isn't sure, and I start chatting with her. She tells me she's 20 and used to be a tennis player. I ask, "Why did you quit? You're 20. Were you like, 'Kim has a ton of money. Let's stop. Let's eat chocolate and waffles for the rest of our lives.'? I'd be the same way."

She says, "No, I just had some bad injuries. What do you do? Are you a coach?" She probably thought I was some dirty old man trying to chat her up. Kim saw me talking to her sister and she called up from the court, "Hey Vince, stop hitting on my little sister."

AUGUST 29
Flushing Meadows, New York

Start spreading the news, if I can make it here, I can make it anywhere. It's up to me, U.S. Open, U.S. Open. Not very original, granted, but it's the truth. I lost to Feliciano Lopez in a tough, three-set match in New Haven, and now here I am. All I need to do is win my next seven matches and my dreams will come true. In tennis, you don't have to beat all 128 players in the draw to win the tournament, just the seven you face. It may sound easy, but it's close to a mission impossible.

The U.S. Open; players are hoping, women are scoping, I'm jump roping, what's with all these players doping?? I gotta start fixing cause I feel broken, in two, losing four first rounds and I'm paying for my shoes. I've paid my dues, but for all the wrong reasons I've made the news. Skies are blue, so is my emotion, I have to find the victory potion, use better sun tan lotion, do sprints in the ocean, whatever it takes, even if I have to fake it til I make it, confidence feels naked.

Arriving in New York City. If you're not pretty, you won't get any pity, if you're not smart, you'll end up pushing a shopping cart, 'cause no matter who you are, what city or nation, this city has no patience for anyone who isn't amazin'.

The symmetry of my life conflicts with the imagery of my strife, that's why winning the U.S. Open title is just so vital, at least I hope to make it to the final, play it out like a piano recital, I feel the same age as vinyl and Billy Idol. Being American with hopefully no arrogance, I lost my Prada glasses, and I bought a new pair again. But my tennis is not as replaceable, my belief has gotta be traceable, to my years of the Top 20, U.S. Open and Vinny go together like Abraham Lincoln and the penny.

How many Opens do I have left? Time's whistling like a ref, cutting down like a chef, I've got the adrenaline of playing at Wimbledon, nerves are meddling, but more than any kind of groping, moping, feeling crazier than eloping, I'm ready to give my best, to this U.S. Open.

Since I've been 15, I've been coming here once a year playing in the juniors, and then the qualifying tournament, all the way to my best performance beating Kafelnikov and getting to the fourth round in 1995. The smell of the city, the restaurants, noise, buildings and people — the melting pot of the world — this is the smell of the U.S. Open. The Open is crazy, packed with ridiculous numbers of people, players, fans, agents, staff, groupies, young and old, a nonstop shuffle of thousands in the grounds, along the outside courts, and in the stadiums. The players' area is magnificent, with two stories of locker rooms, trainer's rooms, a cafeteria, administrative offices, gyms, media centers, medical center, and a hair salon. It's overwhelming. The most important thing for a player is to focus on your own agenda. It's easy to end up in ten conversations before practice. It's okay to mingle a bit, but managing my distractions is the key to my success here.

I watched Federer practice the other day. He's nonchalant, casual, relaxed, yet so confident. If he misses, he doesn't care. I play Glenn Weiner, another qualifier, in the first round. I serve big and consistent and my ground strokes are strong, and I win easily, 6–4, 6–2, 6–0. It's the perfect start to the 2005 Open. I don't expend much energy, and Weiner manages to win only one break point against me the entire match.

I see Andre and his son, Jaden, walking out of the locker room as I enter and I say, "Hey Andre, what do you think of this racket?" I hold up my original Prince graphite racket — which I have returned to after my failed experiment with the new tech racket. Andre used to wield the same racket for many years, and he looks at it with real intent while his little boy stands there patiently.

"It's a beauty," he finally says. I notice he is heading out to practice with only two rackets and a small bottle of water. Simplicity and efficiency, that's what the new Andre Agassi is all about and I'd be wise to follow his lead in these two disciplines.

Then I did my post-match press conference. There were four reporters in the room, a U.S. Open press official, and me.

Q. How long did you work together with Markus?

A. About as long as Sampras and Higueras.

Q. What about Coria in your upcoming match?

A. It's a good opportunity for me. I've got nothing to lose.

Q. What do you mean you have "nothing to lose"? If you lose you're out of the tournament.

A. I have nothing to lose. There's no pressure on me to absolutely win like there was today in this match; but I mean, it's just a figure of speech. You got to say it. What do you want me to say: "If I don't win then I'll jump off the Brooklyn Bridge"? [big laughs from reporters] I probably will. That's reality. Coria hasn't had the most stellar summer, so I think we're in the same boat. We're just trying to fight for a few wins.

Q. There are a few good Italian restaurants in this city. Where do you dine?

A. I dine at Cipriani and Serafina. Those are two very solid, very elite Italian restaurants, and they're different in their own way.

Q. What do you normally order?

A. I order spaghetti with tomato sauce, and normally grilled chicken with some light white wine sauce so I get some protein and pasta. That's a very authentic and meaningful dish. It's like an old school, original Italian dish. That's where you find out, in my opinion, what an Italian restaurant is made of. If they can make a good spaghetti and tomato sauce then you're talking about a stellar Italian restaurant all the way through the fish, chicken, and veal dishes.

Q. What about the gourmet dishes? Don't you

ever go beyond the chicken and spaghetti?

A. As Rocky Marciano said, "No new foods when you're getting ready for a big fight." That's the same with the U.S. Open. Remember Rick Leach having clam sauce before the finals of the U.S. Open doubles? He had a bad stomach and had to default. I'm sure those clams tasted good.

Q. Has Pat McEnroe talked to you about possibly playing for the U.S. Davis Cup team against Belgium on clay in September?

A. I haven't spoken to him. I saw him in an elevator the other day in New Haven, and he said, "Finally, you've won a match." I don't think that puts me in the No. 1 position for Davis Cup in 2005. I think he's got a challenge there on clay in Belgium. Blake and Ginepri are coming on strong and they both have the youth that Pat enjoys. I know if I believe in myself, everyone can step aside. But it's bad timing again. It's like the Davis Cup Gods have reared their ugly head again. Every time a Davis Cup tie comes up, I go into a slump.

AUGUST 30

Andy Roddick lost in the first round tonight to Gilles Muller of Luxembourg in three straight set tiebreakers. I saw his "Andy's Mojo" American Express commercials and I think filming them could have taken a lot of energy out of him. I've seen that commercial with five or six different people in it, which means that he had to shoot each one separately. Just shooting one commercial takes a full day's work, at least. These commercials must have taken at least three or four days to shoot, then he probably had to schmooze with the American Express people for a couple of days. I don't know when he found time to do all that and prepare for the tournament.

The first time I saw Andy play as a professional, I was 26 and he was 18 and playing in his first year on the tour. It was a Challenger in Vegas right after the 2000 U.S. Open. I was at rock bottom, having just gone through the losing streak, and was ranked at No. 237. I was in shock, completely uninspired. I saw Roddick and he looked the exact opposite. He was like a raging fire. He was ready to take the Challengers by storm, while I lost that week in the first round.

The next week in Burbank, I made it to the quarters and played Roddick. He killed me. He was this fireball, blazing all cylinders. It kind of woke me up. I thought, "I can't go out and give a good effort anymore. I need to get more revved up and play with the energy this kid has."

At the 2001 U.S. Open, I had to play in the qualifying tournament since my ranking was not high enough to make it directly into the main draw. I lost 6–0, 7–5, in the last round to this Argentinean teenager I'd never heard of named David Nalbandian. I was up 5–2 in the second set and he won five straight games. Two years before, I'd been in the fourth round of the Open, losing to Richard Krajicek in Arthur Ashe Stadium and here I was losing in the last round of the qualifiers.

I picked up my $5,000 or so prize winnings, packed up my tennis bag, and left Flushing Meadows. Back at my hotel, the UN Plaza — I was paying $250 a night because qualifying players do not have their living expenses covered at the Open — I decided to check out and stay with my sister that night at her apartment in SoHo. I was going to hang around the city for a few days and then on September 1, 2001, I was going to fly home with my sister to spend the Labor Day weekend in Florida.

My dad was in the hospital at the time for 11 days. It was a somewhat serious condition he had, but not life-threatening. Even so, it had shaken me up. Here was the guy who had taken care of me my whole life. I started thinking that you can't depend on people even though they are willing to give their all. I needed to take charge because here I was 27 years old and still mostly depending on my parents for tennis support.

On September 1, I got on the plane with my sister and I thought, "This isn't right." You know sometimes when you have that feeling? I didn't feel right about going back to Florida. I thought something is going on here and I've got to figure it out before I go home.

The flight was supposed to take off at around 10 that night, but the pilot came over the intercom and said there was something wrong with the plane and we had to get off. I thought, "Wow, this is my escape." Something was happening for a reason. I thought it was a sign I had to follow.

I waited in the airport with Luanne, and 45 minutes later, they told us that the problem was fixed and we could board the plane again. But I told Luanne I wasn't going on the plane, that I wasn't comfortable going. My sister was disappointed, but she threw her keys at me and told me to stay in her apartment. I took a cab back to her place and stayed until September 10th, when I took a flight back to Florida.

I spent those days in SoHo roaming the streets and reflecting. I had no direction or purpose. I was just people-watching and feeling very, very down. I went to Foot Locker and a vintage store to buy some clothes because I had none with me — all my bags were on the plane. I tried to talk to people on the street. I remember seeing Natalie Portman walking across Spring Street. I tried to ask her a question, and she looked at me like she was going to call the police, like I was violating her space. I saw the lead singer for the Red Hot Chili Peppers, Anthony Kiedis. It was 10 in the morning and the streets were deserted. I tried to ask him a question, but he had a CD in his hand and he seemed like he was on a mission. He didn't stop. Even in New York City, I thought, people wonder when they see a guy wandering around on his own.

I ended up sitting in a café by myself, trying to reach out to more people and getting shut down. I went there to meet actresses and models, but unfortunately, none of them would talk to me. I thought, "Geez, man, what is my life coming to?" I was supposed to be living the good life, but I didn't have anything to say to anybody. I'd already bragged about my good years, and now I had fallen flat on the skid row of pro tennis. I decided that it was time for me to start fresh and gain the passion once more. I felt like there was a lot out there for the taking. The world wasn't giving me an inch, so I needed to go out and take it.

"What do I want to do?" I asked myself. "What am I great at?"

I started thinking of some of the people I knew in the tennis world, people who could inspire me, who I could reach out to for help. I jotted names down on a napkin and got so excited that I started calling them right away. I called Jim Pierce first. He's a great inspirational speaker. When I told him my circumstances, he told me, "If I had your body, your life, your opportunities and youth, there would be no one who could beat me. I would be out there every morning, at the crack of dawn. I'd kiss the ground, kiss the tennis court, and thank God every day that I had this opportunity. I would go out and train myself into the ground.

"You don't even understand what you have. You only have one chance to go through this life and it's up to you to see how bright your candle will shine. It's all in your hands. This is your life. You can make a comeback if you want it badly enough. You can do it."

I called Pete Fischer next. I knew Pete was a demanding coach, but I had been working with my father for so many years — I knew about demanding coaches. I was at the point where I felt uncomfortable with having my father coach me. He was my father, but I was his employer. Which relationship came first? And if one relationship ends, would the other still be okay? I was dealing with some difficult feelings.

I described my situation to Fischer over the phone. "You're having a tennis nervous breakdown," he bluntly told me. "You've got a brain cramp. It's time to tell your father that you need to make a change in coaches. Fly out to California and let me look at your game." Three years later, at the age of 30, I was back in the Top 20.

AUGUST 31

I play Guillermo Coria today on the Louis Armstrong Stadium court in front of a really ardent New York crowd. I've had a rough year and a killer summer, but if I can beat Coria, the No. 8 seed, playing in front of this sensational, loud, and energetic New York crowd, I can forget it all. There's a nice summer breeze going as we step on the court at four in the afternoon. I hear a couple of "Spadea, ain't afraid a ya" calls from the crowd. They're ready.

The first set turns out to be a heartless one for me. I make errors, but I can hit no winners against Coria, who is on a mission. He's not missing anything, and he's running down balls with legs wiry and sturdy as a whippet's. I get broken on my first two service games, but the packed crowd is still behind me and they cheer for a comeback.

Here's where I'm supposed to step up and rally to a big win. I try to jump-start my offensive game in the second set, but Guillermo runs down all my shots and passes me with angles that are hard to believe. I try to come to net, but I feel slow, and my defense falls short to one of the fastest and steadiest players on tour. I can't overpower him and I can't out-steady him. I'm caught between, as the Rolling Stones sing, "a rock and a hard place." Everything I do, Coria has an answer for, and he closes me out, 6–2, 6–3, 6–2.

I felt like I was playing Marcelo Rios, who ran faster than me, took the ball earlier, and manipulated me on the court. When I tried to get aggressive, Coria ran all my shots down. He slipped passing shots through my pockets. I wasn't able to get any grasp, hold, or bite on him. When I got passive, he dominated me with heavy down-the-line backhands.

Going into the match, I felt confident, like I was going to win. I thought he had lost some of his pizzazz, but I was wrong. Once I started playing, I felt run-down, a little nervous, and had low energy.

In the third set, I hit a drop volley crosscourt, for what appeared to be an outright winner. People were already clapping, but Coria ran it down and hit a winner off the tops of his shoes. He played like a super-human. He seemed fresh as a daisy.

In the press conference after the match, the few reporters who show up, mostly from South Florida newspapers, don't ask me so much about my match as they do about Andre's chances and Roddick's shocking first-round loss to Muller. It's like they look at me as a guy who's been around so long that I'm not really a player anymore, just an expert in the field. When someone finally asks me about myself, the question is: "At your age, Vince, how many Opens do you think you have left in your tank?"

White Plains, New York

Coria and Massu got into it in their five-set, fourth-round match. Coria came back to win the last two sets and as he was doing it, he mocked Massu, who was cramping, by mimicking his limping and hobbling. It's just two South American guys taunting each other and getting carried away. It shows their competitiveness. Neither one wants to be shown up or ridiculed because of the Argentinean-Chilean rivalry.

The South American players are very strong these days with five players in the Top 17: Coria, Puerta, Nalbandian, Gaston Gaudio, and Fernando Gonzales. Canas had been in the Top 10 before he was suspended and Massu won the gold medal at the Olympics and was in the Top 10 in 2004. The economy in Argentina was practically nonexistent for a while and it's still struggling. Money doesn't come too easily. So the players are a lot hungrier and more invested, and they train hard. They follow the Guillermo Vilas work ethic. The South Americans have followed the Australians and the Russians in working hard to beat the rest of the tennis world.

A lot of the South American players are difficult. It started with Marcelo Rios of Chile. He and I grew up together in the juniors. While I got along with him, I could see he was a difficult character. He was apathetic about everything and always had a snarl on his face. My mom is Colombian, and she says sometimes in South America —

and I don't want to generalize here — the men have this macho trip. They're taught to be tough and sometimes their attitude is misunderstood as arrogant and condescending. Rios was callous and mad, but amusing. Sometimes he crossed the line, just like Coria and Massu did the other day. Now, Coria will play Ginepri, and Blake plays Agassi to reach the semifinals. Ginepri and Blake have similar games —they either play great tennis or get into funks where they can't get any rhythm to their games and can't win consistently. Motivation is a question for both of them. But right now, they're both highly motivated. Fitness and focus come into play even more in these big matches. The Agassis, Hewitts, Beckers, and Edbergs really rose on these high-stakes occasions and won the big titles.

It's great for American tennis. People have been waiting for a breakthrough of American players other than Agassi and Roddick at the U.S. Open. Now there are two more players, Blake and Ginepri, both having career-making tournaments, months, and years. And I'm not even in the mix.

I don't feel insanely jealous, but I do wish I was the one doing so well, and not them. My initial thought is, "Gosh, why do I want these guys to lose when I should really hope that they win?" I try to overcome that shortcoming but that's how I honestly feel. I think it's human nature to feel envy when you see your peers doing well. I have this competitive edge. I've felt it with Agassi and Roddick, and even more so with Blake and Ginepri, because I've beaten both of them this year and was at their level of competition until a few months ago.

But at this point, I'm just another spectator. Everyone has their own journey, and I really can't do anything about their success, so why get stressed out about it? If anything, I should be happy about their success because it's making tennis more visible in America.

I called up Pete Fischer today and asked him, "So what's going on here with James Blake being the biggest thing in tennis? Is he better than Sampras?" [Big laughter on Fischer's end of the line.]

"Blake is fast; he's playing awfully well."

"Do you think he's going to win the tournament against Federer?"

"What!?"

"No. Do you think he'll beat Agassi tonight?"

"If Andre plays badly, it might be a close match."

"The odds are for Agassi then? This guy Ginepri is the next Courier, they say." [Fischer laughs.]

"They said that about you, too. But Ginepri's eight years younger than you."

"You don't think these guys are going to be Grand Slam champions and the next Changs and Lendls? [More laughter.] So you think that these guys are just going through a hot Spadea week, like at Indian Wells in 2003 or the 1999 Australian Open?"

"That's my guess. They're not that good."

"Geez. I'm sitting by a pool here in Westchester County, New York, and I feel like I should just quit and start giving lessons. Should I go to Bangkok and Tokyo? I'm really not excited about my travel schedule. But after Delray I'm going to be ranked No. 55 and will have 200 points to defend for the fall. So if I go to sleep and wake up December 31st, it won't be New Year's it'll be my New Careers. I'll be No. 105. So I've got to play everywhere?"

"Yep, I'm afraid so. Here's the deal, you're expecting to work yourself harder and get to the Top 10 where you never were. My game plan for you is that you always have to be somewhat realistic. When we started working together you were No. 240 — and had Jason Applebaum as your traveling coach. My goal for that year was for you to make it to No. 50, and you actually finished No. 53, which wasn't bad. The next year, I set a goal of No. 30 for you, but you made it to No. 29."

"But you have to start out unrealistic and have something to climb for, right? So if I go unrealistic at this point and say Top 10, maybe I'll make it to the Top 15."

"But this year instead of going for the Top 20 or 30 again, you got injured and you could wind up now outside the Top 100. You've lost half-a-million bucks, which you haven't appreciated."

"Right."

"In the two or three years that you have left, I just don't see you taking a chance of getting injured for the sake of something that may not happen. You are 31 and your body is starting to tell you that you have to play differently. From my viewpoint, you've gone as far as you're going to as a purely defensive player. You've got to maintain your defense. Even though you're never going to be a great offensive player or develop a weapon at 31, what I'd like to see you do is get enough offense so you can win a few more points easily and translate that into winning a few more matches. You're never going to be Top 10, but if you can get back to the Top 20 again, that would be a great accomplishment."

SEPTEMBER 11
Boca Raton

Federer beat Agassi in four sets to win his second U.S. Open and his sixth major. One more and he's halfway to tying Sampras' record of winnng 14 Grand Slam tournaments. He's 24, so if he wins two majors a year for the next four years, he'll tie Sampras. I think he'll win more than 10 majors, but will fall short of winning 14. There are just too many variables — a slump, a big injury, the emergence of young players like Nadal, Andy Murray, and Gasquet to challenge him. It's going to be fun to see if he can beat the odds.

NOVEMBER 3
Los Angeles

I finished out the year losing 6–1 and 6–2 to Dmitry Tursunov in the first round of the Paris Masters. The week before in Lyon, I had beaten Ljubicic 7–5, 7–6, to become the only player besides Nadal to beat the Croat in his past 17 matches. In the quarters I played Fabrice Santoro, with a chance — if I beat him — to play Roddick in the semis. But I was run down and the French magician beat me easily.

I started out the year as the 19th-ranked player and I end it 10 months later at No. 77. At the beginning of the year, I was the third highest ranked American, but now I am number seven. My 22–26 win-loss record over 26 tournaments in 2005 is my first losing season since 2002. In four Grand Slam tournaments I won but two matches, and in the seven Masters Series events I played, I won just one match.

My statistics for the season reflect why my results were so dismal. I converted only 43 percent of my break point chances, compared to the leader in that stat, Nicolas Kiefer, who converted on 47 percent. I won only 53 percent of points when returning a second serve, compared to the leader Nadal, who won 57 percent. I won only 73 percent of my service games, compared to the leader Roddick, who won 93 percent, and I won only 25 percent of my return of serve games, compared to Nadal, who topped the charts at 38 percent returning games won.

Injuries, a malaise, or depression — I'm not even sure now what it was — female fandangos, coaching mishaps. All of it led to my season of despair. But I'm still optimistic. There's no quit in this kid. I believe I can still compete at the highest level. Call me crazy, but I do.

In fact, after the U.S. Open, I issued a guarantee to both the *Miami Herald* and *Tennis Week Magazine* that before I retire, I will achieve my highest ranking and break into the Top 10 players in the world. The *Herald*'s headline was "Spadea Issues Guarantee." I got the idea from Joe Namath's guarantee back in 1969 that the New York Jets would win the Super Bowl. If Joe could make his vow a reality, so can I. A lot of papers across the country, and even *The Financial Times* in London, picked up the story, and I got so much press attention I felt like James Blake. But my mother came up to me and said, "Vince, what's up with this?"

At this point, I know there are two ways of looking at my career, and I see it from both perspectives. The optimistic way is to say, "Here's Spadea — living the dream. He made it to the Top 20, a two-time Olympian. He crashed and was buried, suffering the longest losing streak ever, dropping down to No. 237 before making it back to No. 18. He regained more ranking positions than Andre Agassi did in his comeback."

Then there's the pessimistic side: "Spadea was heralded as the next Agassi, but never made it. He's an underachiever. He only briefly made it to the Top 20. He's like an American Xavier Malisse: big expectations but sketchy results. He's had many coaching changes, including his father, whom people felt created controversy and didn't help to maximize his son's potential. Spadea never won a major or made it to the semis of one. He won his first and only pro title after playing in 223 tournaments. His losing streak was unparalleled in the history of the game. He's had a long, rocky, roller-coaster career." Where some see achievement, others see instability.

I want to continue playing on tour and setting big goals because I still love the life. There's so much action. It's the action that still stirs me. It's the feeling of landing after you've been on an airplane for who knows how many hours and knowing that the transportation is going to pick you up. There's somebody there who respects what you're doing and is going to give you props and privileges. He's going to take you to a hotel where you can stay for free. He's going to make you feel your hard work is worth something. It's a great feeling when you're landing and you think, "I can't believe I'm in freaking Bangkok, man. This is wild. This is some weird, wild stuff."

Then I get to go straight out to the practice courts and start training. When you look at the harsh realities of real life, playing pro tennis helps me escape from everything. It's a great passion. I really look at it as a full-time retirement job. Ask people the first thing they want to do when they retire, and they'll say, "Travel." What else? "I want to quit my job and just play tennis." Well, that's my job, traveling and playing tennis, and I have no intention of giving it up until I feel like I've lost my edge and my ability to win the big matches.

In the future, if I become a television tennis commentator or a coach, it's not going to be the same feeling as being the man, the player, the reason why all these people come out and fill the stands. I still want to be the player the people all respect and come out to see.

I saw John Elway eating at a restaurant in South Beach last week so I went up to him and started a conversation. He told me, "If I didn't play football after the age of 30, I never would have won a Super Bowl." The bottom line is I want to be happy. I know happiness is not a permanent state of being; it's a continual process, something you work towards. My biggest thrills in life have come from pursuing my goals and dreams. It's not about winning money or getting fame, it's about striving, struggling, and doing something I love.

This year I learned that I couldn't do a lot of things well and play great tennis. Every cell in my body has to be focused on winning a match. My will to win has to be strong; my dedication to winning matches the main drive of my life. So I'm going to pick up the pieces from my 2005 tennis breakdown, and get back to the love. I love tennis. In essence, it's the game of life. The future is good. It's all good, baby, baby.

APPENDIX A

2005 Tournament Season

Auckland, New Zealand International Series 10/01/05 Outdoor Hard Draw: 32

Round	Opponent	Country	Rank	Score
R32	Sanchez, David	(ESP)	56	6–0 6–0
R16	Ginepri, Robby	(USA)	56	5–7 3–6

Points: 3   New Indesit ATP Race Position: N/A   Prize Money: US $7000

Australian Open, Australia Grand Slam 17/01/05 O Hard Draw: 128

Round	Opponent	Country	Rank	Score
R128	Stepanek, Radek	(CZE)	15	3–6 7–5 6–4 5–7 3–6

Points: 1   New Indesit ATP Race Position: 60   Prize Money: US $13754

Delray Beach, FL, U.S.A. International Series 31/01/05 O Hard Draw: 32

Round	Opponent	Country	Rank	Score
R32	Armando, Hugo	(USA)	N/A	6–2 6–3
R16	Gabashvili, Teimuraz	(RUS)	N/A	4–6 7–5 6–3
Q	Kim, Kevin	(USA)	35	7–5 6–7 6–4
S	Malisse, Xavier	(BEL)	86	5–7 4–6

Points: 15   New Indesit ATP Race Position: 93   Prize Money: US $18000

San Jose, CA, U.S.A. International Series 7/02/05 Indoor Hard Draw: 32

Round	Opponent	Country	Rank	Score
R32	Dupuis, Antony	(FRA)	137	5–7 6–3 6–2
R16	Blake, James	(USA)	74	6–3 6–0
Q	Saulnier, Cyril	(FRA)	81	2–6 4–6

Points: 8   New Indesit ATP Race Position: 39   Prize Money: US $ 10600

Memphis, TN, U.S.A. International Series Gold 14/02/05 I Hard Draw: 32

Round	Opponent	Country	Rank	Score
R32	Enqvist, Thomas	(SWE)	54	7–5 6–2
R16	Dupuis, Antony	(FRA)	138	5–7 2

Points: 5   New Indesit ATP Race Position: 37   Prize Money: US $ 9800

Scottsdale, AZ, U.S.A. International Series 21/02/05 O Hard Draw: 32

Round	Opponent	Country	Rank	Score
R32	Reynolds, Bobby	(USA)	60	1–6 7–6(4) 7–6(2)
R16	Tipsarevic, Janko	(SCG)	84	6–4 4–6 6–4
Q	Blake, James	(USA)	79	7–6(6) 6–1
S	Ancic, Mario	(CRO)	16	1–6 4–6

Points: 15   New Indesit ATP Race Position: 39   Prize Money: US $ 18000

Indian Wells, California, USA ATP Tennis Masters Series 7/03/05 O Hard Draw: 96

Round	Opponent	Country	Rank	Score
R128	Bye,	()	N/A	
R64	Hernych, Jan	(CZE)	57	2–6 6–1 6–7(6)

Points: 1   New Indesit ATP Race Position: 28   Prize Money: US $ 8700

Miami, FL, U.S.A. ATP Tennis Masters Series 21/03/05 O Hard Draw: 96

Round	Opponent	Country	Rank	Score
R128	Bye,	()	N/A	
R64	Ginepri, Robby	(USA)	56	6–3 6–4
R32	Ljubicic, Ivan	(CRO)	5	3–6 6–4 6–7(3)

Points: 7   New Indesit ATP Race Position: 35   Prize Money: US $ 19730

Monte Carlo, Monaco ATP Tennis Masters Series 11/04/05 O Clay Draw: 64

Round	Opponent	Country	Rank	Score
R64	Stepanek, Radek	(CZE)	18	6 5–7

Points: 1   New Indesit ATP Race Position: 35   Prize Money: US $ 7500

Hamburg, Germany ATP Tennis Masters Series 9/05/05 O Clay Draw: 64

Round	Opponent	Country	Rank	Score
R64	Coria, Guillermo	(ARG)	6	6 2–6

Points: 1   New Indesit ATP Race Position: 49   Prize Money: US $ 7500

Dusseldorf, Germany World Team Championship 16/05/05 O Clay Draw: 32

Round	Opponent	Country	Rank	Score
RR	Haas, Tommy	(GER)	35	4–6 2–6
RR	Robredo, Tommy	(ESP)	23	3–6 6–2 3–6
RR	Johansson, Joachim	(SWE)	20	6–3 6–4

Points: 0   New Indesit ATP Race Position: 50   Prize Money: US $ 14410

Roland Garros, France Grand Slam 23/05/05 O Clay Draw: 128

Round	Opponent	Country	Rank	Score
R128	Costa, Albert	(ESP)	45	6–4 7–6(6) 6–2
R64	Haas, Tommy	(GER)	36	4–6 3–6

Points: 7   New Indesit ATP Race Position: 51   Prize Money: US $ 27342

Wimbledon, England Grand Slam 20/06/05 O Grass Draw: 128

Round	Opponent	Country	Rank	Score
R128	Nadal, Rafael	(ESP)	2	4-6 3-6 6

Points: 1   New Indesit ATP Race Position: 53   Prize Money: US $ 17295

Newport, RI, U.S.A. International Series 4/07/05 O Grass Draw: 32

Round	Opponent	Country	Rank	Score
R32	Popp, Alexander	(GER)	118	4-6 6-3 6-2
R16	Kucera, Karol	(SVK)	165	6-1 6-4
Q	Vemic, Dusan	(SCG)	N/A	6-3 6-4
S	Goldstein, Paul	(USA)	134	7-6(6) 6-2
F	Rusedski, Greg	(GBR)	82	6-7(3) 6-2 4-6

Points: 24   New Indesit ATP Race Position: 57   Prize Money: US $ 30600

Indianapolis, IN, U.S.A. International Series 18/07/05 O Hard Draw: 48

Round	Opponent	Country	Rank	Score
R64	Bye,	()	N/A	
R32	Ginepri, Robby	(USA)	85	4-6 3-6

Points: 1   New Indesit ATP Race Position: 42   Prize Money: US $ 5225

Los Angeles, CA, U.S.A. International Series 25/07/05 O Hard Draw: 32

Round	Opponent	Country	Rank	Score
R32	Fleishman, Zack	(USA)	N/A	6-4 2-6 4-6

Points: 1   New Indesit ATP Race Position: 46   Prize Money: US $ 3650

Montreal, Canada Tennis Masters Series 8/08/05 O Hard Draw: 64

Round	Opponent	Country	Rank	Score
R64	Bjorkman, Jonas	(SWE)	89	3-6 2-6

Points: 1   New Indesit ATP Race Position: 53   Prize Money: US $ 7500

Cincinnati, OH, USA ATP Tennis Masters Series 15/09/05 O Hard Draw: 64

Round	Opponent	Country	Rank	Score
R64	Simon, Gilles	(FRA)	134	6-2 2-6 3-6

Points: 1   New Indesit ATP Race Position: 55   Prize Money: US $ 7500

New Haven, CT, USA International Series 22/08/05 O Hard Draw: 48

Round	Opponent	Country	Rank	Score
R64	Bye,	()	N/A	
R32	Seppi, Andreas	(ITA)	68	6-3 7-5
R16	Lopez, Feliciano	(ESP)	30	7-6(5) 3-6 4-6

Points: 4   New Indesit ATP Race Position: 55   Prize Money: US $ 10050

U.S. Open, NY, U.S.A. Grand Slam 29/08/05 O Hard Draw: 128

Round	Opponent	Country	Rank	Score
R128	Weiner, Glenn	(USA)	160	6–4 6–2 6–0
R64	Coria, Guillermo	(ARG)	6	2–6 3–6 2–6

Points: 7   New Indesit ATP Race Position: 56   Prize Money: US $ 25000

Tokyo, Japan International Series Gold 3/10/05 O Hard Draw: 48

Round	Opponent	Country	Rank	Score
R64	Bye,	()	N/A	
R32	Phau, Bjorn	(GER)	111	4–6 5–7

Points: 1   New Indesit ATP Race Position: 60   Prize Money: US $ 4750

Stockholm, Sweden International Series 10/10/05 I Hard Draw: 32

Round	Opponent	Country	Rank	Score
R32	Chela, Juan Ignacio	(ARG)	38	6–2 4–6 6–1
R16	Johansson, Thomas	(SWE)	16	3–6 4–6

Points: 4   New Indesit ATP Race Position: 63   Prize Money: US $ 13500

Madrid, Spain ATP Tennis Masters Series 17/10/05 I Hard Draw: 48

Round	Opponent	Country	Rank	Score
R64	Melzer, Jurgen	(AUT)	50	6–3 4–6 4–6

Points: 1, New Indesit ATP Race Position: 64, Prize Money: US $ 7500

Lyon, France International Series 24/10/05 I Carpet Draw: 32

Round	Opponent	Country	Rank	Score
R32	Ljubicic, Ivan	(CRO)	8	7–6(5) 7–5
R16	Llodra, Michael	(FRA)	98	6–4 6–3
Q	Santoro, Fabrice	(FRA)	78	2–6 2–6

Points: 11   New Indesit ATP Race Position: 66   Prize Money: US $ 23000

Paris, France ATP Tennis Masters Series 31/10/05 I Carpet Draw: 48

Round	Opponent	Country	Rank	Score
R64	Tursunov, Dmitry	(RUS)	73	1–6 2–6

Points: 1   New Indesit ATP Race Position: 61   Prize Money: US $ 7500

Vince Spadea's ATP Player Profile
(as of March 2006)

Birthdate: 19 July 1974

Birthplace: Chicago, Illinois, USA

Residence: Boca Raton, Florida, USA

Height: 6'0" (182 cm)

Weight: 170 lbs (77 kg)

Plays: Right-handed

Turned Pro: 1993

Career High INDESIT ATP Ranking — Singles: 18 (2/28/2005)

Career High Stanford ATP Ranking — Doubles: 114 (2/27/2006)

Career Singles Record: 263–284

Singles Titles: 1 (Scottsdale, 2004)

Doubles Titles: 3 (Orlando and Tashkent, 1997; Buenos Aires, 1995)

Prize Money: $4,094,789